▼ ▼ ▼ ▼ ▼

JACK
IN TWO
WORLDS

▼ ▼ ▼ ▼ ▼

Publications of the
American Folklore Society,
New Series
General Editor
Patrick B. Mullen

EDITED BY

WILLIAM BERNARD

McCARTHY

▼ ▼ ▼ ▼ ▼

WITH TALES EDITED BY

WILLIAM BERNARD McCARTHY

CHERYL OXFORD

JOSEPH DANIEL SOBOL

JACK
IN TWO
WORLDS

▼ ▼ ▼ ▼ ▼

CONTEMPORARY
NORTH AMERICAN
TALES AND THEIR
TELLERS

▼ ▼ ▼ ▼ ▼

The

University of North Carolina Press

Chapel Hill & London

© 1994 The University of
North Carolina Press
All rights reserved
Manufactured in the United States of America

The paper in this book meets the guidelines for
permanence and durability of the Committee on
Production Guidelines for Book Longevity of the
Council on Library Resources.

Library of Congress
Cataloging-in-Publication Data
Jack in two worlds : contemporary North American
tales and their tellers / edited by William Bernard
McCarthy ; with tales edited by William Bernard
McCarthy, Cheryl Oxford, Joseph Daniel Sobol.
p. cm.—(Publications of the American Folklore
Society. New series)
Includes bibliographical references and index.
ISBN 0-8078-2135-7 (cloth : alk. paper).—
ISBN 0-8078-4443-8 (pbk. : alk. paper)
1. Jack tales—United States. 2. Storytelling—
Appalachian Region, Southern. 3. Storytelling—
United States. 4. Folklore—Performance.
I. McCarthy, William Bernard, 1939–
II. Oxford, Cheryl. III. Sobol, Joseph Daniel.
IV. Series: Publications of the American Folklore
Society. New series (Unnumbered)
GR105.37.J32J33 1994
398.21—dc20 93-35592
CIP

98 97 96 95 94   5 4 3 2 1

To all our families

and to all who tell and

listen to these stories

CONTENTS

▼ ▼ ▼ ▼ ▼

Preface, ix
William Bernard McCarthy

Introduction, xiii
Jacks: The Name, the Tales, the American Traditions
Carl Lindahl

Note on the Texts, xxxv
Transcribing Jack Tales in Performance
Bill Ellis and William Bernard McCarthy

PART 1
The Hicks-Harmon (Beech Mountain) Jack Tale Tradition

Chapter One
Jack in the Raw: Ray Hicks, 3
Joseph Daniel Sobol
Hardy Hard-Ass, 10
Ray Hicks

Chapter Two
Jack, My Father, and Uncle Ray: Frank Proffitt, Jr., 27
Carl Lindahl
Jack and the Old Rich Man, 34
Frank Proffitt, Jr.

Chapter Three
The Storyteller as Curator: Marshall Ward, 56
Cheryl Oxford
Jack in the Lions' Den, 70
Marshall Ward

Chapter Four
The Gentry-Long Tradition and Roots of Revivalism:
Maud Gentry Long, 93
Bill Ellis
Jack and the Heifer Hide, 107
Maud Gentry Long

Chapter Five
The Teller and the Tale: Storytelling on Beech Mountain, 123
W. F. H. Nicolaisen

PART 2
Jack in the Storytelling Revival

Chapter Six
The Tellers and the Tales: Revivalist Storytelling, 153
Ruth Stotter and William Bernard McCarthy

Chapter Seven
What Jack Learned at School: Leonard Roberts, 168
William Bernard McCarthy
Raglif Jaglif Tetartlif Pole, 180
Leonard Roberts

Chapter Eight
Between Worlds: Donald Davis, 204
Joseph Daniel Sobol
Jack's Biggest Tale, 213
Donald Davis

Chapter Nine
A Jack Tale Tradition in Pennsylvania's Northern Tier:
Bonelyn Lugg Kyofski, 229
Kenneth A. Thigpen
Grandma Hess's Story about Jack, Bill, and Tom, 237
Bonelyn Lugg Kyofski

Chapter Ten
Jack's Adventures in Toronto: Stewart Cameron, 250
Kay Stone, with Stewart Cameron
Jack and the Three Feathers, 257
Stewart Cameron

References, 273

Indexes: Tale and Song, 281; Place and Name, 283; Subject, 288

PREFACE

▼ ▼ ▼ ▼ ▼

William Bernard
McCarthy

Once bitten, folklorists and storytellers alike find it
hard to resist the Jack Tale. The three Bills represented in this volume, all bitten, agreed to organize a panel on Jack for the 1987 American Folklore Society meeting in Albuquerque. Under Bill Ellis's
leadership we brought together folklorists and professional storytellers to share insights into this irresistible trickster. At the end of that
packed session, as people lingered to discuss points with us or among
themselves, we knew that what we had done in bringing together
scholars and storytellers must be preserved. Work on this volume
began immediately under the general editorship of Bill Ellis. Carl
Lindahl agreed to develop a paper he had presented at another panel
of the Albuquerque meeting into an introductory essay. Joseph Sobol
and Ken Thigpen, hearing of the project through the grapevine,
volunteered additional stories and storytellers.

We found that in the fifty years since Richard Chase published his
collection, *The Jack Tales* (see Introduction), many Jack texts have
been collected and many published in anthologies or journals, but
only one slim—but very revealing—volume has appeared dedicated
entirely to Jack (Perdue 1987). The present collection goes beyond
Chase, both forward and backward. It goes back beyond Chase to the
North Carolina family from whom Chase had collected tales, to present the tales in the words of the family members (not in Chase's

recomposed versions) and in one case to present a tale that the family
had not seen fit to entrust to Chase. It goes forward beyond Chase to
present tales from professional storytellers inspired, at least in part,
by Chase's original book. It also goes beyond Chase in a third way,
including an essay about the story and storyteller to accompany each
tale.

As the book took shape, we realized we had four storytellers representative of the Beech Mountain tradition that Richard Chase had
tapped (including two of his original sources) and four storytellers
progressively further removed from Beech Mountain and the Appalachian oral tradition. All eight storytellers, however, have partici-
pated in varying degrees in the storytelling revival, that is to say, in
the conscious cultivation of storytelling as a North American traditional art form. This cultivation of storytelling has its roots in the
Federal Writers' Project of the 1930s and has flowered into a garland of annual festivals stretching from Jonesborough, Tennessee, to
Whitehorse, Yukon.

As we worked, certain themes asserted themselves again and again:
the fecundity of the Jack tradition, the creative freedom of the individual artist within that tradition, the adaptability of Jack Tales to
many contexts and especially to the classroom, the need for carefully
transcribed texts, the special place these tales have assumed in the
storytelling revival, and the tension between seeing Jack as a single
universal figure and appreciating the distinct personality of each
storyteller's and each listener's own Jack. But many issues had to be
passed over or touched on only lightly: the Jack Tales as a cycle; the
contribution of Scotland, Ireland, and Germany to the American
tradition; the definition of tradition in the first place; the question of
genre and "authenticity"; the influence of collectors—and festivals—
on taletelling; and so on and on. Nor was there room to discuss the
relevance to this material of the work of many scholars who have
deeply influenced our thinking. All this must wait for future articles
and books. We have had to content ourselves here with a sketch,
hardly more than a sketch of the Jack Tale in North America since
World War II, and especially as told today.

When Bill Ellis was forced to withdraw from the editorship, I assumed that position. Much that is best in the volume, however, is
owing to Bill's determination that American Jack Tale texts should be
presented in a new and better way. A number of people worked on

the textual transcriptions, but we did not reach unanimity about what that better way should be. Consequently I assumed responsibility for working out the final details of format, to some extent a series of compromises. We recognize that our practice still subjects the reader to the discretion of an editor. But we recognize, as well, that an editor is to some extent subject to the sufferance of potential readers: we cannot produce a text that is insufferably opaque for contemporary readers, however adept future readers may prove to be.

We owe thanks to many people: first, to all of our families; then to the Folk Narrative Section of the American Folklore Society, which sponsored the original panel from which the book grew; to Herbert Halpert for his careful critique of an early draft of Carl Lindahl's introduction; to the DuBois Educational Foundation and the Office of Undergraduate Education of the Pennsylvania State University for funding; to faculty secretary Lisa Taylor, who did much of the re-typing, photocopying, collating, and encouraging; to research assistants Betty Patrick, Lisa Brouse, and Deborah Kohler; to James W. Thompson for the genealogical charts in Chapter 5; and to Thomas McGowan, Jane Douglas, Dianne Cameron, and Edith Roberts for information about and photographs of Marshall Ward, Maud Long, Stewart Cameron, and Leonard Roberts, respectively.

DuBois, Pennsylvania
Twelfth Night 1993

INTRODUCTION

▼ ▼ ▼ ▼ ▼

JACKS: THE NAME, THE TALES, THE AMERICAN TRADITIONS

▼ ▼ ▼ ▼ ▼

Carl Lindahl

This book brings together eight Jack Tales collected from performance since World War II. All the performers have their feet planted firmly in traditional soil, yet all have been affected to some degree by popular notions and scholarly attitudes toward *The Jack Tales*, published fifty years ago by Richard Chase. Maud Long, for instance, grew up with Jack Tales in pre–World War I Appalachia but went on to become a close friend of Chase and to record her versions for the Library of Congress. Leonard Roberts was born in a log cabin at the head of a Kentucky hollow but went on to become a folktale collector and editor who viewed *The Jack Tales* as "an American folktale classic" (Roberts 1969, 20).

In the last fifty years, Jack Tales have come to occupy a privileged position for scholarly analysts of folklore, for popular purveyors of folklore, and even for folk themselves. Before turning to individual stories and storytellers, we might well ask, Who is this boy Jack? In what forms has he existed before—and beyond—the work of Richard Chase? How and in what ways has British Jack became American?

And how has one particular strand of English-speaking oral tradition been elevated to folk self-image for an entire nation?

The Name: Fragments from Far-Flung Traditions

As far back as English-language folktales can be traced, there are stories about Jack. From the fifteenth century, when "Jack and His Step-Dame" was set down in rhyme in England, to the present, when Ray Hicks's rendition of "Jack and the Three Steers" dominates the National Storytelling Festival, one name above all others has been associated with magic tales in the British-American tradition. Yet the relation between the earlier Jacks and the most recent is difficult to trace, since no oral Jack Tales have survived from distant centuries. But a handful of texts provide essential, if fragmentary, clues about the nature of the stories told by long-dead raconteurs. The earliest written versions of the fantasy tales that scholars call märchen were most often rendered in rhyme and hand-copied on manuscripts. Later tales, printed in prose and priced for a popular audience, were known as chapbooks. Jacks populate both forms.

The oldest known version of the international tale type, "The Dance among Thorns" (AT 592),[1] is an early fifteenth-century English poem titled "Jack and His Stepdame," in which Jack is an only child abused by his stepmother. He shares food with an old beggar, who grants him three magic wishes: a bow and arrows that never miss their mark, a pipe whose music compels all that hear it to dance, and a spell that forces his stepmother to fart explosively whenever she looks angrily at Jack. With these gifts Jack punishes the stepmother as well as a friar whom she has recruited to beat him (Furrow 1985, 67–156; Bolte and Polívka 1913–32, 2:491). Because so many recent editors have attempted to sell Jack exclusively to children, obscene and scatological elements of his tradition have long been suppressed. Yet "Jack and His Stepdame" testifies that Jack's name has figured in off-color adventures for nearly six centuries, and Appalachian tales just now finding their way into print (including the tales of Ray Hicks and Marshall Ward in this book) affirm that the Jack of oral tradition is sometimes a character shared by adults but off-limits to children, enjoyed among men but largely concealed from women.

Sixteenth- and seventeenth-century texts provide hints of Jack's better-known and more heroic role. The first scraps of giant-killer tales appear in English Renaissance drama. The rhyme

Fy, fa and fum,
I smell the bloud of an Englishman

—now so closely associated with tales of Jack and the giants—appears in Thomas Nashe's *Haue with You to Saffron-Walden* (1596) and a little later, with variations, in Shakespeare's *King Lear* (ca. 1605). When Nashe wrote, the rhyme was already old, for he warns that only a pedant would search for "the first inuention" of "Fy, fa and fum." Apparently then, by 1600 the giant had long been on the scene, but we cannot prove that Jack was: nowhere in these records is he mentioned as the giant's foe (Opie and Opie 1974, 58–60; Bolte and Polívka 1913–32, 4:72–73). Jack's major appearance in Renaissance drama, as a character in George Peele's *The Old Wives' Tale*, seems to be in a role that parodies his traditional status as boy-hero (see Hook 1970, 319–41). We must wait until the early eighteenth century for the oldest surviving Jack-and-giant tales, "The History of Jack and the Giants" (Newcastle, 1711) and "The History of Jack and the Bean-Stalk" (AT 328; London, 1734). Read and told throughout Britain, these would become in effect the signature stories of the English storybook tradition that flowered in the nineteenth century.

"Jack and the Giants" (known in nineteenth-century storybooks as "Jack the Giant-Killer") presents a boy, the only child of a Cornish farmer, who saves Cornwall from a giant by trapping him in a pit and killing him with a pickax. The boy strangles two other giants and kills a fourth by tricking him into cutting his stomach open (AT 1088). He lures a fifth giant into a cell to hide from an imaginary enemy, locks him up, and then steals his magic objects (AT 328 IIa, e; Opie and Opie 1974, 62–71). It is tempting to see in "Jack and the Giants" traces of ancient British legend. For instance, the earliest surviving biography of King Arthur (Geoffrey of Monmouth's *History of the Kings of Britain* [1136]) pits the young king against a fierce giant in a battle near Land's End—precisely the locale where, six centuries later, chapbook Jack will kill the giant Corinoran. Has the legendary British king traded his crown for a hoe and become a working-class hero? We cannot answer that question, but it is true that the eighteenth-century farmer Jack, like Arthur before him, became a kind of national, and then an international, hero. Popular with all classes of English people, his tales stirred even the literary giants of the day, including those then inventing the novel. Henry Fielding, in the first chapter of *Joseph Andrews*, asserts that the story of the giant-killer—which he'd heard as a child—was "finely calculated to sow the seeds of virtue in youth." James Boswell—and even Samuel Johnson, that arbiter of British literary culture—also praised Jack. The most intensive education seems to have provided no certain cure for fascination with this character, for Nicholas Amherst complained in 1721 that too many history professors "never read any thing" other than stories of Jack and Tom Thumb. As the cheaply priced chapbooks of the eighteenth century became the elaborate storybooks of the nineteenth, the farmer's son invaded the nurseries of wealthy Victorians. All English people knew something of Jack (Opie and Opie 1974, 60–62).

By the eighteenth century it is clear that Jack had become the John Doe of English oral tradition. Even more numerous than tales are surviving nursery rhymes in which Jack is by far the favored name for male characters.[2] No consistent figure emerges in the boys portrayed in "Jack and Jill," "Jack Horner," and "Jack Sprat." But because both the nursery rhymes and the chapbooks first appear in broad distribution early in the eighteenth century, and because such rhymes and tales are the most popular published forms of oral entertainment dating from the era, we can reasonably assume that Jack was the most commonly voiced name in the nursery.

Beyond England's borders other Jacks thrived. In Scotland and Ireland, even among Gaelic-speaking narrators, Jacks figure prominently in the earliest printed folktales. In Robert Chambers's *Popular Rhymes of Scotland* (1826) Jack appears in his Scots form as Jock, and in the Highland tales collected by John Francis Campbell of Islay, Gaelic-speaking tellers often call him Jake. Among the most prolific Jack Tale tellers today are the "traveling people," migratory families of Scotland. Storyteller Duncan Williamson declares Jack a hero to the travelers, who often change the names of figures in borrowed tales to create new adventures and greater fame for Jack (Williamson 1983, xvii–xxi; Williamson and McDermitt 1978, 141–48; Williamson and Williamson 1987, 20–21).

Jack's popularity grew throughout Britain and Ireland at the same time that Britain was colonizing the world. Immigrants from Britain and Ireland brought Jack to the imperial colonies, including the Caribbean, where Jack is the most popular human character among black Bahamian tellers (Edwards 1895, no. 34; Crowley 1966, esp. 29). In some Jamaican traditions Jack appears in every tale, not as a character, but as the archetypal listener. Narrators close each tale by saying, "Jack Mantora, me no choose any"—which means, roughly, "By Jack Mandora [listening at heaven's gate], don't blame me for the tale I've just told" (Jekyll 1907, xi).

The focus of the present inquiry is on North American Jacks, who first surface in historical records before 1800. Samuel Kercheval, remembering his early experiences in backcountry Virginia, recalled that settlers told tales of Jack and the giants and wandering knights— all characters popular in chapbooks circulating throughout the English-speaking world at the time. "Many of those tales were lengthy, and embraced a considerable range of incident . . . and were so arranged as to the different incidents of narration, that they were easily committed to memory. They certainly have been handed down from generation to generation from time immemorial" (Kercheval 1902, 285–86). Kercheval's brief sketch indicates a vital oral tradition and accompanying aesthetic.

Some recently published American tales retain clear traces of English chapbook influence, and some narrators today continue to insist on the English background of Jack Tales.[3] Yet Scottish and Irish settlers brought their Jacks as well, and these oral traditions too would find expression in American tales. Indeed, several streams of English, Scottish, and Irish storytelling must have fed the body of American märchen. Between the rare revolutionary-war-era references and the recent popularity of these tales, however, lies an enormous, scantly documented gap. On one side of the void lies a rich tradition, both written and oral, reaching across an ocean and back through centuries. On the other side stands one book, by Richard Chase; one family, the Harmons of North Carolina; and a company of contemporary storytellers in their thousands and listeners in their millions who have been influenced by this book and this family.

Most contemporary narratives known as Jack Tales, and most of their tellers, owe much to Chase's 1943 collection, *The Jack Tales*. Across the country, librarians and members of storytellers' guilds lead listeners and students to this one book, easily the best selling and most influential collection of American folktales that has yet appeared. In *The Jack Tales*, Chase purported to present a localized and unique hero with a well-developed personality, the creation of a single family from the Beech Mountain region of North Carolina. But no matter how localized the original range of these stories, and how small their audience, *The Jack Tales* was adopted by Americans as a national tradition. How did this happen?

American Märchen-telling Styles

To begin to understand how diverse Jack Tales with many different regional and cultural styles merged into one small body of narrative about a national folk hero, it is necessary to consider some facts about storytelling in the Old and New worlds, beginning with some information about the magic tale itself. The typical märchen presents a tension between home and the road. Beginning in a quiet, unremarkable place—such as the simple hearth where poor Jack and his widowed mother worry about their next meal—the story only gradually opens to the magic world. Taking to the road to make his fortune, the hero finds more magic the farther he travels from home. Usually—especially in European traditions—Jack ends his tale by coming home and settling down. The märchen is a magic sandwich, in which the miraculous events of the hero's travels are framed by mundane beginnings and endings, the simplicities of home.

The double-faceted märchen world—both homely and exotic—mirrors the two-stranded storytelling tradition that developed the märchen. Linda Dégh (1969, 63–93) has established that the great European märchen tellers were not homebodies, but travelers by profession and inclination. Like the heroes of the tales they narrated, these men (for such narrators were principally male) were wanderers through the world—tinkers, soldiers, woodmen, and migratory farm workers. A great teller would often end his tale by pretending to have been present during the action of the story: "As I was there when all that happened, they sent me here to relate it to you. I have finished" (Saucier 1962, 103). Thus the teller represented himself as an emissary from the magic world of the open road, and because he was a traveler, his audience sometimes playfully acknowledged that he was indeed closer to the magic than they were (Lindahl 1987, 39–43).

If the greatest narrators learned and told their greatest stories on the road, they also brought them to homes. As their stories were retold in such relatively quiet settings, it would seem, there developed the special regional and cultural variations of particular tales—the oikotypes—so richly reflective of the groups that share them. It was this cross-fertilization of traveling and domestic traditions that made the märchen such a vital genre, once upon a time. Thus the märchen-narrating world, like the märchen itself, presents a tension between the adventure of the open road and the gravitational pull toward the settled life of home. Misappropriating the language of Robert Redfield, I term the traveling narrative world the great tradition and the domestic narrative world the little tradition—more to reflect the performance scale and geographic scale each embraces than to imply any judgment on the relative quality of the two forms of artistry.[4]

Ironically, it was in America—that archetypally mobile society—that the märchen quit the road and settled down. The great tradition gave way to the little tradition. American frontiers were too fluid and print-oriented to sustain the communities of traveling storytellers that had thrived in Europe, so the bulk of märchen narration has been confined to homes and passed down largely within families in a series of little traditions. These lack the theatrics and scale of the performances of Europe's great public narrators but are no less worthy of study, especially as American märchen are guarded and cherished within the family unit and are often considered too valuable to share with outsiders. Historically, these little märchen traditions have been shy.

American märchen traditions can be characterized as little and shy at least in part because of two facets of British-American performance style. First, according to märchen listeners and tellers I've interviewed, storytelling is viewed as an exercise in sensory deprivation. Like the Irish tellers described by James Delargy, who turn their backs to the audience or even speak, audible but invisible, from another room, British-American storytellers tend to speak out, but not to act out, their tales, eschewing gesture and confining drama to the voice. For their part, listeners tend not to watch storytellers. Informants have told me that they listened in the dark—or in front of a fire, staring at the flames, to become hypnotic subjects in an environment where only the voice mattered. As a girl, Ozark storyteller Mim Nerelich listened to quilters telling tales. She would lie on her back under the quilting frame and stare upward intently at the slowly changing sewn patterns until, self-hypnotized, she sensed only the voice of the storyteller ringing in her head. Ray Hicks seems to be getting at something similar when he describes his childhood experience of stories at the beginning of "Hardy Hard-Ass," in this book. And in the Donald Davis tale included here, in which Jack tells stories to the king, the king repeatedly responds, "Ah, I can just see it now," or conversely, "Tell me a little bit more about it, so I can sort of see it a little better." Thus, all stimuli are channeled into speech, all responses evoked through hearing: a great energy transfer for those who participate, but an environment antithetical to the sensory over-load that characterizes contemporary American public life. (See the firsthand accounts of Maud Long's narrative style in Chapter 4.) Unfortunately, most folklorists, knowingly or otherwise, have incor-porated the loud, public life into their collecting aesthetics. Conse-quently, the shyer world of the lone, quiet voice figures too rarely in folkloric performance studies.

Second, most British-American narrative traditions are not merely focused tightly on the voice; they are also voiced mildly. The under-statement dominant in the diction and the inflection of American jokes and tall tales also prevails in märchen performances. In "The Celebrated Jumping Frog of Calaveras County," Mark Twain's flaw-less written adaptation of American tall-tale style, narrator Simon Wheeler "never smiled, he never frowned, he never changed his voice from the gentle-flowing key to which he tuned his initial sentence [and] never betrayed the slightest suspicion of enthusiasm." Sim-ilarly, Edgar A. Ashley's telling of "Billy Peg and his Bull" is an extended understatement, performed without laughter or vocal mod-ulation.[5] This quiet tone reflects a pervasive aesthetic attitude in the culture. Compared with other American ethnic groups, British-Americans are shy about their art. Henry Glassie has commented on the tendency of Appalachian basket weavers to stress the utility rather than the beauty of their craft. Yet, says Glassie, these artists are continually producing "unnecessarily beautiful" artifacts. Quilters stress proficiency of stitching, not beauty of design, privileging the practical skill over aesthetics. What is true for material culture is equally true for oral art: both media mask artistry with claims of practicality. The tall-tale teller contends that his skill is one of deceit—his aim is to fool people rather than to entertain them. The artist plays the role of competitor, calling attention away from his art. The dominant styles of British-American oral art involve understatement. To laugh while telling a joke, to vary pitch on the punchline, or to deliver a tall tale in an excited tone is to compromise the story. Thus British-American folk culture calls attention away from its art; but the märchen, an unmasked fantasy, cannot hide its impossibilities in claims of truth, so the teller tends to turn it into a tall tale or a legend or a joke, or tells it only to children, in private.

The märchen tellers I have met are participants in little traditions. Most often, they are women who received their stories from parents and grandparents and are now passing them on to children and grandchildren. Thus, in another sense, the American tradition is a little one—the auditors are little, generally young children. In my fieldwork, I have found the parent-child storytelling chain of transmission so strong and exclusive that it has often taken the child's intervention to get the parent to share a tale with an outsider.

The small scale of New World märchen performances—and the small size of their listeners—are evident in the fact that public school classrooms were the sites of the largest storytelling gatherings.[6] Although such narrators happily shared their stories with young listeners, they have often been embarrassed to tell them to collectors.

In one final respect, the English-language märchen is a little tradition. It has too long been trivialized, even dismissed, by people having little regard for its internal rules, or it has been warped into a dramatic form by storytelling circuit performers wishing to realize their own distorted notions of its scale and grandeur. Yet these little traditions live, sometimes even thrive, as they await the fair treatment of folklorists.

Returning now to Jack Tales, we find that twentieth-century collectors discovered a series of little traditions shared by families, principally in the Appalachian and Blue Ridge mountains. In 1925 Isabel Gordon Carter published several of Jane Gentry's "old Jack, Will, and Tom" tales, in which Jack is the third son, left behind when his brothers seek adventure. Jack follows his brothers, and when they are tested by hosts and donors, it is Jack who passes the tests for all of them. The climactic test is often a series of thefts of magical objects from the giant; Jack's success is rewarded with marriage. It would later be revealed that Gentry's family tradition overlapped that which Richard Chase would tap—and alter—in *The Jack Tales*.

Nevertheless, the research of Leonard Roberts in Kentucky and Vance Randolph in the Ozarks demonstrates a much broader range of Jack Tales than was once supposed. Stories featuring Jacks appear not only in North Carolina but also in Virginia, West Virginia, Tennessee, Kentucky, Pennsylvania, New York, Missouri, Arkansas, and elsewhere.[7] Beyond Beech Mountain, however, Jack is often just another name for a folktale character. His personality is not consistent, nor does it dominate the tales as in Chase's book.

Even within Appalachia the consistency found in the Chase collection is not characteristic. Leonard Roberts's fine folktale anthologies

South from Hell-fer-Sartin and *Old Greasybeard* offer a more representative sample. About 10 percent of the tales in these books contain a
character named Jack. In about one-fifth of these tales, however, Jack
is a dupe or an opponent rather than a hero. Jack is an only child in
approximately half of the tales, and one of three children in the others. He is most often the youngest child, but sometimes the oldest.
Mountain storytellers clearly had many and varied ideas of who Jack
was. Yet, in spite of such diversity, one Jack eventually grew to ob-
scure the others. How did a series of little traditions become the giant
tradition, the industry that Jack Tales now comprise?

The Giant-Killer Becomes the Giant

The rise of Chase's Jack must be traced through a myriad of social
patterns connecting the isolated hearths at which folktales were once
told to the broad arenas of politics, economics, and nationalist fervor.

In the 1930s the United States began a process of intense national
introspection as historians and literary critics sought to discover the
defining properties of American culture. The Great Depression, the
Second World War, America's postwar dominance of world economy and politics—each of these massive realities spurred the impulse
to identify and understand the inner workings of a "national mind."
Scholars believed that "the American experience was indeed exceptional, and that it was best understood as involving a refusal, upon
principle, of the values derived from history and society" (Donoghue
1987, 7). Hence, the secret of America's sovereignty lay in its rejection of its European past.

Integral to this search for a national soul was the attempt to find
the folk roots of our "cultural personality." During the thirty years
framed by Constance Rourke's *American Humor* (1931) and Daniel
Hoffman's *Form and Fable in American Fiction* (1961) literary and
cultural critics set themselves the task of identifying folk heroes. Was
there a single folk figure that both condensed and crystallized the
national character? Rourke, Dixon Webster, Leo Gurko, Richard V.
Chase (not the Jack Tale man), and Richard M. Dorson had all
played with this question by 1961, when Hoffman defined an American folk hero with a distinct personality and assured all Americans
that it was our own. Hoffman examined a handful of nineteenth-
century heroes straddling the boundaries of print and oral culture—

Davy Crockett, Mike Fink, and Sam Patch. From them he created a composite creature that he held up as a mirror for Americans, faithful to the country's ideals because "the heroes of folklore and of popular culture inevitably display those qualities of character that their celebrants admire" (Hoffman 1961, 51). Hoffman's piecemeal hero was, he said, quintessentially and uniquely American, ours and ours alone: "The American Hero is startlingly different from most of the great heroes of myths or of märchen. Unlike them, the American has no parents. He has no past, no patrimony, no siblings, no family, and no life cycle, because he never marries or has children. He seldom dies. If death does overtake him, it proves to be merely a stage in his transformation to still another identity" (Hoffman 1961, 78). This biographical pattern succinctly expressed an American rejection of Old World values. With no ties to culture, family, or other human beings, this new man was free to re-create the world as he pleased.

While Hoffman and other intellectuals were seeking to define a national folk hero, however, Richard Chase produced one. *The Jack Tales* (1943) instantly became our most famous collection of British-American folktales, a distinction it continues to enjoy. Chase's work was also, in its time, the largest published collection of American märchen, presenting more than twice as many as any of its predecessors. His subsequent books, *Grandfather Tales* (1948) and *American Folk Tales and Songs* (1956), enlarged his collection and his reputation. Only Vance Randolph and Leonard Roberts have published more extensive American märchen collections.

Anticipating Hoffman, Chase claimed that the protagonist of *The Jack Tales* was a true American hero, distinctly different from English Jacks: "Our Appalachian giant-killer has acquired the easy-going, unpretentious rural American manners that make him so different from his English cousin, the cocksure, dashing young hero of the 'fairy tale' "; Jack is "the unassuming representative of a very large portion of the American people" (R. Chase 1943, ix, xii). Many readers concurred. "Jack Tales reflect the true spirit of American folklore as it exists in the Southern Appalachians," said Joseph Carrière (1946, 76), and Leonard Roberts (1969, 20) pronounced the book "an American folktale classic." Apparently Chase had succeeded in transforming the little tradition of Beech Mountain into a great American tradition.

At first glance, *The Jack Tales* does seem to offer independent confirmation that the American folk hero is a new man shaped by a new land. If we set Hoffman's characterization next to Appalachian Jack, there is a clear correspondence. Often Jack enters his tale from the woods; the audience hears nothing of his parents or family. Of those tales that do give Jack a family, a considerable percentage abandon his parents before the story's end, subverting the final family reunion found in European märchen. Tales typically end with Jack's material success. He marries very infrequently by European standards, only about half of the time.[8] The defining trait of Chase's and Hoffman's hero is his isolation, expressed in his separation from home and parents, his traveling and working alone, and his self-reliance and lack of interest in a mate.

So in Chase's stories Jack is set apart. But he has been isolated still further by the American scholarly community, which—consciously or otherwise—has used three strategies to give Jack the appearance of uniqueness, namely, cutting Jack off from his forebears, accepting Chase's Jack at face value, and abstracting Jack semiotically. First, we cut Jack off from his forebears, the protagonists of Scottish, English, and Scots-Irish tales. Any claim that the American heroes differ substantially from European heroes should be bolstered by a close comparison of tales, yet proponents of Jack's uniqueness never subjected their claims to such study.[9] But weren't these isolationists correct? Had not Chase discovered a uniquely American hero? Yes and no. Though Chase collected his tales in one of the country's more conservative regions, he was from the beginning influenced by the same cultural trends that had created the search for the American hero. He began his fieldwork as a cultural outsider. Inspired by the romantic vision of a folk past cultivated at such elite schools as Harvard and Wellesley, he sought to impose that vision on Appalachian culture (Whisnant 1983, 202–4). He became an employee of the Federal Writers' Project, a service created by the Roosevelt administration to limit the negative effects of the Depression. Among its many functions, the Federal Writers' Project provided employment for authors, who collected, rewrote, and published all types of lore, attempting to turn the nation's attention away from its economic troubles and back to its (sometimes newly invented) folkloric past. So it is not surprising that Chase, a government employee assigned to a task of national self-celebration, should alter folktales in an effort to create a national folk hero. Like other "individualist" intellectuals in his time, he was working with a self-fulfilling prophecy. He sought a unique folk hero, and a unique folk hero was what he found.

When Chase and Hoffman wrote, this strategy of isolation was a good deal more understandable than it is now. There were few authentically collected English-language tales from Britain with which the American tales could be compared. Now, however, collections on both sides of the Atlantic are large enough to permit a thorough comparison. In Britain one anthology alone, Katharine Briggs's *Dictionary of British Folk-Tales* (1970), doubles the number of variants that were available to American scholars in the 1950s. Taking Ernest Baughman's *Type and Motif Index of the Folktales of England and North America* (1966, but including no tales published after 1958) as a gauge of what was available to Chase and comparing it with Briggs's dictionary, we find a dramatic increase in material. Four tales crucial to a British-American comparison are "The Boy Steals the Giant's Treasure" (AT 328), "The Little Red Ox" (AT 511A), "The Table, the Ass, and the Stick" (AT 563), and "The Master Thief" (AT 1525). Baughman finds only nine British variants, but with Briggs the number leaps to twenty-two. A similar growth has occurred in the Appalachians, where nineteen variants of the four tales were listed by 1958. Since that time just five collections by four men (Glassie 1964; McGowan 1978; Perdue 1987; Roberts 1969 and 1974) have increased the number to forty-two. (Unpublished works by McDermitt [1986], Oxford [1987], and Sobol [1987] augment that number substantially.) These recent collections support some preliminary conclusions. Set against the British tales, the American stories reveal a remarkably similar Jack, confirming W. F. H. Nicolaisen's (1978) early, insightful study of the two heroes. The qualities that Hoffman finds most conspicuous in the American hero ("self-assertive independence," "self-reliance," "innocence"), traits he elsewhere presents as "all the strengths and weaknesses of youth" [Hoffman 1961, 78]), are found in British Jack as well. These characteristics are arguably fundamental to the märchen hero in whatever cultural context he may appear. The personalities projected by the two Jacks are, in fact, almost identical.

A second sense in which the scholarly community isolated Jack was in accepting Chase's book at face value, not realizing Chase was promoting pseudotraditional tales at the expense of authentic ones.

By his own admission Chase was more interested in performing and rewriting tales than in faithfully rendering them. Not until the appearance of a remarkable study by Charles Perdue, however, was it clear how drastically Chase had altered his oral sources. Perdue shows that Chase "borrowed" and rewrote tales collected by co-workers. Though it has been continually claimed that the published Jack Tales came exclusively from the New World, Chase admitted having taken at least one motif from European sources, and as "it would appear to be impossible ever to discover all the changes made by Chase" (Perdue 1987, 113), he probably borrowed more. Though we cannot be certain what Chase did, it does seem—paradoxically—that when his published texts diverge from authentic Appalachian tales, they tend to follow Old World rather than New World patterns. For example, the nuclear family is even less important in Appalachian tales collected by Chase's co-workers in the Federal Writers' Project than in Chase's text. In the sources studied by Perdue, only eight of the twenty-five märchen mention parents, and only one-fifth have a strong family setting. But in over half of Chase's published texts, Jack's parents are mentioned, and in one-third they figure prominently. Thus Chase obscured the distinctiveness of the American tale at the same time that he was proclaiming it.

In any case, Chase should not take all the blame. It is not his fault but the default of others who left Appalachian oral tales uncollected so long. Before the publications of Roberts, Glassie, and Perdue, only Marie Campbell's unrepresentative collection competed with Chase's books. Folklorists allowed one man's version of Appalachian narrative to persist almost unchallenged for decades.

A third way in which scholars have isolated Jack is semiotically. He has been separated from the other aspects of the tales in which he appears. Scholars who extolled the uniqueness of American culture were so anxious to see it embodied in one individualistic hero that they did not consider the hero's environment within the tale or his relationships with other characters. Yet the important cultural indicators in the Jack Tales are not to be found in the hero's personality but, rather, in his surroundings. As Hoffman himself had suggested, the hero's lack of family background is distinctive. Though Appalachian Jack's personality may not be unique, his homelessness does set him apart from British Jack.

Furthermore, examining Jack's relationships with other characters, and the nature of those characters, I have identified what I believe to be two other important differences between American Jack Tales and their British antecedents, differences in who wields magic and in who plays the role of donor. The first difference is a matter of wonder. By my count British and American tales contain similar quantities of fantasy elements—talking animals, giants, magical powers obtained from seemingly unremarkable objects. Yet there is a great difference in the ways that the forces of fantasy are deployed. In British tales, most magical elements provide help for the hero—for example, an animal that Jack has saved gives him a magic weapon. In American tales, however, the most common fantasy elements comprise magic used against the hero. By far the most common supernormal element is the giant, Jack's special enemy for at least three centuries, who is the villain in nearly one-third of the American stories. In nearly all of these Jack has no magic help against his monstrous foe.

Märchen magic, however, is an equalizer, functioning to fill the gap between one's resources and one's needs. British Jack, like most European heroes, must have magic if he is to survive against the powerful forces of his enemy, the king. But among the most popular Appalachian tales there are only two in which the hero's magic help-ers are instrumental to the plot: "The Little Red Ox" (AT 511A) and "The Table, the Ass, and the Ox" (AT 563).[10] The more common situation by far is one in which Jack—aided only by his mental re-sources and sometimes by the encouragement of another mortal—confronts and defeats his magic foe. If märchen magic indeed serves to offset perceptions of social helplessness, the American Jack Tale is one of the most optimistic forms of folk expression to be found any-where. Its premise is that Jack's antagonists, not Jack, need magic to survive. There is no gap between Jack's resources and his needs—an idea consonant with the "folk idea" of unlimited opportunity found so prominently in American lore (Dundes 1972, 93–105).

A second important difference between the American and the British tales lies in the identity of the donor. In Britain, the donor is usually a magical being—a dwarf or, more often, a white-haired "beg-gar" with magic powers. Jack passes a test of virtue, usually by giving the last of his food to the man, who then rewards Jack with a magic gift to help defeat the evil king or giant. In America, though magical helpers are rare, the donor survives in a new form. (Examples of the "new" American donor can be found in Carter 1925 and Glassie

1964.) The typical American donor is a rich landed man. Jack works to earn money from this man or—far more rarely—to win the man's daughter as a wife. The donor has no magic to lend Jack but normally provides food, clothes, weapons, or money. It often happens that Jack ultimately gives his donor more valuable help than the donor has given him. A rich man may give Jack a thousand dollars and some food if Jack kills the giant, but when Jack succeeds, the donor prospers more than Jack does.

The differences between American and British narratives may be explained, in part, with reference to a dialectic involving two assumptions that have dominated American views of society. The first is the concept of equality, with its fantasy of a perfect utopian democracy on the frontier. Intertwined with this fantasy is the second concept, that of the primacy of the individual, the idea that American social freedoms created the conditions for a Jeffersonian "natural aristocracy" that allowed resourceful individuals to rise to the top. Despite inherent conflicts in these concepts (how is it, for example, that a utopian democracy can possess an aristocracy?), the two models have persisted, even thrived, side by side. As Arthur M. Schlesinger, Jr., explains:

> The struggle is between capitalist values—the sanctity of private property, the maximization of profit, the cult of the free market, the survival of the fittest—and democratic values—equality, freedom, social responsibility and the general welfare, ends to be promoted when necessary by public action regulating property and restricting profit. This remains a tension rather than a mortal antagonism. Capitalism and democracy began as allies in the revolution against monarchy and feudal aristocracy, and they continue to share a faith in individual freedom, popular sovereignty, limited government and equality before the law. In America capitalism includes democracy, and democracy includes capitalism. Yet the two creeds point in different directions[:] those most firmly attached to democratic values exhibit least support for capitalism and those most firmly attached to capitalist values exhibit least support for democracy. (Schlesinger 1986, 25–26)

The two perspectives, once united in opposition to British feudalism, have since grown ever farther apart. During the Great Depression, when the Federal Writers' Project and Chase began collecting folktales, lessons of democracy and interdependence were strongly stressed: the U.S. government has never come closer to socialism than between 1932 and 1945. It is not surprising that Chase's tales provided a compensation fantasy for a public longing for more individual opportunities. In preparing them he emphasized individual freedom and capitalism and retained only as a vestige Jack's dependence upon donors. In examining oral texts, however, I have found that this capitalistic emphasis preceded Chase—American tales have long suppressed democratic aspects.

American Jack's reliance on capitalism emerges in a comparison of American and British versions of "The Master Thief" (AT 1525), an amoral tale with a moral hero. Jack—normally the embodiment of his society's positive values—is in this story asked to act as a sociopath, performing a series of robberies. Most narrators sense the dilemma of forcing a hero into a criminal's role, and they tend to offer apologies and rationalizations for Jack's crimes. Hence variants of this story contain a greater number of subjective statements and narrative asides than most Jack Tales. This interpretive imperative helps make the tale more volatile, allowing cultural differences to emerge more quickly and clearly in "The Master Thief" than in other tale types.

In most of the ten British versions of "The Master Thief" found in Briggs's dictionary the focal antagonism is class struggle.[11] Jack is a servant or apprentice pitted against a superior, usually his master. The British narrators justify Jack's theft by pointing out the moral inferiority of the man he robs. The villain usually wants to kill Jack, and their rivalry becomes so vicious that in one variant Jack ruthlessly kills his master and his master's wife and children and still emerges the hero. In two texts Jack plays the role of Robin Hood, giving to the poor the money he has stolen from the rich man. Narrative asides usually emphasize the victim's evil. In one tale, after Jack's thefts have driven the villain to insanity, the moralizing narrator concludes: "Many a covetous wretch that loved his good better than God . . . by the right judgement of God ofttimes cometh to a miserable and shameful end" (K. Briggs 1970, 2:270). Such tales assert that Jack's victim, and not Jack, is the real thief.

Six Appalachian versions, on the other hand, present a struggle between a moral thief and a moral victim, a good-natured game rather than a fight to the death.[12] Tellers pose themselves the question, How can one be moral and a thief at the same time? These are the most popular answers: 1) Jack is captured by robbers who will kill him if he does not steal, and 2) the money that Jack steals is used to serve his needy family. Far more difficult to explain is Jack's relationship with his victim. In the British tale the victim is the man responsible for Jack's poverty, so poetic justice prevails when the man becomes a victim of theft, the same crime he has practiced against Jack. But in the New World there is a less antagonistic relationship between Jack and his victim. In Ray Hicks's story, for instance, we never get to know the victim, but Hicks presents no reason for us to dislike the man. Jack never talks to his opponent, but Hicks assures us that Jack has no bad intentions. Planning his theft, Jack says, "I might fool that old man and not have to hurt nobody. . . . I don't believe in hurting no one" (McGowan 1978, 75–76). In some variants Jack's friendship with his opponent stretches beyond all credibility. The plot demands that the dupe try to kill Jack, but narrators insist on the villain's goodness. Tellers work hard to justify a bad act by an essentially good character. This "tension of essences" grows greater than most tellers can handle: Cornelius Allen, for example, introduces the donor as "a kindly rich old feller" who likes Jack. But when Jack tries to steal a sheet from his bed, the dupe says, "That Jack is disturbing my peace. He's already got a lot of my money. . . . I believe I'll slip out and kill him and get all my money back" (Roberts 1969, 150–51). The sudden conversion from kindly feller to would-be killer seems to trouble the narrator, who abruptly abandons the donor after this scene. Thus, American narrators stretch the plot as far as they can not only to explain Jack's crimes but also to portray a friendly relationship between Jack and the victim, a relationship in which the rich man becomes both dupe and donor.

This transatlantic comparison of versions of "Master Thief" tales reveals a remarkable transformation. A bitter British class struggle has become a playful American test of skills. British Jack is a Robin Hood who defends the poor. Though American Jack steals to help his mother in one of the six Appalachian texts, his principal beneficiary is himself. The British tale celebrates the lower classes; the American tale celebrates Jack.

How has a British democrat evolved into an American capitalist? The simplest answers would express boundless optimism ("lacking an oppressor class, the United States stopped producing tales of villainous tyrants") or extreme cynicism ("without a real villain there can be no real hero"). A better answer, I believe, is that the continual, if subtle, presence of the donor allows each teller some interpretive choice. There are at least three readings. First, the friendly rivalry of Jack and the donor may be developed as a democratic statement (this seems to be the rarest narrative solution). Second, Jack and the capitalism he stands for have no need to make enemies—and no one need make enemies with them—in a limitlessly wealthy land (this self-congratulatory reading may be used to relieve the guilt attending self-serving actions). Third (perhaps the most deeply buried reading), behind Jack's seeming independence is a need for social support. The American hero is put in a position of debt to a power structure for which he must work in order to succeed, but if he works he will succeed. The donor serves as Jack's tutor, instructing him in the arts of acquisition. Read in the starkest Proppian terms, British and American donors are indistinguishable in function. If the content of the tales means anything, however, we see in these donors a clear development. The old magic world of the British tale has been invaded by a tutelary figure that compromises our notion of an infinitely self-reliant hero. The American tales—perhaps like American culture in general—foreground the individual, but not without offering him a social order that ensures his success.

One question remains unanswered. Do these "American" changes reflect a national aesthetic, or do they represent only the regional aesthetic of Appalachia, which—although it holds a very special place in America's mythology about its past—differs greatly from the rest of the country in demography, economy, religion, and other matters?

The first American trait is the lack of magic under Jack's control. If we interpret this trait as reflecting Americans' faith in their ability to control their destinies, the Jack Tales are both regional and national, for the conviction that life holds limitless possibility seems to play a part in both national and regional value systems.

The second trait, trust in authority, belongs to the national aesthetic but has not always expressed itself in the same fashion in Appalachia. Particularly in coal mining areas, where corporate power and local values have clashed head-on, certain kinds of authority have long been challenged among the folk that told Jack Tales. Is Jack's trust in the farmers and landowners who put him to work a value that has been imposed on the region hegemonically, or is it a regional value as well?

In *Albion's Seed: Four British Folkways in America* (1989), David H. Fischer suggests an answer. He shows that the backcountry immigration that settled the Appalachians and the Blue Ridge came predominantly from the borders of northern Britain. Whether English, Scottish, or Scots-Irish, the immigrants were transplanted members of feuding clan societies that harbored great distrust of external authority but extraordinary trust in local authority. Appalachian Jack may assault the alien giant, but he will trust and serve the local landowner for whom he works. Regional ethics require such loyalty. Fischer points out that Andrew Jackson, the first president elected from the backcountry, modeled his politics after those of Scottish clan chieftains. For Jackson and his followers, freedom was incomprehensible without a complementary and absolute loyalty to one's chieftain.

Fischer's explanation may appear too simple, but it goes some way to explain the tension between the region's almost anarchic, freedom-loving democracy and its half-blind trust in authority. Such a tension, then, though differently derived, seems to be part of both the regional culture of the Appalachians and the broader national culture of America. When extended by a taleteller in North Carolina, Jack's trust is part of a familial network of mutual obligation; when imparted at a festival in California, that trust serves a more abstract network of capitalism. The trusting nature of Jack belongs to a national profile; yet, because different narrators have arrived separately at their varied notions of trust, they are portraying more than one Jack.

Indeed, there have always been many Jacks, though Richard Chase and his more dogmatic followers on the storytelling circuits have tried to give us only one, a national personality. A risqué Jack has prospered for more than 500 years in spite of editors' attempts to clean him up. Jack the oldest son, Jack the youngest son, and Jack the only son have thrived side by side. Chase's Jack is aided by magic, while most American Jacks rely on their wits to fight the giant. In my survey of these other Jacks, born in the Old World and still enjoying their boyhood in the New, I have tried to call attention to the myriads of little traditions, gifted narrators, and special circumstances that nurtured these boys and shaped them into diverse heroes before Chase published *The Jack Tales*. As the following tales and essays attest, these little Jacks did not die, and today's scholars, listeners, and—most especially—storytellers make themselves delightfully busy freeing their Jacks from the giant shadow of one boy who has grown too big.

NOTES

1. AT numbers refer to items in *The Types of the Folktale,* an index of fundamental folktale plots developed by Antti Aarne and expanded by Stith Thompson.

2. In *The Oxford Dictionary of Nursery Rhymes* (Opie and Opie 1951) Jack occurs as a principal name 16 times. The only other male names occurring more than 5 times are Tom (12), Robin (8), and John (8).

3. One tale clearly based on the British chapbook and storybook tradition is "Jack the Giant Killer" as given in Roberts 1969, 75. Stanley Hicks and Frank Proffitt, Jr., are among the narrators who feel that their tale traditions go back to England (see Oxford 1987, 75–76).

4. I first made the point of the great and little traditions in a paper presented at the 1989 congress of the International Society for Folk Narrative Research, Budapest. There it was brought to my attention that Gerald Thomas (1983) has made a similar point, likewise citing two narrative traditions.

5. Ashley's "Billy Peg" (AT 411A/530) is printed in Glassie 1964, 97–102; the recording is found in the Archives of Traditional Music, Indiana University, Bloomington.

6. In fact, four of the narrators in this volume, Maud Long, Marshall Ward, Leonard Roberts, and Bonelyn Kyofski, were teachers at some point in their lives, and Hicks, Davis, and Proffitt have also told stories to students in schools.

7. See the collections of Glassie, Perdue, Roberts, Randolph, and Carter listed in the references.

8. In at least half of Chase's eighteen tales 1) Jack's parents are not prominent, 2) the action begins away from Jack's home, and 3) Jack does not marry. These percentages are uncharacteristic of English tales. Compare the cognate tales in an English collection: Jacobs 1890, 59–68, 102–16, 159–61, 215–19.

9. At the time Chase and Hoffman were promoting the idea of a unique American hero, Richard M. Dorson, the preeminent American folklore scholar, was likewise stressing the uniqueness of American lore (Dorson 1959, 197–242; 1972, 45–53). Dorson's "hemispheric theory" was born in the same era and from the same impulse as the ideal of an isolated individualist hero.

10. Magic helpers appear in five of the stories in this book, all of them somewhat rare and included for that very reason. Three of the five are Appalachian, and in one, "Raglif Jaglif Tetartlif Pole," Jack succeeds by turning

the magic of the magician against him or by stealing a magic resource (the horse) from him. The heroine, however, needs magic to win Jack back when he magically forgets her.

11. The ten variants are listed at K. Briggs 1970, 1:59; the five cited here are 2:170; 2:253; 2:393; 2:408; 2:413.

12. The six variants are found in R. Chase 1943, 114–26, 195–97; McGowan 1978, 75–78; Perdue 1987, 76–79; Roberts 1969, no. 39; Roberts 1974, no. 113.

NOTE ON
THE TEXTS

▼ ▼ ▼ ▼ ▼

TRANSCRIBING
JACK TALES IN
PERFORMANCE

▼ ▼ ▼ ▼ ▼

Bill Ellis and
William Bernard
McCarthy

The early collections by Charles Perrault (1697) and the Brothers Grimm (1812–15) made no effort to present folktales exactly as they were told but revised them to make them attractive to audiences used to literary forms. As Jacob Grimm commented, "In order to get to the yolk of an egg, you have to break the shell, but if you do it with care, the yolk will remain intact" (Ward 1981, 2:375). Later collectors tried to be more faithful to the oral traditions they documented, but frequently they fell afoul of Grimm's paradox.

Alan Dundes (1980, 20–32) suggests that oral traditions actually have three dimensions: the text, or literal content; the texture, or style of performance; and the context, especially the significance of the tradition. Rephrasing Grimm's analogy in Dundes's terms, we might say he felt one had to falsify the literal text (break the egg) in order to construct a literary version that "feels like" the texture of the original or suggests the lost context (preserves the yolk). Alternatively, one can preserve the literal text (keep the eggshells) and lose the social context (throw away the yolk) that gives the tales flavor. Both options risk falsifying the tales. The literary version may replace a talented narrator's oral aesthetics with the romantic, idealized aesthetic of popular literature. The more foreign this aesthetic to the subculture documented, the more likely this process will replace the actual texture of the tales with one based on racial and social stereotypes. However loving the "translation" is, the result distorts the tradition. But even a "literal" version, though it preserve the words made by the narrator on a given occasion, may in fact be a mere abstract of the text. Without some effort to represent the performance's texture or explain its context, the reader will have no clue as to dynamics, import, or impact. Ironically, the result may again lead readers to dismiss poorly transcribed tales as unartistic and childish.

In this volume we adopt a third strategy: refusing to break the egg. That is, we argue that the text, texture, and context of the performance compose a living entity—a fertile egg. We can preserve all three, and in the process of preserving them gain a fuller understanding of the social processes that create and guide the folktale.

This approach still begins with a text. To be sure, it has always been a difficult battle to record the exact text of a given teller. The stop-and-start process of dictation has often inhibited tellers, and in any case transcription as prose effaces many performance details clearly audible to an audience in the subculture. Collectors familiar with a subculture, such as Vance Randolph, could use memory as their primary means of recording: they would hear a tale, then write it down at their earliest convenience, trying to retain the details of the original. But such a text, however close to the mark the collector feels it comes, replaces the aesthetics of the storyteller with those of the collector. When memorial transcription is done with care, we can sometimes infer the dynamics of the original; but the danger is always that the collector might use informants' materials for artistic creations of his own, as did Frank Cushing with the Zuni narratives he reshaped according to nineteenth-century literary expectations (see Tedlock 1972b, 115–18).

Early forms of mechanical recording, such as the aluminum disk cutters used by the Library of Congress during the 1930s and 1940s, made the exact words and dynamics available to collectors. At first, though, these obtrusive devices turned informal contexts into charged recording sessions. Miniature cassette recorders have, in recent years, minimized intrusion and made accurate texts theoretically available. But the difficulty remains: how do we use recorded versions of oral tales to make texts that accurately represent texture and context?

Because this problem was first engaged with Native American material, subsequent work has dealt with this dilemma in non-Western cultures. To counter the inevitable loss of meaning in transcribing and translating Native American narratives, ethnographers like Dell Hymes (1981) and Dennis Tedlock (1972b; 1983) agree that we must consider oral narratives as essentially dramatic in nature. Erving Goffman (1974) has likewise argued that narratives in natural context are best described not as stories but as drama: performers do not simply relate narratives, they enact them. In his words, "We spend most of our time not engaged in giving information but in giving shows" (Goffman 1974, 508). Hymes and Tedlock come to different conclusions about how to "realize" oral narrative in print: Hymes, often dealing with transcriptions made decades ago, uses verbal cues, such as initial particles and syntactic relationships, to reconstruct poetic "stanzas" that in turn give form to the performance. Tedlock, using field audio and video recordings, takes pauses and audible intonations as a pragmatic basis for line breaks and other orthographic devices. Both techniques have their advantages, but Tedlock's method, being more immediately adaptable to differing linguistic traditions, has proved the more influential.

Since Tedlock's collection of Zuni narratives (*Finding the Center*, 1972a) appeared, several folklorists have applied and extended his methodology. Barre Toelken, drawing on earlier work (Toelken 1969), produced a detailed transcription and analysis of a Navaho coyote tale (Toelken 1979, 93–103). John H. McDowell observed how differently the same informant could tell the same narrative when asked to simulate an actual performance (McDowell 1974). Charles L. Briggs (1988, 1990) produced detailed performance-oriented texts of Hispanic narratives from New Mexico. In addition, Richard Bauman has produced in *Verbal Art as Performance* (1984 [1977]) a clear statement of the implications of a performance-centered approach to oral narrative. Indeed, some form of the performance-based transcription is now standard, particularly among Native American ethnographers, as it is obvious that many myths and tales cannot be comprehended by outsiders without re-creating their dynamics and context.

Yet, in collections of Anglo-American tales, old-fashioned methods have remained the norm. With the Jack Tales, in particular, we remain caught in Grimm's dilemma: we may choose anthologies of "folksy" recreations, or authentic but dry verbatim texts. We need to apply performance-based transcription to English-language materials. Herbert Halpert and J. D. A. Widdowson (1986) have summed up the failures of previous transcribers and the challenges faced in preparing to publish Newfoundland tales. In particular, they decry the unexamined way in which collectors silently edit their texts, removing performance details that they presume to be secondary to the text. But we omit those details at the cost of preserving only a fraction of what our informants' voices are saying.

How, then, do we get the texture right? Henry Glassie (1982) has experimented with Tedlock's methods in transcribing Irish historical narratives. Elizabeth Fine (1984) has constructed a detailed model for transcribing oral narrative, using a variety of devices to denote pitch, falsetto, rasp, and sustain as well as posture and hand motions.

Fine's work stresses that even the most uncomplicated transcription is in fact a translation of a text from one medium of communication into another. While some details inevitably disappear in the transfer from oral intonation to cold type, however, other clever details of performance may not stand out until the transcriber has to deal with rendering them in print. Hence the act of reproducing a text's texture may lead to a deeper, more exact understanding of performance aesthetics.

An example from the present study will make the last point clear. Careful attention to line pause revealed that the basic rhythms of the storytellers in this volume varied considerably. The line lengths of Donald Davis and Maud Long, for example, maintained remarkable consistency from beginning to end of their respective stories, supported the syntactic and grammatical structures of their sentences, and compared favorably with each other. But the line lengths of Ray Hicks and Frank Proffitt often worked in counterpoint to the grammatical structure and varied tremendously over the course of their stories, from but a word or two to great long leaps of sound. Varied though these line structures were, they could be identified in the speech of the first six storytellers, all of whom grew up listening to southern Appalachian storytelling. All six were speaking in a kind of free verse—in the case of Hicks and Proffitt that verse even being emphasized by an intonation toward the end of each line. When we tried a similar analysis of the discourse of the remaining two storytellers, however, we found it did not work. They were speaking true prose, the units of utterance corresponding exactly with the syntactic and grammatical units. Because the pauses served only grammatical or rhetorical purposes, it made no sense to try to break their discourse into lines. In fact, such a presentation obscured rather than clarified the story. This discovery came as a complete surprise. We did not think we would discover two such distinct mediums for storytelling. The first six storytellers gave us incantation; the last two, oratory. Probably the last two spoke true prose because in their formative years they heard prose exclusively in all public discourse, including radio and television, classroom teaching, and pulpit oratory, and had little or no exposure to rhythmic incantation.

More importantly, Fine has stressed that even the most detailed transcription cannot make the text "speak for itself." The reader must learn something about the normal performing situation and the larger significance of motifs and allusions. For this reason, she argues that a "record" of the tale's text and texture must be accompanied by a "report" incorporating information about the performer and his or her subculture. A purely text-centered approach to narratives, however detailed, is incomplete. We cannot assume that texts, tale types, motifs, and such are irrelevant because each performance is totally unique (see Georges 1969; Jones 1979). As Lee Haring (1972) has argued with respect to African material, however, tales cannot be understood purely in terms of historical-geographical norms either. The circumstances of telling—and especially of collecting—deeply influence what text and texture emerge. In fact, as Haring, Tedlock (1983, 287), and Toelken (1979, 100) observe, the tale can even become a comment on the ethnographer, who is always part of the performance context.

In brief, folklorists and ethnographers dealing with foreign cultures have struggled to capture the words, style, and social setting of the tales they collect. With few exceptions, however, these methodological advances remain untested on English-language material. As a result, we have many Jack Tale texts but know little about their textures or contexts. We keep trying to make omelets out of eggshells.

Jack Tales have been performed in the Appalachians for over 200 years (Kercheval 1902, 285–86; Perdue 1987, 97). Their British analogs were anthologized by pioneering folklorists such as Joseph Jacobs, S. O. Addy, and Andrew Lang. But these British folklorists, like their Continental predecessors, collated and normalized texts to make them more easily readable as "fairy tales" in the Grimm tradition. American folklorists, starting with W. W. Newell (1888), recognized the value of these tales and were more cautious about presenting "authentic" texts. In line with the early historical-geographical emphasis, however, they were content with publishing bare texts with little in the way of cultural or biographical information.

Isabel Gordon Carter's (1925) important collection of Jack Tales from Jane Gentry first called attention to the Hicks-Harmon (Beech Mountain) tradition. These texts are sketchy and probably reflect the stop-and-go dynamics of dictation, but Carter was careful to reflect Gentry's changing use of dialect pronunciation and also recorded many of her asides commenting on the tale. Despite the lack of more than a few sentences of context, these transcriptions were, for more than half a century, the best available documentation of southern mountain Jack Tale texture.

Revivalist and popular author Richard Chase soon came to the Beech Mountain area, and his work made these tales known nationally. But Chase, like Jacobs and older collectors, considered it his duty to break the shells of the "raw" tradition and scramble the yolks more aesthetically for a broad popular audience. As Charles Perdue has discovered, his method of collecting was to listen to several different versions, then practice telling the tale himself, adding elements and subtracting them according to his own sense of "folksiness" (Perdue 1987, 113). Examination of the records from which Chase worked shows that he bowdlerized sexual and scatological details and collated versions to such an extent that tales such as "Jack and the Bull" (R. Chase 1943, 21–30) are practically his own invention. Nevertheless, Chase's work has dominated the field.

Other Jack Tales appear in Leonard Roberts's three folktale collections from Kentucky (1955; 1969; 1974). John Burrison's *Storytellers* (1989) includes some tales from northern Georgia. But these "prose" collections include no descriptions of performance, and neither do Perdue's (1987) rediscovered WPA texts from Wise County, Virginia. A fresh presentation of Jack Tales is therefore overdue.

In this volume, the contributors present several English-language narratives as text, texture, and context. We try not to break the eggs but preserve them as living entities nestled within specific social settings. As Fine has suggested, we approach the Jack Tales through a detailed record of the text and texture in performance and through a report, in the form of an accompanying essay, on the culture from which the text emerged.

To convey the texture, we employ many of the devices suggested by Tedlock to represent performance details. Our texts are accurate in recording the exact words of the speakers: all have been checked by at least two transcribers, and in some cases by three. We have listened to each tape, at a conservative estimate, twenty to thirty times, and to difficult places on the tapes many more times than that. Beyond the basic conventions of written English (periods, question marks, capital letters, and so forth) we have restricted orthographic markings to empirically determinable elements. Pauses in the first six stories are marked by line breaks, making the texts closer to free verse than prose and also approximating the pace or speed of the performance. Most other orthographic devices are familiar from their literary use:

increase in volume: capital letters ("a BIG day");

drawing out a word: adding hyphens ("a b-i-g day");

drawing out a phrase: adding dashes ("back—and—forth");

running words together: joining them with hyphens ("what-are-you-doing-there?");

word stress: italics (used sparingly);

interruption of thought, or self correction: a dash;

words added by editor for clarification: brackets ([Jack] said);

editorial descriptions of vocal quality or physical action: brackets and italics;

words of audience: brackets and indication of speaker ([*Children:* Yeah]);

a sound unit longer than a line of type: indentation of the next line;

change of speakers within a sound line: dropping down a line and indenting to the break (standard poetic convention);

editorial comment on the part of the storyteller: parentheses and indentation of the comment;

a run: indentation of the entire run;

audience laughter: exclamation points inside brackets; the number of exclamation points varies with the degree and length of the response, though we have not felt it necessary to indicate every chuckle or guffaw ([!!!!]).

Dialectical spellings are used only sparingly to indicate the slurs or dropped sounds common to oral discourse. Thus, *and* is usually to be understood as pronounced *'n*, *-ing* as *-in'*, *of* as *o'* (or, rarely, *'f*), *wasn't* as *wadn't*, and *them* as *'em*, the dialectical spellings being reserved for places where a reminder seemed helpful. "Eye spelling" such as *wuz* for *was* is avoided altogether as demeaning to the performers.

Elizabeth Fine proposes a script that will enable the reader to re-create vocally and physically the original performance with its changes of pace, inflection, and vocal quality and its iconic movements, postures, and gestures. Such a transcription is performance oriented because it captures the text and texture of a performance and because it demands that the reader re-perform the story, assuming the original performer's posture, speaking the words out loud, and accompanying them with the appropriate actions. We, like Tedlock, have settled for texts suitable for silent as well as audible reading, but readers should not stop there. Both tellers and collectors hope these tales will be read aloud and retold, in private and in public. We have tried not to multiply orthographic devices to record every audible intonation, while still meeting our responsibility to discern and record the essential texture. In short, we have tried to make the tale both easy to read and immediately comprehensible as drama.

In the reports, we relate the tales to their historical backgrounds, but not merely as rare butterflies are pinned and classified. In varying ways, we consider how the tales are the performers' artistic creations. We describe how the texts incorporate details and emphases from family or community history. We describe how the individuals' artistic choices interact with the broader tradition of Anglo-American taletelling. Finally, we relate significant features in the text and texture to circumstances surrounding the actual performances.

The performance-based texts can be read independently of the contextual essays (and vice versa). Performance and context coexist, however, so texts and essays together describe these narratives as living things. Together they introduce readers to the Jack who is part of each storyteller who brings him to life, and part as well of Everyman, Everywoman, and Everychild.

*Ray Hicks (right) and Frank Proffitt, Jr., at home on Beech Mountain
(photograph courtesy of Frank Proffitt, Jr.).*

(Above) Marshall Ward in action (photograph by Thomas McGowan); (left) Maud Gentry Long (photograph courtesy of Jane Douglas).

Opposite page: (Top left) Leonard Roberts (photograph courtesy of Edith Roberts); (top right) Donald Davis publicity shot (photograph © by Donald Davis); (bottom) Bonelyn Lugg Kyofsky demonstrating how it hurts to have an ear cut off (photograph by Kenneth Thigpen).

*Stewart Cameron performing at a festival
(photograph courtesy of Dianne Cameron).*

I

▼ ▼ ▼ ▼ ▼

THE HICKS-
HARMON
(BEECH
MOUNTAIN)
JACK TALE
TRADITION

CHAPTER 1

JACK IN THE RAW

▼ ▼ ▼ ▼ ▼

RAY HICKS

▼ ▼ ▼ ▼ ▼

Joseph Daniel Sobol

Though he rarely leaves his home on top of Beech Mountain in western North Carolina, Ray Hicks is surely among the most influential storytellers in North America. His art is a window into a realm of knowing far older than books or writing. Aspiring tellers, scholars, and enthusiasts from all over the English-speaking world have made the pilgrimage up the rocky road to Ray's house, their ears popping and their cars' suspensions rattling, to bask for a while in the light of that older world. To illuminate the nature of Jack Tales in performance, it may be helpful to share some images from a few of those journeys.

I first visited Beech Mountain in the fall of 1984. As a volunteer for the National Storytelling Festival, in nearby Jonesborough, Tennessee, I was the driver designated to take Ray and his wife, Rosa, back and forth across the mountains. Ray has been invited to tell at Jonesborough every year since the festival's inception in 1973, the only storyteller to be so featured. His Saturday appearances, a Jonesborough trademark, make up a significant part of that event's claim to preeminence in the storytelling revival.

When I arrived at Ray's house that Saturday morning, I found him sitting on a bed in the parlor, rolling himself a cigarette out of a Prince Albert tin, and telling stories to his nephew, Frank Proffitt, Jr. Ray barely interrupted himself when I knocked. He just hollered, "Come in," allowed me to introduce myself and state my purpose, nodded to include me in the gathering, and went on with his story.

Till then I had been conditioned to recognize storytellers as stage magicians of the imagination, dressed in motley costumes and juggling more or less memorized routines with which they mesmerized large groups of strangers. My first conscious shock that morning, which sprang from the sensory shock of the old plank floors buffed only by sixty-five years of all-weather scuffing, of the woodstove with its tin pipe bristling with lidless tin cans ("to spread the heat around," explained Ray; "some feller said I ought to patent that"), and of the wild and domestic smells that impregnated the house—cornbread and lard, hand-rolled tobacco, and drying "yarbs"—was the recognition that the overalls Ray was wearing were exactly like those I'd seen in photos of him performing at Jonesborough. But this was no costume. It was Ray.

The shock that followed, for me that morning, was the visceral realization that this milieu—Ray's parlor with his wife and his nephew and whosoever happened by—was the real source and home place of Ray's art. The stage at Jonesborough was for him, at best, a translation, an explosion of the natural intimacy and at-homeness of his stories into a gigantic artificial frame, which was only borne and transcended year after year through a leap of faith and love on Ray's part and on the part of his audience.[1]

The Hicks house is a traditional two-story frame farmhouse, one room deep with a kitchen ell in back. It was built by Ray's father in 1919. Ray was born in it three years later. He absorbed his stories in that house, or in others like it, not as performance events separated from the daily rhythms of life but as part of the imaginative ecology of his elders' world. Thus Ray Hicks's relationship to Jack is much more intimate than that between a reader and a character in a written story. The oral tales speak to Ray in the voices of his grandfather and grandmother and of their grandfathers and grandmothers stretching back as far as their packed genealogies will take him. But at the end of the chain of oral transmission, all the voices fold back into his own.

Thus the stories grow out of an active, functioning communal and personal mythos. Ray's mythos is not so much a matter of belief, in the intellectual sense, as it is a thorough assimilation of the ethical, spiritual, and creative resources of the tales into the fabric of his identity. The sense of being filled and empowered by the example of Jack is naturally amplified by the experience of transmitting—by the power to embody the stories. Ray has expressed it this way:

> That's the way it was when I growed up. . . . When you git like I tell it, *I'm* Jack. Everybody can be Jack. Jack ain't dead. He's a-livin. Jack can be anybody. . . . Like I tell 'em sometimes, I'm Jack. I've been Jack. I mean in different ways. Now I ain't everything Jack has done in the tales, but still I've been Jack in a lot of ways. It takes Jack to live. Now I wouldn't have been livin, probably, if I'd not been Jack's friend. (McDermitt 1983, 9)

The following June I went back to visit the Hickses. This time I brought a friend, Kathleen Zundell, a professional storyteller, who had grown up in Los Angeles and still lives there. We arrived in the late afternoon. Ray was in the parlor again, talking with a neighbor, a distant cousin (as are most of his neighbors) about ten years younger than Ray. After greetings and introductions, I went back into the kitchen to visit with Rosa. She was sorting through a bowl of wild strawberries, the first of the season—tiny scarlet droplets that made painfully brief bursts of tartness on the tongue—and lining up provender for the final rush to supper. Kathleen stayed in the parlor, a baptism by immersion.

After a while I went to check on her. She was sitting with her mouth open, in a kind of dazed rapture. Ray was telling about the days when there were no fences on Beech Mountain and stock grazed free. People had been known to shoot each other's cattle, or each other, over the damage. He told about the early Primitive Baptist churches, one in particular that he helped to build, where an important part of the building's design was "the Devil's Corner." That was an area in the back of the church where no lantern shone, where the unregenerate could come just to hear the preaching without ever stepping forward into the light of judgment. "Hadn't been for that corner, that church would've been empty," Ray said. Then he drifted onto the subject of Jack, as if talking about a neighbor or an old friend, and told the story of Jack and the animal bride, which he calls "Cat and Mouse."

Kathleen told me later that she barely understood a word of Ray's dialect in that first hour, but she was drinking in the atmosphere through every pore. Meanwhile, Rosa went into overdrive back in the kitchen, and soon there were plates and bowls of cornbread and vegetables all over the table, along with slices of the ham we'd brought, and strong coffee that Ray poured over his cornbread and ate as mush. He kept talking all through supper, and Kathleen said that somewhere between the collards and greenbeans and the cornbread and coffee and wild strawberries, something fused in her cerebral cortex and she suddenly understood him fluently.

It was during supper that Ray began talking about the Jack Tale that Richard Chase had written down in the 1940s from Ray's family tradition and had called "Hardy Hardhead."

"That's not the way they told it," Ray asserted. "He took out the rough parts, to put it in the book. 'Hardy Hard-Ass' is how they told it when I was a kid."

He seemed to be testing the waters, fishing for signs of interest and of openness to the rough parts, and we, of course, chased at the bait. Like any folklorist, I am fascinated by the process of change in traditional story performance; Kathleen was fascinated by everything. So, supper over, we went back to the parlor, I turned the tape recorder on, and Ray began.

"This hyer Hardy Hardhead—," he started.

I broke in: "Um, Ray—what were you saying before about . . . ?"

He immediately corrected himself: "Hardy Hard-Ass. This hyer Hardy Hard-Ass—this's the name of it, Hardy Hard-Ass." With the magical third repetition of "Hardy Hard-Ass," Kathleen came apart altogether, and so did I. Rosa and the neighbor joined in the uncontrollable laughter, and Ray himself, while orchestrating the laughter and never missing a beat of his tale, nearly turned himself inside out with grinning.

It must be emphasized that the text as printed here is, at best, a translation, far more problematic than the translation from the parlor to the Jonesborough stage. The typographic version is an entire change of medium, and change of medium, as McLuhan points out, inverts the order of the senses. Through the silently gliding eye, the reader can have only an oblique relationship with the sensory experience of being told, or telling, a traditional tale. The story is meant to live on the breath, in the interiority of sound, and in the warmth of the group imagination. The poetic rendering here, representing the rhythms of the performance as recaptured from the tape, is our attempt to render the problem visible, perhaps, more than to solve it. So, too, are the battalions of exclamation points marching across the page to represent our laughter, for laughter was one of the essential organizing principles of this performance. But ah! If only you could have heard it!

Ray has been telling the "cleaned-up" version, "Hardy Hardhead," for many years at festivals and at local schools, as well as for folklorists who lacked the Jacklike luck to catch him in just the right mood. But the "original" has always been alive inside him, and like any living folklore, it craves release. The key and tempo of this particular performance were set by that release. The telling modulated effortlessly between rollicking obscenities and comic-strip violence, at one pole of expression, and magical hush at the other. Far from obscuring the mythic themes of the tale, however, the obscenity and violence actually seemed, by intensified contrast, to heighten their power and mystery. The actions in this version are all more vivid than we have seen before in print, either in Richard Chase (1943, 96–105) or Carter (1925, 346–49). Will and Tom's transgressions are more crass, their punishments more brutal; Jack's spiritual receptivity is more emphatic, and his magical rewards more explicitly sublime.

Due to the prudery of early collectors, publishers, and readers, we are only recently admitting the erotic and scatological sides of Jack's folkloric nature into our image of him. These are the elements that comprise the tales that scholars genteelly label fabliaux, after a racy style of thirteenth- and fourteenth-century French comic verse based largely on oral traditional motifs (Sobol 1987, 85–89). Chaucer, Boccaccio, and La Fontaine drew on the same traditional story stock as the fabliau poets, and a significant number of these floating tales and jests made the crossing to America and emerged as naturalized Appalachian folktales. The title character of the fabliau "Le Moine Segretain" ("The Sacristan Monk," Brians 1972, 108) is none other than the ineluctable preacher of "Old Dry Frye" (R. Chase 1948, 100). The stories Richard Chase recorded in *American Folk Tales and Songs* (1956) as "The Man in the Kraut Tub" and "Pack Down the Big Chest" are fabliaux. Still other fabliaux turn up directly as Jack Tales in the repertoire of Donald Davis, who grew up about seventy miles down the Blue Ridge from Ray. The story of the thieving miller and his wife, for example, is the fabliau "Le Meunier et Les Deux Clers" ("The Miller and the Two Clerks," Hellman and O'Gorman 1965, 51; it is also "The Reeve's Tale" from Chaucer's *Canterbury Tales*). In Donald's Jack Tale version the clerics' roles are split between Jack, as the trickster, and the brothers Will and Tom, as the dupes. Ray Hicks has told me a local Beech Mountain courting joke, of which I later discovered a thirteenth-century fabliau variant ("Berangier of the Long Ass," Duval and Eichman 1982, 47).

There are episodes of latent erotic content, sublimated fabliaux in fact, in several published trickster Jack Tales. In "Jack and the Heifer Hide" (a version is included in this volume), the adulterous lover is trapped in the hope chest. In the "Master Thief" cycle ("Jack and the Doctor's Girl" in R. Chase 1943; "Jack and the Old Rich Man" in this volume), Jack has to steal the "shimmy" off a man's wife while she is in bed. In "Big Jack and Little Jack," Jack tells the rich farmer's wife that her husband has ordered her to "kiss" him while her husband hangs in the apple tree. In the magic tale that Chase calls "Fill, Bowl, Fill," (R. Chase 1943, 89–95), when the king orders Jack to "sing this bowl full of lies for me," Jack's song consists of sexual bragging on himself and the king's wife and daughters.

We can assume that all these motifs might have been expressed more explicitly than they were in earlier printed versions, had the context been congenial. Vance Randolph's Ozark versions of "Fill, Bowl, Fill" (Randolph 1976, 47–50; Randolph 1952, 17–19, 185–87) provide perfect illustrations. Randolph's storyteller, he says, had one version of the story for mixed audiences and another version for men only. Here is the mixed audience version of the bragging song:

> Oh the oldest daughter she came out
> All to buy my drill.
> I fooled around her, kissed her well.
> Fill, bowl, fill.

Then the "men only" version, from *Pissing in the Snow and Other Ozark Folktales*:

> The next to come was the king's own daughter,
> To steal away my skill.
> I laid her down and honed her off.
> Fill, bowl, fill.

Ray was emphatic in answering the question of which "Hardy" was the original: the "Hard-Ass." In the absolute sense, perhaps, there never is an original form of a folktale any more than there is a final form, outside the whited sepulcher of print. Nor is there any one set of meanings or morals to be drawn from a tale. Meanings and morals, like levels of language, violence, sexuality, and spirituality, and like the structural elements of length and density of motifs, are modulated by master tellers in the spontaneous play of performance. Evidence is pretty clear, however, that sexual and scatological mischief has always been a part of the trickster's repertoire and thus a part of the character complex we know as Jack. In this respect, Jack Tales have a strong affinity with the Native-American Coyote tales, in which the sacred and profane are also inseparably bound. Jack, like Coyote, plays the fool in some tales, the trickster in others, and in still others the hero-savior. In "Hardy Hard-Ass" the functions are split: Jack gets to play the initiate, and Will and Tom are left (literally) to play the butts.

Within a traditional storytelling event, each person present would hear what they were willing or able to hear. If the children did not understand a certain reference, that was fine: there was plenty of action elsewhere to keep them busy. If certain strands of the story had outworn their magic for other listeners, they might discover new threads and follow the journey afresh. In a setting in which culture depends more on the inclusiveness of orality than on the discriminations of literacy—in which Jack can go from fool to trickster to saint in the course of one all-embracing journey—instruction and entertainment, child and adult, and sacred and profane can all coexist without shame, conflict, or constraint, within the magical time-space of the wonder tale.

NOTE

1. For the effect of festival audiences, especially at Jonesborough, on another storyteller, see Mullen 1981.

HARDY HARD-ASS

as told by Ray Hicks

Ray Hicks told this version of "The Land and Water Ship" (AT 513B) at his home on Beech Mountain, North Carolina, on 16 June 1985. It was recorded by Joseph Daniel Sobol. Also present at the telling were Ray's wife, Rosa; Kathleen Zundell, a storyteller friend of the collector, from Los Angeles, California; and another man in his fifties, a neighbor of the Hickses. The version of this story in Richard Chase's The Jack Tales (1943) is titled "Hardy Hard-Head," and it is in reference to that kind of bowdlerizing that Hicks, at the beginning, makes such a point about the "true" name of the story. The telling is punctuated by much helpless laughter from Hicks himself and from all four listeners, particularly from Kathleen and the collector.

Hicks often runs phrases or sentences together without a pause and, conversely, pauses in mid-sentence. To represent accurately in transcription this characteristic of his style, the line breaks, as nearly as possible, correspond only to pauses, and not to breaks in the sense. Almost every line has one word that is emphasized with strong pitch modulation. A representative sampling of these words has been indicated with italics, but too many italics seemed to detract from the clarity of the transcription. To capture Hicks's characteristic pronunciations it seemed advisable to use a number of specialized spellings. The word Gawd—*pronounced like* God *drawn out—is almost always said very softly, as if in amazement and wonder. Indeed, characteristic of Hicks's style is a soft tone of breathless awe as he narrates—as if for the first time—the more wondrous parts of his story.*

▼ ▼ ▼

Hardy Hard-Ass.
This h'yer Hardy Hard-Ass—
(This's the name of it, Hardy Hard-*Ass*.) [!!!!!]
An' this h'yer witch—[!!!!!]
This h'yer—
(Hardy Hard-*Ass* is the name of it. [!!!!!]

Not Hardy Hard-*head*, the way *they* told it.
It's Hardy Hard-*Ass*, is the name of it.
An' I've heared 'em an' laughed, when I 'as a kid—
Gawd, you talk about gettin' a kid. [!!]
An' then they'd cuss in it.
Gawd. [!!!]
Cuss along in it, with the cuss words.
An' them old men in beard—
an' boy that made a young'un—I'd crawl on my breast
an' didn't know night was a-passin'.
Heck, I coulda—
Hell, I coulda stayed all night
with it, then.
I'd crawl up on my Grandfather's lap,
an' watch his lips work,
through the beard.)

An'—
an' so, uh,
uh,
this h'yer witch
had a,
a 'chant-ment on a beautiful girl,
an' she couldn't be got out of it till somebody broke 'at.
An' so *all* the other boys,
of the other neighbors
in the country,
went,
each, one at a time.
An',
an' got killed
on the *hackerd* [hackle].
She put out a hackerd.
    (That's a *hackerd*, is a thing that they used back at that time,
    that had steel points in it,
    sharp as a needle;
    an' *steel* points
    an' was in it, that they used, uh,

to lint out lint—*flax* with,
you see.
Comb through.
   [*Inaudible comment from Kathleen.*]
Ye-ah.
What they called a hackerd was a brush,
thing about that big around, had a handle on it, where it was in
   wood,
   see . . . ?)
An' she'd lay that up, at the stump
an' say, uh, bet with 'em,
an' say, "One-two-three-go."
An' that witch'd get up on that stump,
an' say [*high pitched here and throughout story*],
   "TOORALOODLOODLOODLOO!"
an' she'd give about a six, eight somerset an' hit her ass down on that
   hackerd, [!!!]
an' never even knocked a hair out of it. Said,
   "WOODLOODLOODLEE!
Good as it ever was!" [!!!!!]

An' so this boy got up an' he sunk his ass down on it, he just tore it
   all to pieces.
Gawd.
An' he drug off in the woods an' died.
His whole ass was tore out. [!!!!!!!!!!!!!!!]

An' so—[!!!!!]
so the other'ns went an' they all of 'em the same thing, an' got killed,
their asses tore out, an' they was asses all through the woods. [!!!!!!!!]
Gawd sakes. Panthers a-eatin' 'em. [!!!!!]
Blood strowed where they'd bled—their asses bled out all through
   where they'd crawled. [!!!!!!!]

So it wound up,
Will an' Tom an' Jack
was three brothers.
An' Will kept *beggin'*.

He said, "Mama,
let me go!"

     She said, "Son,
you know how that tears peoples' asses out!" [!!!!!!!!!]
[!!!!!!!!!!!!!!!!]
Said, said, "You won't make it."
Said, "You hain't tough enough!" [!!!!]
Said, "It's gonna take a tough—" [!!!]
Said, "It's gonna take a tough asshole to stand that!" [!!!!!!!!!!!!!!!!]

     (That's the way they told it, then!) [!!!!!!!!!!!!!]

So,
so Will, to make it hard on him, she said, "Son,
you go to that branch,
an' take this meal-sifter
an' carry enough water to bake two pones o' bread."
Thought it'd bluff him.

Will got there,
an' this little bird come over, tryin' to tell him, an' he's a-runnin'
    with drops in it, tryin' to run an' shake it out in a bottle.
An' the bird'd say each time [*high-pitched voice*], "Spread-it-w'-moss
an'-daub-it-w'-mud, an'-it'll-hold-water!"

               He said, "You little devil,
    you get your ass away from h'yer." Said, "You've aggra-*va*-tin'
    me." Said, "I'll have to *do* somethin' to git this water."
So he finally got enough dripped out an' baked two pones.
Took off to go to the witch's palace.

An' he walked,
an' come to a,
a oak tree.
An' there sit a,
a long-gray-bearded man
with a hat on,

an' he said,
"Young man, would you give me somethin' to eat?"

He says, "I hain't got enough for myself, let alone givin' it to a thing
like you!" [!!!]
[*As usual, very soft:*] Gawd.

So he went on. The witch—
he hollered an' the witch come out.
Said, "I'm come h'yer
to break a 'chant-ment
if I can, to git that daughter out of it,
an' git her, maybe."

Old witch brought out the hackerd,
an' betted him fifteen guineas apiece,
that she'd beat him, an'
she got up there, "TOODLOODLOODLOODLOO-DOO-
DOO!"
An' went over, an'
hit her ass on it an' never knocked a hair out. [!!!!!!!!!!!!!!!!]

Will got up,
give us four-five-or-six somersets an' tore his ass up good!
  [!!!!!!!!!!!!!!!!!]
He drug off an' died. [!!!!!!!!!!!!!!!!!!!!!]
[!!!!!!!!!!!!!!!]

An' so . . .
Tom—
that made it real hard on him, bein' that Will's ass tore out like that.
  [!!!!!!!!!!!!!!!!!!!!!!!!]
She said, "GAWD!
Will's ass is tore out." Said, "He hain't come in. Gotta lose you, i'
faith?"

So he kept beggin'. An' she said, "You go carry enough water in that
sifter to make *three* pones o' bread."

Will, uh, Tom went.
That Robin-bird come over, an' said,
"Spread-it-w'-moss, daub-it-w'-mud, an'-it'll-hold-water."

Said, he said, "You little devil you, you little ass!" [!!!!] Said,
    "Gawd!"
Said, "You be a-flutterin' around my eye,
a-ruinin' me!"
Said, "I'm gonna have to run
till my tongue hangs out,
to get this water shook out."
He run, an' finally got it,
an' she baked three pones.
He took off—
An' sent a bottle of water—
He got a bottle of water an'
three pones of bread an' he come to that tree.
An' each one didn't know, seein' the man, y' see.

An' there he was, with the beard, an' the hat on,
an' he said, "Young man,
would you give me somethin' to eat?"

                    An' Tom said,
"The way I've carried water
to get this three pones o' bread, a thing like you hain't gonna get to
    eat none of it." [!!!]
An' he went on,
an' got to the witch's house an' told her,
an' he betted her
fifteen guineas agin' the witch's fifteen that he could
out her on the hackerd.

                    An' she brought it out
an' went "Tootootoot"
on it, an' didn't knock a hair out of her ass. [!!!!]

Tom got up an', boy, he just *ripped his*. [!!!!!!!!!!!!!!]
He hit it sideways! [!!!!!!!!!!!!!!!!!!!!!!!!!]

He hit it sideways an' tore every bit out. [!!!!!!!!!!!!!!!!!!!!!]
He drug off an' died an' never come in. [!!!!!!!!!!!!!!!!!!]

Went on a few days.
Jack, he was younger, an' he said, "Mama, [!!!!!!!!!!!]
I believe I can—"
Said, "I believe I can do the job."

She said, "Yeah, you'll just get your ass tore out an' die!"
[!!!!!!!!!!!!!!!!!!!!]

He kept beggin', an' she put it up to *five* pones.
Thought she'd bluff him with the sifter.

He went.
Carried one load.
An' that little bird was a-flutterin', sayin',
"Spread-it-w'-moss, an'-daub-it-w'-mud." An' he was interested an'
    never meant—an' never caught what it meant.
An' the second load,
it was a-flutterin' an' come right down in his face,
said, "Spread-it-w'-moss!"
A-goin', it sounded like that:
"Spread-it-w'-moss, an'-daub-it-w'-mud, an'-it'll-hold-water." An'
    Jack filled it again,
an' it came into his face.

[*Soft:*] "'That's what it's a-sayin':
'Spread it with moss an' daub it with mud.'"
An' he went out in the branch—
side o' the branch—dug him some mud.
Spread it over them sifter holes,
an' then put moss over the sifter holes,
an' then daubed it with mud,
an' went in an' was enough to—
one load, an' had water left!
Gawd.

An' she said, "Gawd, Son, you brought her in fast!"
An' he said—she said, "What caused you?"

He said, "Mama,
a little bird told me [!!]
how to do it."

Well, she filled his bottle up with water,
an' he took off,
an' come to this h'yer oak tree an' there sit that *man*,
but *he* hadn't never seed him before; none of 'em [had].
He said, "Young man, would you give me somethin' to eat,"

an' Jack said, "Yeah, bedad, you've obliged to half of it,
or if you hain't had n'ary a meal, an' me had one, you can eat it *all!*"

An' so, *you know what?*
[*Awe struck voice:*]
[When] they sit down there eatin' them pones o' bread, startin',
hit turned to a big cake!
A big cake—an' the water a-drinkin' out o' the bottle, turned to wine!
An' every time they'd drink out, it would fill back.
Gawd.
Cut a piece out o' the cake an' it'd grow back,
while they's a-eatin'.
Fill the cake back every time.
Couldn't get it dry—
couldn't get the bottle dry.
Drunk wine, it'd fill back up.

[*Resume normal voice:*]
Well, as he got full, all he could eat,
he said, "Young man,
I know where you've a-goin'."
An' said, "You're all the man 't's ever treated me right,
that's come by here."
Said, "All the others has sassed me.
Said they wasn't gonna give nothin' to eat to a thing like me."
An' he said, "Up in there is a b'ilin' spring,"
an' he hewed out a stick,
an' he said, "If you've got faith,
I can help ye."

An' he hewed the stick out,
re'ch it to Jack,
an' said, "If you can turn that spring to wine,
you've got faith."
Said, "Take this stick up there an' stir in it."

An' Jack got up there—
just him, is all he seed there—
an' he stirred an' stirred.
His arm—changed hands, his arm was a-givin' out an' he says,
    "Bedads,"
He says, "Don't seem like I've got much faith." About that time,
he thought it looked a little pink,
an' that just made it turn to wine *that quick.*

Then when it turned, there stood the man.
Said, "*Gawd Give!*
You've got faith, Son—Young man."
He said, "Now I can help ye."
An' he said, "I've got a ship h'yer, down h'yer,
a dry-land ship."
An' said, "You can carry it under your arm,
fold it up,
or you can unspread it an' hook it together an' fly,
over the tree-tops,
an' light down in the field, every time you call on it,
an' back up."
An' he said, "You pick up
every man you see from here to the witch's palace." Said, "Don't
    you miss n'ary a one, now."
Said, "You pick every man up."

An' he got on out a-walkin' with it under his arm an' unfolded it an'
    hooked her up an' called on it, "Fly, Ship, fly!"
An' it just 'gin to wave an' flutter an' up it went!
An' him a-floatin' in it all over the tree-tops.
An' he hadn't went too fur,
till he seed a man a-comin' down off a mountain an' his,
an' his *ass,* [!!]

he was a-bumpin' trees down with his *ass*,
knocking rock, an' they'd roll,
jump in a bunch o' thorns an' gougin' his ass an' it wasn't a hair
   knocked out. [!!!!!]
An'
so he got on out to where he was at an' he said,
"What's your name, sir?"

He said, "My name's Hardy Hard-Ass, sir." [!!!]

He said, "Hardy Ass—
Hardy Hard-Ass you are! Into my ship."
He lowered it to the ground. Hardy Hard-Ass got in it,
an' his ass was so tough an' big it was a-wreckin' the ship,
an' Jack had to get him to get over in the middle. [!!!]
An' his head was big as a washin' tub.
Gawd, what a man. [!!!!!!!]
An' a tree, an' a rock, nor nothin', didn't *budge* his ass. [!!!!!!!!]
Gawd, nothin' hurt his'n. [!!!!]

An' so he,
he went on,
an' wasn't long,
till he seed a man
come into a branch,
come into a branch, was thirsty,
an' he drunk that branch dry,
an' hit a creek an' nearly had hit dry 'time
Jack,
uh, hollered at him,
Jack hollered, said, "Hello there!
What's yer—"

       An' he said, "Hush-hush-hush-hush!"
Said, "I was fixin' to drink the *river* up!"

Said, "What's *your* name?"

Said, "Drink-well, sir."

Said, "Drink-well, in my ship."
So Drink-well got in, an' he floated it,
said, "Fly, Ship, fly," an' it went on up.

Went on.
An' he seed a man a-comin' out in a sheep field.
An' Gawd, he run up an' swallered a sheep whole, it wool an' all!
An' Jack says, "What's *your* name?"

                              He says, "Eat-well, sir,"
an' he had a—
an' he done got onto a cow, had a hind leg,
started down to eatin' it, [!!!!!]
'time Jack hollered.
Said, "Eat-well, sir."

Said, "Eat-well, into my ship."
An' Eat-well got in it.

An' he went on.
An' out come a man out o' the woods into a broom-sage field,
an' he's runnin' through there, an' a bunny-rabbit jumped up.
An' they said he picked that rabbit up,
an' hit a-runnin' hard as it could run,
an' [he] just hittin' one foot every now an' then.
An' picked it up in his right hand an' went on.
An' Jack hollered an' said, "What's *your* name, sir?"

He said, "Run-well."

He said, "Run-well, you must be in my ship."
An' he lowered it an' got him in it.
Riz it back up,
got on, an'
he seed a man
with oh! big years [ears],
Gawd, they's as big as saucers,
plates, his years was, an' he's a holdin' it, an'

[*hand to ear, listening*]
[Jack] said, "*Hello there*, what's yer—"

Said, "Hush-hush-hush-hush-
hush-hush-hush!" [!!!]
Said, "I'm a-listenin' to them there—
listenin' to them g-nats up in the air
grit their teeth."

Said, "Gosh." Said, "Hear-well you are! Must be in my ship."
Hear-well got in it.

He went on.
Seed a man a-lookin',
lookin' up through to the ely-ments,
an' said, "What's *your* name?"

Said, "Hush-hush-hush-hush-hush!"
 [!!!!!]
Said, "I'm watchin' that
hawk up there catch g-nats in the air."
Said, "I get a—"
Said, "I get a good feelin' out o' watchin' that an' hear 'em grit their
teeth." [!!!!]
(Good Gawd.)
He said, "Don't mock me out."

An' Jack said, "Well, what's yer name?"

An' said, "See-well, sir." [!!!!]

Said, "See-well, into my ship."

So it went on,
with them, an'
he seed another one with a hog-rifle,
a-sightin'.

Said, "*Hello there!*" Said, "What's *your* name?"

He said, "Oh Gawd, hush-hush-hush-hush!"
He said, "I'm a-fixin' to knock a squirrel's eye out over in Scotland!"
[!!!!!!!!!]

He said—[!!!!!!!!!!!!!]
An' Jack waited till he shot the squirrel, [!!!!!]
An' he said, "What's your name?"

He said, "*Shoot*-well, sir."

He said, "Shoot-well, you must be into my ship."
He got it lowered an' got in an' said, "Fly, Ship, fly."
An' he went on.
An' he figured he didn't see n'ary another one; he must have got 'em
    all.

An' he got on into the witch's palace.
An' he said, "Lower, Ship."
It went right down a-floatin' an' lit right in,
next to where the stump was at.

An' he called 'em all, took 'em all out,
hit 'em with a hand an' got 'em all out,
an' hollered.

Witch come out, an' she said, "You here?"

He said, "Yeah, I'm here,
for my men to try
breakin' that 'chant-ment."

She said, "Well." An' she went an' got that hackerd, [!!!]
an' put it down beside the stump an' betted Jack fifteen guineas agin'
    fifteen. Jack pulled it out an' laid it there.
An' the old witch got up an', "TOODLOODLOODLOODLOO!"
five-or-six-or-seven somersets, an',
an' hit her ass on that, never even knocked a hair out of it. [!!!!!!!]
Gawd.

Bounced off, an'
said, "I bet you hain't got n'ary a man can beat that!"

He said, "Hardy Hard-Ass!"

"Here, sir!" [!!!!!!!!!!!!!!!!!!!]
Hardy Hard-Ass got up on that,
an' he give a big round somerset an' timed his ass,
[*one breath:*] an' hit come over an' struck right down on that hackerd
 an' they said it wasn't a piece of it found nowhere an' not a hair
 knocked off o' his ass! [!!!!!!!!!!!!!!!!!!!!!!!!!]

Said
[*crone's voice*], "Well well well!" Said, "You beat me on that 'un!"
[*Resume normal voice:*] Said, "I bet you hain't got n'ary a man can
 out-drink me!"

Jack says, "Drink-well!"

"Here, sir!" [!!!]
Drink-well come, an' they betted again, an'
above that.

An' she took him out to a branch.
An' said, "One-two-three-go."
An' Drink-well had drunk his branch up an' had the creek about dry
 before the witch had got her'n even
dried down much.
Said, "Just *quit!*" Said, "You've done outed me!"
An' they walked back, an' she said, "I bet you hain't got n'ary a man
 can out-*eat* me!"

He said, "*Eat*-well!"

"Here, sir!"

Eat-well come out, an' the old witch went an' got a sheep apiece,
An' said, "One-two-three-go,"
an' they betted, she betted again with Jack an' said,

"One-two-three-go,"
An' Eat-well swallered a sheep,
an' had a cow goin' down 'fore the witch was
tryin' to part the wool to get started. [!!!]

"Well," she said, "You beat me on that one again,
the third one."
Said, "I bet you hain't got n'ary a man that can out-run me."

He said, "Run-well!"

"Here, sir."

An' Run-well—
She went to the henhouse an' got a eggshell
apiece.
Broke the egg an' let the goody run out of it an' said, "Now the
    ocean water's salty."
An' said, "That'll prove that you've got
water from the ocean."
Said, "We'll go on a run,
an' see who beats who." Betted with Jack
on that, and it was gettin' higher all the time.

An' so her an' Run-well took off.
Gosh, they was a-cuttin'.
An' Run-well got started,
an' he left that witch like she was a-standin' still.
An' so,
Run-well had got to the ocean an' got his eggshell full of water an'
    run back an' met her on a *halfway run*!
She was just half-way there, an' she said [*crone voice*], "*O-h-h!*
Gosh, man," said, "hain't no use to be in that big a hurry." Said, "Sit
    down h'yer,
an' let's take a little chat!"
Run-well, neg-lectin', sit down with her under a tree—oak tree.
An' spoke to her,
an' that ended it: she witched him,

put a skull-bone under his head,
an' long as that skull-bone 'as there he'd sleep.

Jack kept waitin' there with his other men,
an' he said, "Somethin's happened to Run-well."

He said, "Hear-well!"

       "Here, sir." [!!]
Hear-well got down one o' them big ears,
an' hit his hand on it an' he said, "Oh, yeah!"
He said, "I hear him a-snorin' yonder,
sounds like about half-way to the ocean."

He says, "See-well!"

       "Here, sir!"
See-well got down. He said, "*Yeah, I see him.*"
Said, "He's met her on a half-way run,
an' he's took a chat with her an' she's witched him an' put a skull-
    bone under his head." An' said,
"She's smashed his eggshell o' water,
too!
Smashed it up.
The hull's a-layin' there." He could see the hull a-layin'. [!!!]

Said, "Shoot-well!"

       "Here, sir!"
Shoot-well
got down
with that rifle,
an' cut down an' the bullet knocked that skull-bone out from under
    Run-well's head an' it dazed him, an' he jumped up,
with his mind dazed,
an' went around in a three-to-six circles,
an' didn't know what he 'as a-doin'. An' Gawd, when he come back
    enough to see that eggshell smashed,
he flew so mad,

till he took back toward the witch's henhouse,
an' got another eggshell out o' the henhouse an' poured the goody
    out o' it an' went back,
fast as he could go an', 'time he got there, the old witch had just
    stooped over to *get* her'n,
just stooped over to get her'n full to come back with it,
to beat Run-well.
Thought she had it.
He pushed her in an' held her an' drowned her. [!!!]

An' Jack—
Out come the girl, back like she was an', said, Jack
took her in,
an' married her, an' was a beautiful—an' lived a happy life.
[!!!]
An' that's uh "Hardy Hard-Ass." [!!!!!!! *Sounds of four pairs of hands
    clapping.*]

CHAPTER 2

JACK,
MY FATHER,
AND
UNCLE RAY

▼ ▼ ▼ ▼ ▼

FRANK PROFFITT, JR.

▼ ▼ ▼ ▼ ▼

Carl Lindahl

"Jack and the Old Rich Man," as told by Frank Proffitt, Jr., one of the longest and finest Jack Tales in the American repertoire, is the product of a series of social changes that have transformed an old, "shy" tradition of storytelling into a more dramatic and public one.

Born in 1946 in Watauga County, North Carolina, Frank Proffitt, Jr., is a lifelong resident of the Blue Ridge region. He belongs to the extended Beech Mountain family that made the Jack Tales famous. Nephew of Ray Hicks, the best known and most imitated Jack Tale teller, Frank is a younger relative of "the descendants of Council Harmon" who told Richard Chase most of the stories that appeared in his book *The Jack Tales*.

Indeed, Frank owes his fondness for this tale to Richard Chase's book. Although "Jack and the Old Rich Man" was part of his family tradition, it was not often told. Frank, Sr., wrote down a version from the recitation of his father, Wiley Proffitt. Richard Chase obtained a copy of this written tale and printed it word for word, with minor punctuation changes, in the appendix of *The Jack Tales*.

Frank, Sr., told this story to his son once and also recorded a version that Frank, Jr., has heard.[1] But the recording, made on primitive equipment in 1937, is of poor quality and is difficult to follow because—in the words of Frank, Jr., "My father talks so fast on that tape that he sounds like a chipmunk. I'd never have liked the tale if all I'd heard was that recording." Frank, Jr., grew to love "Jack and the Old Rich Man" by reading the written version that appeared in *The Jack Tales*. He credits Richard Chase with keeping Frank, Sr.'s, story alive.

The role of writing in preserving this tale may make some old-fashioned folklorists feel funny about it. Nevertheless, "Jack and the Old Rich Man" is in some ways the most authentic text in *The Jack Tales*. Richard Chase had already collected a related version of the same tale type, "The Master Thief" (AT 1525), from R. M. Ward and Ben Hicks. The Ward-Hicks version appeared as "Jack and the Doctor's Girl" in *The Jack Tales*. Like the other featured stories in the collection, "Jack and the Doctor's Girl" was substantially edited by Chase. But "Jack and the Old Rich Man," relegated to the appendix, survived without serious changes, in the form that Frank, Sr., had copied from Wiley Proffitt's dictation. As "Jack and the Doctor's Girl" became popular on the storytelling circuit, "Jack and the Old Rich Man" remained quietly in the Proffitt family. Thus, although Chase's alterations have significantly affected certain American storytelling traditions, the performance by Frank Proffitt, Jr., of this tale is more strongly shaped by family tradition and neighborhood values.

That "Jack and the Old Rich Man" continues to exist in oral form is rather remarkable, as the Proffitts have been known as musicians rather than storytellers. Although the family shared a wealth of narratives, their stories stayed at home. Frank, Sr., was a subsistence farmer whose talent with the banjo and knowledge of traditional songs brought him fame only near the end of his life. Although his formal education did not take him beyond the sixth grade, he was "interested in everything," according to his son, "thirsty for knowledge"—a man whose many interests were reflected in the variety of tales he told. He passed his treasured songs and stories to Frank, Jr., during work breaks, as when father and son had finished hoeing one section of field and were about to begin another. Work was hard, and the older Proffitt was not always talkative. "He was a quiet person 'til he got started," his son remembers. When larger family groups assembled to share stories on Beech Mountain, Frank, Sr., would sometimes tell his stories, but he was far more comfortable as a musician. Toward the end of his life, as he began to perform at folk festivals, he would happily play and sing, but he did not generally tell tales. In the words of his son:

> [Frank Proffitt, Sr.,] was not what you would call a storyteller, as compared to Ray [Hicks]. He could tell a good story and knew lots of them—mostly stories to go with the songs and ballads. There were, for example, many Civil War stories he learned from his father, handed down through the family from my great-grandfather, John Proffitt, a "Southern Yankee" who served with the 13th Tennessee Cavalry, USA. He also heard many of them from his Uncle Noah. In other words, my father would hardly tell stories unless prompted in relation to a song or ballad. Ray tells them, or insists on telling them, on the spot, while my father was shy that way. He was more comfortable telling facts rather than fiction. He was a great "Fact" or "True" storyteller—although he could be a fairly good liar when he wanted to.

Clearly, Frank Proffitt, Sr., represented the shy tradition of family storytellers that I have described in the introduction. Although he was an accomplished oral artist and had the talents to tell fictional tales, he did not do so in large gatherings.

Frank, Jr., began his artistic career by imitating his father. He learned the family traditions of performing banjo and dulcimer music, and he often accompanied his public performances with brief tales about the history of the songs that he sang. Only after he had been performing some years did he begin to make Jack Tales part of his public performance repertoire. Frank writes,

> I started telling [stories] around 1976 during the Bicentennial, because I always enjoyed hearing [stories] and wanted to try telling them to add to my repertoire. In other words, I guess the main thing was that I got tired of singing all the time. When I told my first one in front of an audience and saw how they reacted and

enjoyed it, I decided I enjoyed it also. Besides, storytelling was becoming very popular at this time and I thought why not get "on the train" and tell them! It was part of my heritage and I wanted to share it and help preserve it! "Jack and Ole Rich Man" was not the very first one I told in public.

As the tales' audience shifted from family and friends to large-scale gatherings around festival stages, Frank, Jr., effected some concomitant changes in style. Although the plot and even some of the vocabulary and sentence structure of "Jack and the Old Rich Man" come directly from Frank's father and grandfather, his vocal style does not. Frank, Jr., knew that he would have to make some stylistic changes in his father's tradition if he was to be a successful stage performer of folktales. Accordingly, he adopted the narrative style of his uncle, Ray Hicks, the one Beech Mountain narrator who had been successful in transforming the North Carolina märchen into a large-scale attraction:

> I tell "Jack and the Old Rich Man" in this style from my Uncle Ray Hicks, though I never heard him tell it either. He tells "Jack and the Doctor's Girl," which is similar in the last half. I try—or really do it without thinking. I use Ray's accent to a degree, because I have heard him so much and I am part Hicks, and it comes naturally I guess. My father never deviated from his natural voice in telling a tale.

According to Frank, Jr., Ray Hicks had always dominated taletelling on Beech Mountain. With a style more flamboyant than those of the Wards and Proffitts, he could speak nonstop at family gatherings. "My father wouldn't get a word in edgewise," recalls Frank, Jr. When Ray would finish a performance of "Jack and the Doctor's Girl," Frank, Sr., would say, "My dad knew one like that, but it's a little different; we called it 'Jack and the Old Rich Man.' " But Frank, Sr., would never tell the tale.

Frank's decision to tell his father's story in his uncle's style proved highly successful. In the process of many retellings, it has become uniquely the property of Frank Proffitt, Jr. The favorite tale in his now-extensive repertoire, "Jack and the Old Rich Man" is also the longest. Many words and phrases found in the version written by Frank, Sr., are repeated exactly in the oral tellings. For example, the Old Rich Man's phrases, "I'll have you hung or shot certain" and "I

gray Jack got it" belong to both father and son. Yet Frank, Jr., greatly
enlarges his father's telling by dwelling on the tale's details. The text
printed in *The Jack Tales* takes about ten minutes to read aloud, but
the oral version transcribed below was a twenty-eight-minute performance. Frank says for him the length depends on the audience. He,
too, once told "Jack and the Old Rich Man" in about ten minutes to
an audience of schoolchildren, but, he says, "I almost had to work to
tell it that fast. It wasn't satisfying." He prefers the much more leisurely pace apparent in the version included here, recorded at his
home by Scottish folklorist Barbara McDermitt in an intimate setting
of five listeners: McDermitt, a friend, and Frank's wife and two children. Frank recalls feeling comfortable with this small group, and
he credits Barbara McDermitt with a role in shaping a fine performance. "Barbara's a wonderful listener. She hangs on every word. I
tell my best stories when someone's there who really loves to hear
them."

The nature and extent of Frank's additions to the written original
are apparent in a comparison of the two versions of the Brother
Dickie episode. This is the longest episode in the story. In the written
version, Brother Dickie and his wife exchange few words: the woman's part is limited to four brief sentences. But the oral tale develops
both the characters of Brother Dickie and his wife and their quarrel:
the woman speaks twenty sentences that serve to underline her husband's foolishness and enhance the comic effect of the scene. In addition to being foolish, Brother Dickie is stingy; both of these aspects of
character are contributed by Frank, Jr. Further additions occur when
Brother Dickie is discovered; the men who find him wriggling in the
sack in the pigpen believe that he is a "booger"—a monster or ghost.
When Brother Dickie gets out of the sack, he has arrived—not in
heaven, but in "hog heaven." These two comic touches by Frank, Jr.,
inspire the most laughter during the performance.

Although some of the scenes are so drawn out that they threaten to
make listeners lose the thread of the plot, Frank holds the tale together by stressing the formulaic phrases—"I gray Jack got it"; "not
your'n, but MINE"; "I'll have you hung or shot certain"; "If I do, is
it mine?"—that his father and grandfather had used to conclude each
of the theft scenes and to begin each new contest between Jack and
the rich man. Like his forebears, Frank lengthens this ritualistic exchange each time he repeats it, but Frank's additions also serve to

develop the personalities—as well as the rivalry—of Jack and the rich man. In Wiley Proffitt's version the last challenge dialogue between the rich man and Jack is 87 words long, but Frank, Jr., lengthens this to 357, adding—among many other touches—the line in which the old man, in a teary voice, complains, "Well, DAD BLAME it, Jack, you about cleaned me out of everything now." Through such additions, Frank, Jr., vividly depicts the escalating rage and eventual helplessness of Jack's foe.

"Jack and the Old Rich Man" belongs to the internationally known tale type "The Master Thief" (AT 1525). In one respect this telling diverges notably from all other published American versions. As I have explained in the introduction to this volume, the major difference between British and American examples of this tale type has to do with the relationship between the thief and his rich victim. In British versions, the old man is cruel and Jack is a punishing Robin Hood figure; in the United States, however, the two men engage in a strangely friendly rivalry that often becomes a point of tension for narrators who have trouble conceiving or explaining why two such good, friendly characters would do such cruel things to each other. In its depiction of the relationship between Jack and the Old Rich Man, the version of Frank Proffitt, Jr., clearly comes closer to the Old World tales than does any other British-American variation. From the beginning, the old man's cruelty is stressed. Jack and his mother are honest and hardworking, but they are cheated and pushed to the edge of starvation by the old man. This antagonism is central to Frank's interpretation of the tale: "The Old Rich Man got what he deserved for being so stingy, treating Jack and his mother like he did. While I don't condone thievery, Jack had to do it, because it was forced on him. He did it to survive." Frank, Jr., believes that his father's life and philosophy may have influenced this particular aspect of "Jack and the Old Rich Man." Frank, Sr., a poor, hardworking man all his life, was deeply concerned about issues of social justice. Among the songs he recorded were ballads of the Great Depression. Although Frank, Sr., was fond of saying that "it was always the Depression in the mountains," he felt great compassion for all people who suffered from poverty, and he expressed anger concerning social conditions that cause people to struggle to survive. His strong sense of social justice survives in his son's telling of this tale.

The performance of Frank Proffitt, Jr., thus blends two traditions as a shy, family process and a more public one converge. Similarly, "Jack and the Old Rich Man" bears the stamp of three strong personalities. Both Frank Proffitt, Sr., and Frank Proffitt, Jr., are present in the words and philosophy of the tale, and Ray Hicks's powerful and flamboyant style emerges in performance.

When I'm watching Uncle Ray tell a tale, I get hypnotized. He becomes Jack when he's telling. And when I watch him, we both become Jack. I love that man.

NOTE

1. The original aluminum disk is in the Frank C. Brown Collection at Duke University. The University of North Carolina has a cassette copy.

JACK AND THE OLD RICH MAN

as told by Frank Proffitt, Jr.

Frank Proffitt remembers hearing his father tell this story only once. He himself learned it from a 2,100-word version written out by the senior Proffitt that ultimately found its way into the appendix of Richard Chase's The Jack Tales. *Though characteristic phrases of that version persist intact in the present version (recorded by Barbara McDermitt in 1982), Frank Proffitt, Jr., has so developed the story, especially the conversations, that, at 5,450 words, it is the longest Beech Mountain tale in this volume.*

Like Ray Hicks, Frank Proffitt often runs sentences together in long, loping bounds of sound. He also speaks a little more rapidly than most of the other Beech Mountain storytellers, sometimes with only the briefest pauses. These two qualities of his style make it more difficult for the transcriber to discern breaks between lines. Fortunately, Proffitt provides an additional cue: generally speaking, his lines end with an upward, almost questioning inflection on the last accent or last accented word. That inflection provides a very sure empirical basis for determining line breaks. We have indicated these inflections with italics in the first ten lines and in a representative sampling of lines thereafter. This stylistic feature is especially marked during excited passages, and in such passages the last line may end, instead, with a downward inflection. A very clear example of this variation on Proffitt's style occurs in the description of Jack scaring the cattle herders. In that passage we have indicated every upward inflection with italics and the final downward inflection with small capitals.

▼ ▼ ▼

Well, this one's *about*
where Jack and his mother worked for an Old Rich *Man*,
and Jack, he found out where the Old Rich Man kept his *money*,
and he concluded he's going to help hisself to *some* of it,
since the old man hadn't been paying him and his mother nothing
   hardly, just barely enough to eat, and not, not nothing, no money
   on the side hardly, just a little penny every now and *then*.

He decided he'd get him some back *wages.*

Well, he got two fellers to go along, and he found out when the Old
Rich Man, when he's going to leave his *home,*

and he found out when he's going to be *gone.*

He got two fellers to go up [*laughing*] to the Old Rich Man's house
with him

to stand *guard*

on the outside, one on one side of the house and the other one on the
other'n

while he went in and stole

the Old Rich Man's *money* and stuff.

And he told them fellers, if he got in there and got caught,

that he would stomp his foot and whistle.

And that was a *warning* to them.

And said if anybody come around, for them to warn *him*

—what they're supposed to do. He got in there

and found a key

to the old man's bureau drawer where he hid his money

a-lock, had it locked up—

unlocked that bureau drawer.

And he was holding a kerosene lamp and there was so much gold
and silver and money, all kinds of paper money, and jewels and
everything all mixed in together. And hit was *a-glittering*

in that *light.*

And Jack [*laughing*], he got so excited, he started stomping his foot
and a-whistling,

[*Gives a whistle:*] "LORD HAVE MERCY! I never seen so much
money in my life," he thought.

And them fellers heared Jack on the outside and thought he'd got
caught,

cause he's a whistling and stomping his foot [*laughing*]. And they—
it's a sight to see them fellers get out of there. They just gone—

tearing brush down, running into fences.

And Jack, he's just scooped all that up in a hemp sack he had there
with him—a big old sack, flour sack or somp'n, and

toted it 'cross his shoulder and went on *home.*

And didn't even share it with them two fellers he was supposed to
share it with and they ran off.

Old Rich Man [*laughing*] come down to Jack's house next *morning*,
said, "Bedad," said, "Jack."
Said, "Where's Jack at?" (He wasn't there; Jack wasn't there.) He
asked his mother, he said, "Where's Jack at?"
(Jack didn't go to work for two or three days.
Didn't need to.)

She said, "*We*'re just as independent as you are." Said,
"We don't need to work for you anymore."

He said, "Why?"

She said, "Because Jack's become a highway robber. That's why."

He said, "He is?"—rich man—"He is?"

She said, "YES. He's robbing everything that moves—and part of
anything that don't move. [!!!]
He just, he's just, he's a good'n."
Said, "We're doing good now."

And about that time Jack come in and the Old Rich Man just looked
at him and said, "Your mama tells me you've become a highway
robber. Is that *right*?"

Jack said, "Yea-ah."

He said, "You're a pretty good one?"

[Jack] said, "Yeah, I'm doing all
right."

Said, "You think you're the best one—you think you're real
good, don't you?"

Jack said, "I'm a—I told you I was a doing all right."

Said, "You're—
you think you're such a good one," said,
"You stole all my money last night—or about three nights ago."

Jack said, "Not your'n, but MINE."

Old Rich Man flew mad and cussed him up one side and down the
    other and said,
"All right." And said, "Being you think you're such a good robber
and I'm gonna—
there's one thing you've gotta do between now and tomorrow
    morning. You've got to steal
off of me, or I'll have you hung or shot certain."

And Jack said, "If I do, is it mine?"

                                        He said, "Yea-ah.
It's yours if you can steal."

Jack said, "What I got to steal?"

                            He said, "You got to steal my saddle
    horse
out of my stable tonight,
with a saddle on it—
my mare,
out of the stable,
between now and tomorrow morning, or I'll have you hung or shot,
    certain."
Said, "If you do, it's yours."

That night the Old Rich Man placed two guards outside his stable
    door and they built 'em up a fire. And long about twelve o'clock
or one o'clock in the morning,
come an old beardy man along all bent over, nearly *doubled*,
and walking on a *cane*,
a-hobbling *along*.
And Jack—it was Jack!
He was all fixed up and camouflaged and *disguised* [*laughing*].
And he walked up to them two guards, said,
"Could I lay down awhile?" He talked so pitiful, you know, like a—he
    could talk like an old man, you know [*with a quivering voice*]: "Oh,
    Lordy, I been walking twenty miles today." Said, "This makes

about twenty miles." Said, "I'm just about to just give plumb out.
Do you'ns care if I lay down by the fire and rest here and warm
up? I'm cold and hungry."

First the guards told him to go on and get on out of there. Said they
    didn't want to be bothered with him, with him.
Said, "Just get on out of here."
But Jack started to hobble off—the old man did—
and they got to feeling a little sorry fur him.
He was looking so *pitiful*. And they said, "Wait! Here!" They said,
    "You can lay down about five minutes,"
they said, "then you've got to move on.
About five minutes, I reckon we'll let you stay."

Jack [*laughing*]—the old man—laid down there, Jack did, and the—
directly he went to *sleep*,
or made like he was going to sleep—He wasn't really sleeping—
He's a-snoring and that guards thought he was sleeping.
And he turned over *directly*,
and took a bottle of rum out of one of his coat *pockets*,
and made out like he was taking a *dram of it*,
and [*laughs*], and then he laid it down beside of his head and then
    turned back over and started snoring again.
And the guard, one of them guards, seen the bottle of rum—or both
    of 'em did. One of 'em got to it first, said, "That'n's mine."
Both of 'em grabbed at it. That one had longer arms than the other
    and he grabbed it first.
Just took it up and drunk it straight down, about a quart,
just drunk it straight down, there, about two swigs maybe.

Directly Jack he rolled *over*,
he was a snoring—
made like he was asleep again.
In a couple minutes he rolled over
and took out another bottle of rum out of his other coat pocket,
    made out like he was taking a dram, laid it down beside his head,
    and turned back over, started snoring. The other guard seen that
    and said, "That'n's mine."

And the other one wasn't in no shape to grab for it anyway. He'd
    done passed *out—*
or just about was [*laughs*].
He drunk it straight down, the other guard did,
and in a little while both of 'em were just passed out stone-cold
    drunk.
Just had it. They were just sprawled out over the top of each other.

Jack he just got *up*
and took the key off of one of the guards' belt and opened the stable
    door
and took that saddle horse *out*, the mare—or he first, first put the
    saddle on it,
and then he led it out,
and locked the door back
and put the padlock back on the door,
and put the key back
on the guard's belt—[*laughing*] the one that passed out on top of the
    other'n—
and, and rode *off*.

Well, next morning Old Rich Man come down. His guards're
    standing around. They'd woke up, but they were just barely woke
    up, they were a-staggering around. Had the awfulest hangover,
holding their heads.
Said, "What's wrong with you'ns?"

"Oh, I don't know. Got a little headache this morning."
They didn't remember a thing that happened that night,
didn't remember.
Said, "What we supposed to be doing here?"

                              [He] said, "You're
    supposed to be standing guard
outside, my—watching for—"

"Oh, *yeah*."
They said, "Yeah, we, we recollect now.
It's coming back."

[He] said
[*laughing*] (they're in pretty bad shape), said, "OH LORD!" Said,
  "My saddle horse
better still be in that stable or"—said—"I'll give you'ns each thirty
  lashes apiece with a bullwhip!"

The guard said—the main, the big guard there, he just spoke for the
  other one and said,
"Oh, it has to be in there." Said, "The key's still on my belt, and you
  can look there and see the door's still locked.
Ain't no way in the world nobody could've got in there and got that
  mare."

He said, "They better not—Let me have the key and let me look."
And
Old Rich Man got the key and opened the doors to the stable,
looked in, and the mare was gone.
Said, "O-h, Lord have mercy, I gray Jack got it.
I gray Jack got it."
Said, "You'ns has had it."
Them guards was looking mighty pitiful. Gave em thirty lashes
  apiece then
—or had somebody to do it. Boy, he just whipped 'em to death, near'y.

Went down to Jack's house then
—Jack was outside a-currying that mare, a-brushing it down; he was
  so proud, he looked so happy—
and said, "You stole my saddle horse last night, did you, Jack?"

Jack said, "Not your'n, but MINE."

Old Rich Man flew mad and cussed him up one side and down the
  other'n
and said, "You—you think you're such a good *robber*?"

Jack said, "I've done pretty good, ain't I?"

Said, "Well, just one more thing [*laughs, makes inaudible comment*]
you gotta steal between now and tomorrow morning,
or I'll have you hung or shot certain."

Jack said, "What's that?"

And said, "You gotta steal all my Brother Dickie's money or I'll have
     you hung or shot certain."

                              Jack said, "If I do, is it mine?"

Said, "Yea-ah.
It's your'n.
But you'll never *get* it
cause he watches his *money*
like a chicken hawk."
Said, "He's a stingy rascal.
He's stingier than I am. You'll never get it."

Jack said, "Well, I'll see—we'll see about that."

And that night—there was a meeting house pretty close to Brother
     Dickie's
     (and that's why they called him "Brother"—he was the pastor of
        it)
—just about a hundred feet up the road from, or up the hill behind
     his house.
And, uh, 'bout three o'clock in the morning Brother Dickie woke *up*
and heared, he heared preaching going on up at the meeting *house*,
at three o'clock in the *morning*.
Beat any preaching he ever heared in his life.
Lord have mercy, what preaching!
And he thought, he said, "What in the world is going on up there?
Preaching, three o'clock in the morning?" Said,
"Somebody up there is outpreaching me."
And said [*laughing*], "I got to get up there and check this *out*."
Said, "Something strange is going on here." And he got—he ran on
     up to the meeting house and knocked on the door,
and said, "Who's that in there a-preaching?"

And it was Jack.
And he said, and Jack said, "Hit's the angel Gabriel."

And Brother Dickie ran around, looked in through the meeting
     house winder. And Jack had a robe on, a white robe,
and had a kind of a halo fixed up around his head some way—a halo,
looked like.
And Brother Dickie ran around and knocked on the door again
     —and the door was locked—and tried to get in,
banged on it.
Finally said [*in a moaning, supplicating voice*], "Oh, Lordy, Angel
     Gabriel,
what can I give thee
to let me be in thy place?"

And Angel Gabriel said,
"All thy money,
and you can be in my place."

And Brother Dickie [*laughing*],
he said, "Oh, now I'll go down there and get it." Said, "Don't you
     run off."
Said, "You stay here. Don't you run off nowhere." Said, "I'll be right
     back."
Just—"Oh, I'll get all my money."

And Jack said, "All right"—Or Angel Gabriel—said, "I'll, I'll stay
     here," and started preaching again
and Brother Dickie ran back down to the *house*,
and Jack, he
followed along behind him, you know.
And he ran int' his house. And Jack, he listened outside the winder.
     You know what was a—Him and his wife was in there and they
     was a-having it out.

And Brother Dickie said, "Let—," said, "It's bound to be the Angel
     Gabriel."
Said, "I never heard no such preaching."

She's trying to tell him it was somebody trying to trick him, said,
     "That's somebody trying to fool you,
trying to get all your money or something." Said, "You better watch
     it."

He said, "No!" He said, "No!"
Said, Brother Dicky said, "It's the Angel Gabriel.
And," said—"All I need to go to paradise,
to heaven
—it's a one-way ticket to Gloryland—
is just give him all my money
and I'm on my way." Said, "You been telling me I'll split hell wide
    open. I'll show you."
Said, "I may never get another chance like this."

And she was argu—he was arguing,
they was having it out, you know.
And, finally, she said, "Wait a minute!" He'd started to take all his
    money.

He said, "What?"

                    She said, "Just take half the money. He won't know
    the difference.
Just take half of it."

Said, "He might know the difference."

Said, "No, he won't."

Said, "That's the Angel Gabriel you're talking about. He knows
    everything. He was sent from the Lord."

"Aw, Go ahead and try it, then."

Said, "Well, I reckon I'll go along with you on that." So he took half
    his money out. And
Jack, he ran back up to the meeting house—(he was out listening to
    all that)—and put his robe back on and his halo and started
    preaching again.
And Brother Dickie ran up there with half of his money
in that big old sack,
banged on the door and said, "Angel Gabriel!
Is thee still there?"

He said, "Yes,
I'm here."

Said, "Well, here's all my money. Now let me be in thy place."

And Jack said, "It's not *all* your money,
it's just half.
Go back and get the rest of it.
And then I'll let you be in my place."

And [*laughs*] Brother Dickie said, "Oh Lord!"
Or he thought to hisself and said, "Oh, it is the real thing;
how in the world'd he of knowed
that it was just half of my money,
if it wasn't really the Angel Gabriel?"
Said, "My old woman's wrong—as usual."
Said [*laughing*], "I—I'll just go back." Said, "Wait here a minute
   now." Said,
said, "Don't you run off now.
I'll go back and get the rest of it. Don't you run off on me."

And, uh, Angel Gabriel said
[*deep voice*], "I won't.
I'll be here,
to take thee to paradise."

Brother Dickie ran back down there and Jack followed along behind
   him
and listened outside the winder *again*
—and uh, him and his wife was getting into it again and finally she
   said—
she just got so aggravated with him and said, "Just go on!
And take all your *money*
and take yourself. And just get out of here." Said, "I'm getting tired
   of fooling with you—
and go on to *heaven*,
and," said, "I'll be there soon myself
to join you."
Said, "But you're liable to end up in the other side—" and said, "if
   you don't watch."

And Brother Dickie said, "Now how in the world would he have
knowed? It's bound to be him. He just knowed that I had half my
money there."

And she said, "Well, just go on.
I want you to hush your mouth."

And Jack ran back up there [*laughs*] and started preaching again,
locked the door back,
put his robe back on,
you know, and everything.
Brother Dickie ran back up, back up there with the rest of his *money*
and knocked on the door and said, "Now here's all my money. Let
me be in thy *place*."

And the Angel Gabriel said (or Jack),
"Just one more thing."

Brother Dickie said, "Now *what?*"

He said, "You got to go—
I got to have something to carry you off to heaven in—
And go get a big old sack,
for me to tote you off to heaven in" [*laughs*]. [!!!]

And Brother Dickie said, "Oh, oh yeah, yeah. That's right. Got to
have something. Yeah. Uh.
Now, don't you run off." And he ran back down to his *house*
and got a great old big hemp sack [*laughing*]
or flour sack, or some kind of sack.
And he said, "I got the sack."

Said, "Well, crawl down in it.
And I will take thee to paradise."
And Jack [*laughing*]
had Brother Dickie crawl down in the sack, outside the meeting
house *door*,
on the steps,
on the porch of the meeting house.

And Jack, he ran out
and had him a big old twine of string here, and [*laughing*] tied him
    up in it,
and slung him across his shoulders.
And toted him down to the Old Rich Man's hog *pen*
    (or where he kept his fattening *hogs*, you know,
    his best *hogs*)
and just slung Brother Dickie right over in the middle of it.
He's in hog heaven, then [*laughs*].
And Jack—and, uh, so Jack, he just got all that money and went on
    back home, and—all Brother Dickie's money.

And next morning Old Rich Man come on down to Brother Dickie's
    house,
come in to—his wife was in there, sitting—
and said, "Where's Brother Dickie at?"

                              Said, "Oh, Lord."
Said, "Ain't you heared?"

Said, "Heared what?"

Said, "He went off to heaven last night."

Uh, Old Rich Man said, "Well, did he take anything with him—
besides his clothes?"

Said, "Yeah. He took all his money."

Old Rich Man said, "Oh Lord have mercy, I gray Jack got it. He
    tricked him out of every penny."

                         [She] said, "I tried to tell the
    blamed fool
somebody was trying to trick him. He wouldn't listen to a word I
    said.
The crazy thing. He deserves whatever he got."
Said, "I got to find where he is.
If he ain't in heaven, he's guarant' in some kind of a mess."

And Old Rich Man's servants had come out to feed the hogs that
    morning
and seen Brother—and seen that sack in there [*laughing*] jerking
    around
—where Brother Dickie was in—
and thought it was some kind of booger or somp'n
a-twitching around in there and
—a haint or something hainted.
And ran off.
They wouldn't feed the hogs. Dropped the slop all over everyplace.
    [*Laughs.*] Ran off.
Scared 'em nearly to *death*.

And Old Rich Man, he comes down there and
went over in the hog pen and untied the sack—and out stepped his
    Brother Dickie.
Said, "Yeah, you made it to heaven all right, didn't you."
[*Laughing:*] He was in awful bad looking shape. And, uh,
so Old Rich Man went down to Jack's house, then, and Jack was
    down there counting his money,
counting Brother Dickie's money—or his money then.
And said, "You stole all my Brother Dickie's money last night, did
    you?"

Said, "Not his'n, but MINE."

And the Old Rich Man flew mad and cussed him up one side and
    said,
"Well, you might get to thinking you're a pretty good robber."

Jack said, "I reckon I'll do."

"Well," said, "there's one more thing."

                                    Jack said, "What I got to prove
    to you?" Said, "I done stole two things that you told me to."

                                                            Said,
    "Well, there's one more
thing you got to do or steal.

One more thing you got to steal, or I'll have you hung or shot certain
   by tomorrow morning.
If you don't have it stole by tomorrow morning—"

Jack said, "What's that?"

Said, "You got to steal all my cattle
out of my field.
Three hundred head of cattle—or I'll have you hung or shot certain,
tomorrow morning
—if you don't have them stole by tomorrow morning."

Jack said, "If I do, are they mine?"

                              Said, "Yeah, they're yours.
You got all this other stuff [*laughing*], ain't you?"

So Jack—I mean the Old Rich Man had his
men, you know, that looked after the cattle—had 'em
drive 'em to another *pasture*
because he thought Jack knew pretty sure where they was. And had a
pasture way back in the wilderness, way back in the *woods*
—was a cleared place,
about five miles *away*.

And Jack, he just figured out a way he could, he could *get* 'em.
He killed him a sheep and got him a bladder of *blood*,
and them fellers was driving them cattle along the road and he ran
   ahead of 'em
—and stripped hisself off *naked*
and hung hisself by the heels above the *road*,
and poured that blood all *over* him.
Awful' looking mess you ever seen. Them fellows come *around*
[*laughs*] the curve in the road, see Jack a-hanging *there*
—and it just scared them plumb to *death*,
nearly. And they just turned nearly *white*.
Their hair and everything. Just hair stood straight up—and they ran
   off and left the *cattle*
and Jack just rounded them *up*
and took them and put them in HIS PASTURE.

And the next morning Old Rich Man come down and said, "You
  stole all my cattle last night, did you?"

Said, "Not—not your'n, but MINE."

"Well," said, "Dad blame. There's one more thing you gotta do."

Jack said, "LORD HAVE MERCY!"
Said, "I'm gonna clean you out if you keep this up."

Said, "Clean me out?"
Said, "I'm gonna get everything back and have you hung or shot.
That's what's gonna happen. You ain't gonna clean me out."

So Jack said, "What have I gotta do now?"

Said, "You gotta steal a shimmy
—or my wife's nightgown—
off of her tonight,
while she's in bed. Steal it off of her back.
Off of her body while she's a-sleeping tonight,
or I'll have you hung or shot certain by tomorrow morning."

Jack said, "If I do, is it mine?"

Said, "Yeah [*laughing*], it's your'n."

And that night the old witch—uh, Rich Man stood guard outside his
  winder
with a double-barreled shotgun,
his wife laying in bed, a-sleep.
Had the light out.
And waiting for Jack, standing guard.

And Jack, he
—he went to the graveyard
—and dug up a fresh buried corpse,
where it'd been buried about a day,
and stuck a—yeah, killed him another sheep and got him a bladder
  of blood.

Drug that corpse down to the Old Rich Man's house, and cut him a
    sapling about six feet long, a poplar sapling, and
stuck that through the back of the
coat of the old—of the *corpse,*
and brought it around to the side of the house, right below where the
    Old Rich Man was a *looking.*
    (It had two stories, you know. He's on the second floor of it,
    his bedroom was.)
And he got around there, right below the winder
[*laughing*] where the Old Rich Man was a-watching.
And that stick, poked up through that corpse,
he'd stick the head of it up to the winder,
and yank it back down one time, and then stick it up the second
    time.
Pull it back down. The *third* time
he poked it up, the Old Rich Man let him have it, with both barrels.
Ke-bang!
And Jack dropped the corpse: Ke-thunk.
Ke-thunk on the ground. Old Rich Man said, "LORD HAVE
    MERCY!" Said, "I GOT HIM.
I GOT HIM this time. Jack's had it. I blowed his head plumb off.
Wife," he said, "we, we's shet of that rascal for good."

She said, "I'm so glad. That's all I've heared lately [*in a shrill voice*]:
    'Jack this, Jack that'—that's all I've heared.
Ay, Lordy, I'm glad, too."
She said, "What you going to do with him now?"

"Do with him?"

            "Oh, yeah.
You can't leave him laying out there."

And Jack, you know, when the corpse dropped, he poured that
    bladder of blood all over its face,
and the Old Rich Man said, "Let me go check on him."
And uh, he went down, around the corner of the house and looked.
    And
there was so much blood on its face he couldn't tell it wasn't—
    [*laughs*].

[*Here, story has been interrupted—probably to change tape—then resumes at approximately the same place.*]

So,

The Old Rich Man, he went around the corner of the house where Jack had fell—or he thought it was Jack.

And there was so much blood

he got about—he was holding a lantern, you know. And there was so
   much blood on that corpse's face, he

thought it *was* Jack.

He said, "Ohhh, Lordy, I blowed Jack's head plumb off!"

Said, "I—"

said, "I got to go get two of my trusted best friends to help bury that, bury that rascal

—and then hide it from the law—and everything."

Said, "Oh, Lordy."

And Jack, he was hiding back in the bushes, you know.

Old Rich Man ran off to get two, two of his friends to help bury Jack.

Well, about two minutes after he was gone, Jack, he just snuck out of
   the bushes and went through the door and went upstairs and got
   in bed with the old woman.

And he could talk [*laughing*], he could talk like the Old Rich Man.

And he said, "Oh, Lordy."

Said, "Old lady,"

Said, "We buried him so deep,

nobody'll ever find him. And hid it good."

She said, "You buried him already?"

                     Said, "Yeah. I 'as so happy, we
   buried him quick.

I 'as so happy to be shet of Jack we just dug real quick and shoveled
[*laughs*] and covered him up."

She said, "That's the fastest burying I've ever heared tell of."

Then he, then Jack said, "Oh, Lordy"
   (talking like the Rich Old Man).

She said, "What's wrong?"

He said, "I forgot.
I's been out a-handling Jack
and got blood all over my hands
and I forgot to *wash* 'em.
And I've got blood all over your shimmy."

She said, "Hit don't make no nevermind. I'll just get up and put
    another'n on
and—while you're washing your hands."
And Jack got up a-washing his hands, and she pulled off that bloody
    shimmy—it wasn't, wasn't no blood on it anyway; she just thought
    it was—
and she said, "I'm gonna throw this shimmy over to you."

—No, Jack said—yeah—"Throw it over to me. I'll wash it out for you
    in the wash basin here.
Wash the blood out of it."

She said, "That's a good idee."
Said, "Here."
And she slung it over to Jack, and boy it was a sight to see him get
    out of there [!!!!]
with it.
Soon as he grabbed that, he was gone.
Snuck out, being he could run real light, you know. Bare feet.
She didn't hear him leave, and she put a clean one on,
—a clean shimmy—
and crawled back into bed.

And in about five or ten minutes the Old Rich Man come in and
    said, "Oh, Lordy." Said, "I'm just wore about plumb out." Said,
"I buried Jack, and it was pitiful.
I just blowed his head plumb off, it was, it was just a, just a mess.
But we buried him so deep and covered him up so good, nobody'll
    never—"

She said, "What in the world you talking about?" She said, "You
    buried him twice?" [!!!]
Said, "You crazy thing." [!!!!]

Said, "What are *you* talking about, 'you crazy thing'?" They got into
it.

   Said, "Some blame fool come in here awhile ago that sounded
just like you,
and crawled into bed with me here,
and said they got—he got blood all over my *shimmy*—is what he told
me.
And I got up and put another one on. And he was over there
   a-washing his hands,
and I slung it over to him to wash."

He said [*teary voice*], "Oh, Lord, you crazy old woman." Said, "That
   was *Jack*." Said, "He got my—
he got your shimmy." Said, "I gray *Jack* got it. Lord have mercy.
A man just go off a while. Ever—I don't know what to do."

[*Normal voice:*] And he went back—he went down to Jack's house the
   next *morning*.
And Jack was there, a-holding the shimmy—I mean, he was
   a-washing it out and a-putting it on the clothesline, where he had
   washed it out. And he said, "You got my wife's shimmy last night,
   did you?"

Said, "Not her'n, but MINE,"
Jack said.

[*Teary voice again:*] "Well, dad blame it, Jack, you about cleaned me
   out of everything now."
Said, "But I'll tell you what I'm gonna *do*."
Said, "I'm still gonna have you hung or shot certain."

                                                      Jack said,
"Here we go *again*." Said, "What have I gotta steal now?"

Said, "You ain't gotta steal nothing else."

                                        Said, "Well,
what are you talking about then?"

Said, "Well, you gotta—there's one thing you gotta do 'tween now and tomorrow morning. You don't have to steal nothing."

And so Jack said, "Well, what'll I get,
If I ain't got nothing to steal?"

Said, "I'll give you the deed to half of
my place.
That's what I'll give you,
if you can do what I'm gonna tell you."

Jack said, "What do I gotta
do?"

Said, "You've gotta come here tomorrow morning, neither riding,
neither walking,
a-hopping,
a-skipping,
or a-jumping, or a-flying.
And you got to come here to my house
and neither come in or stay out.
Don't come in the house or stay out, either one."

And Jack said, "Is that all I gotta do?"

He said, "Yeah."

He said, "Well, and I get a deed to half your place?"

Said, "*Yeah*."

And that next morning, Jack, he caught him an old big fat sow,
out of the Old Rich Man's hog pen [*laughing*],
snuck it out and
pulled his shoes off,
and he just went back and forth on its back, from one side to the
other, holding it, and wanting it go from his left arm hanging on
around its neck over to his right arm—it a running up the old—
toward the—and wasn't—he wasn't really riding it or nothing, just
flopping around on it.

Wasn't doing none of them things
that the Old Rich Man said he couldn't do. You'd have to see it to
    believe what he was a-doing,
just a-flopping around over, all over that sow.
And hit a-squalling
and carrying on.
And he come up the Old Rich Man's house,
and up the road,
on that old big sow and Old Rich Man was standing at his gate.
At his fence. The gate—and the gate was locked.
And he was standing on the other side of it. And Jack, he flopped off
    that sow. And
Old Rich Man said, "Hey, Jack." Said,
"Being you're here this early," said, "my old lady's got breakfast on."
    Said, "You're welcome to come in—Come on in and have some
    breakfast." Said, "You look wore out,
messing around with that sow."

Jack, he just,
he just straddled the gate.
And didn't go in or stay out—just straddled the gate [*laughing*]. [!!!]

And the Old Rich Man just stood there with his mouth a-hanging
    open and his eyeballs bulging out, and
said, "Jack, come in and let me sign the deed over."
Went in and signed the deed over to half his *place*.

And the last time I was down there,
Jack and his mother, they was a-doing well.
Extra well. They was a—
they had the Old Rich Man out a-working for them [*laughs*]. [!!!]

CHAPTER 3

THE
STORYTELLER AS
CURATOR

▼ ▼ ▼ ▼ ▼

MARSHALL WARD

▼ ▼ ▼ ▼ ▼

Cheryl Oxford

  The late Marshall Ward was one of the best-known western North Carolina Jack Tale tellers. Born at Beech Creek on 10 December 1906, he was the third of eight children born to Hessie and Miles Ward. A great-grandson of Council Harmon, the patriarch of the Jack cycle preserved on and around Beech Mountain, he explained that the Wards were of German descent and the Harmons were "Dutch," a word that in local parlance often means German.[1] Ward was raised in an intrafamily tradition of storytelling in which older relatives told tales to entertain the children.[2] He readily reminisced about his youth, sharing, among other tidbits, anecdotes about his first years after being born prematurely and not being expected to live. Ward could only have learned these accounts of his infancy through the oral tradition of his immediate family. It seems that Miles Ward's first-born son was a subject of, as well as a rapt listener to, family tales.

  From his father, Ward began to learn stories at an early age. His account of his childhood exposure to storytelling provides an excellent description of the traditional, family-centered context for the performance of Jack Tales.

Dad had made a banjo and a dulcimore. That's all the entertainment we had in the home. He could pick the banjo, he could sing, and he could play the dulcimore. But you know about fifteen to twenty minutes of that singin' and pickin' is all I wanted. I wanted *stories.*

And after supper, now, them cold, long, winter nights, that big fireplace get fired-up, you know, and get warm—I'd get to beggin' my Daddy to tell me a story. He'd get started and he wouldn't quit before midnight. And he'd do this over and over. I knew ever story by heart, and I could tell 'em just as good as he could tell 'em.

Later in his life, when asked by Richard Chase if he knew any old songs from the mountains, Ward replied that he did not. His memory, it seems, was selective. The told tale, not the sung ballad, became his artistic medium.

"I could tell 'em just as good as he could tell 'em," the young Ward had concluded, and apparently he used every opportunity to hone his emerging skill as a yarnspinner. With good humor, he recalled nights spent retelling these stories to listeners his own age. "'Fore I was eight years old I knew ever' one of 'em. And I was telling 'em to ever' boy friend, or anybody come to see me [who] would set and listen—I'd tell 'em these stories. And I'd tell 'em over and over as long as they'd listen to 'em. And my boy friends—now when I went to school, they'd come home with me, stay all night with me. We slept together. And I'd tell 'em these stories till they went to snorin'.'" Not only did adults tell these tales to young members of their own family, but a child might also entertain his peers with accounts of the heroic Jack. Since this narrative cycle seems to have been in the possession of only certain families living on and around Beech Mountain—the Wards, Harmons, Gentrys, Rowlands, and Hickses—some boys might well have heard of Jack's adventures for the first time as they were drifting into sleep while spending the night with young Marshall Ward.

It seems somehow fitting that the prodigy who told these tales to his schoolmates should become a teacher of elementary students. After earning a teaching certificate from Appalachian State Teachers College in nearby Boone, North Carolina, Ward taught the fifth grade in Banner Elk for the next thirty-five years. As might be expected, the Jack cycle became an important part of his curriculum. Every Friday afternoon Mr. Ward's fifth-graders held a club meeting, and their teacher's narrative talent was a featured part of this weekly program.

> I always told 'em a story—a Jack Tale or some other. When I run out of Jack Tales I make 'em up one. They wouldn't know the difference. Sometimes streamline 'em and they liked them better. Up-to-date, modern, you know, modernized. Just as long as it had Jack, Tom, and Will in it. And Jack, he always come out the hero and that's why they liked it, you know. They want to be a Jack, you see.

Thus Marshall Ward found in his students attentive listeners for these tales handed down from his own father. The influence of Ward, a thirty-five-year veteran teacher-storyteller, upon "his children" and the folk heritage around Beech Mountain would be impossible to quantify, but his would likely prove to be a rich legacy.

Perhaps Ward's greatest legacy, however, was his contribution to Richard Chase's 1943 publication of *The Jack Tales*. Ward recollected his first conversation with Chase, back in 1935:

> Well, I met Mr. Chase—he was up at Appalachian State Teachers College, at that time, hunting for old songs and ballots. He called all the teachers that would come in and tell him about 'em. If they knew any song, he'd like to hear their version of it. And they come in. He stayed in there and talked to 'em about thirty minutes. And after the meetin' was over I stayed in and I said, "Mr. Chase, I don't know anything about your songs much. I know a few old songs, heard my mother sing a few, but I don't know much about 'em. But I know a *whole lot* of old stories like you're talking about, handed down stories about Tom, Will, and Jack, called the Jack Tales." He said, "I'd like to know more about 'em." He said, "I'd like to hear you tell some of 'em." I said, "Get me somebody to tell 'em to, and I can do a better job."

Two important points should be noted from Ward's oral history. First, this cycle of tales was already known to the people who told them as "the Jack Tales," having been categorized not by the folk collector but by the folk themselves. Second, the schoolteacher ac-

customed to telling these stories to his students was not as yet comfortable performing without the stimulus of a responsive audience. In
order to do more than merely report basic story plots for a note-
taking collector, Ward needed listeners to "do a better job." Only with
"somebody to tell 'em to" could the storyteller break through into full
performance.

Not only did Chase readily shift his focus from the ballads he had
hoped to find to the folktale tradition that had fortuitously found
its way to him in the person of Marshall Ward, but Chase also provided Ward with the audience required to do a better job with his
storytelling.

> Over here at the Mission Home at Valle Crucis, the Episcopal
> Church had a school over there from kindergarten through the
> high school. They had about seventy-five students. I told four
> stories four days over there. Sixteen stories. And he had a girl take
> 'em down in shorthand. She wrote 'em out for him. Then he re-
> wrote 'em like he thought they ought to be, in his way of doing 'em,
> and he had 'em published in his book. Sixteen of 'em. Then two
> stories [that] he got from other places he put in the book, a little
> different from what I tell.[3] And—that made up his Jack Tale book.
> So, Richard got the stories from me. He tells in the book that that's
> where he got 'em.[4]

Through his association with Chase, Ward collaborated on one of the
major folktale collecting projects in the North Carolina Blue Ridge.
Despite its shortcomings, especially from a performance-oriented
perspective (see introduction), Chase's 1943 publication of these
composite, rewritten narratives remains the largest single corpus of
the North Carolina Jack Tales printed to date.

Ward's partnership with Chase was a source of great pride for the
storyteller, yet he took even greater pleasure in acknowledging the
wider audience his beloved Jack Tales received as a result of the
book's publication.

> I am the o-riginal man that got the Jack Tale books out. But I'm
> glad I did. I tell you—probably if Richard Chase hadn't a-put them
> out, they'd never heard tell of me, they'd never heard tell of the Jack
> Tales. They'd just been like they were in the dormant stages. No-
> body'd a-got any good out of them. I think it's good to have them
> out and let people read them and know about them.

College-educated Marshall Ward believed that "to have them out and let people read them and know about them" was to achieve for these stories a kind of universality and immortality. Far from decrying the disembodied voicelessness of print, the fifth-grade teacher of reading, writing, and history celebrated its liberating powers. "And, you know, I want them to live on and let other people learn them. And the more I give these old stories, the more people will know them, and maybe it'll make somebody else happy."

Marshall Ward gave the story of "Jack in the Lions' Den" to me on 11 July 1981, four months before his death. We held the recording session outdoors in front of his home. The storyteller was seated in a lawn chair under a large shade tree, surrounded by mountains geologists have judged to be among the oldest rock formations in the world. The audience was composed of myself and a technician who operated a ¾-inch color VTR portapack. The recording equipment did not intimidate the teller, however. By this time Ward was used to folklorists and students who wanted to record his stories and other traditional lore.

Marshall Ward had inherited "Jack in the Lions' Den" from his father, Miles Ward, and he promised to tell the story "just like Daddy told it to me *way* back yonder." Readers of Chase's collection have little to prepare them for the overtly sexual and scatological elements found in "Jack in the Lions' Den." Such earthy, off-color features quickly flag this tale as an authentic folk composition rooted in an oral culture that can be both vulgar and violent.

As a storyteller who performed for young children, Ward was sensitive to indelicate elements in his traditional material, changing or omitting them if necessary. For the purpose of this collection, he agreed to present the "o-riginal" version of "Jack in the Lions' Den," yet his performance was remarkable for its innocence. Nowhere did the telling become coarse, crude, or indecent. Perhaps the performance context had, in fact, modified Ward's recital. His tasteful treatment of the story was only what one would have expected from a retired schoolteacher obliging a young female collector he had just met. Indeed, it was somewhat surprising that Ward volunteered to record this particular tale in the first place. Obviously, the aging storyteller very much wanted this previously uncollected tale to be recorded in all its bawdy richness while he could still tell it.

Ward characteristically starts each of his Jack Tales with an introduction, both of himself and of the folk heritage he is about to share (see McGowan 1978). The introduction frames the tale and signals a movement from conversation into performance. Ward's introduction also keys the performance that follows, providing insight into the tone of his tale telling and thereby arousing a specific audience expectancy. For instance, in describing Council Harmon's life as a legendary raconteur, Ward notes the church's disapproval of storytelling. The established religion attempted to censor the Jack cycle by revoking membership for wayward storytellers, yet Ward chuckles as he recalls his famous forebear's troubles with the church. These opening remarks cue his audience that the forthcoming performance probably would not receive the sanction of the old-time religion. Far from incurring disapproval, however, such comments likely serve to build listener suspense, whetting the appetite for whatever worldly parable this secular storyteller has in store. Ward seems confident that his audience in this particular context shares his amusement as he tells of Counce Harmon's repeated "repentances." As his introductory frame segues into the story, Ward shifts his weight forward, leaning toward his listeners and the camera. Moving into closer proximity and rubbing his hands as if in anticipatory delight, the storyteller begins his performance.

The story he tells, "Jack in the Lions' Den", is composed of two discrete episodes: Jack's quest to answer the princess's three questions and Jack's imprisonment in the lions' den. The first part incorporates Motif H507.1.0.1: "Princess defeated in repartee by means of objects accidentally picked up." Two versions of this tale motif have been published by Vance Randolph (1952, 6–7; 1976, 57–58) from his fieldwork in the Ozarks. A third version, from Kentucky, has been published by Leonard Roberts (1969, 147–54). Roberts, in reference to a version that he has chosen not to print, speculates that "because of the obscene parts, the story is probably more in tradition than is revealed by these scattered references" (Roberts 1955, 240).

In the opening exposition of Ward's rendition, the storyteller paints the narrative backdrop for the dramatic action that will follow. The situation is a familiar one in folk literature—an oppressive regime under which the poor suffer. One route of escape from this harsh existence demands craftiness and cunning. The king's subjects are challenged to answer correctly three questions posed by his daughter; failure results in public execution. Goaded by the misery of their condition or by their own ambition, many men lose their lives in this fateful contest, their impaled heads making a mockery of future hopeful contenders. The social order here represented is cruel and violent.

In Ward's telling, however, the grim tone is lightened by laughter. The mean king is not simply capricious; rather, "he wanted to do something to see how many crazy people he had in his kingdom [that] would take a chance on answering these three questions." The storyteller's laughter on this line turns the seemingly sadistic decapitation into a joke. Only "crazy people" would make such a gamble because the stakes are simply too high. Men who take this risk are driven by pride, arrogance, or ambition.

Thus, the character of these successive challengers is the real theme of Ward's narrative. The storyteller is less interested in sociology than he is in psychology. For instance, the old king in the tale is indeed mean to his people and the times are hard, but his feudal villainy is eclipsed by Jack's virtue. To answer the princess's three questions, more than guile is required. An innate goodness is the requisite attribute of the victorious quest hero. Before the youngest-best brother is permitted to try his luck, however, Tom and Will must first exercise their successive rights of primogeniture. Their initial misdeeds provide a foil to Jack's eventual good deed.

Ward's account of the oldest brother, Tom, and his attempt to answer the princess omits the important episode concerning the hungry old man. This meeting is not reported until the second brother, Will, begins his journey. At that point, Ward remembers these important encounters with the starving traveler, encounters that pose the real test of all would-be suitors—the test of charity. The storyteller corrects his original oversight by adding phrases such as "And the same thing with Tom" and "Tom did the same thing," as he tells of brother Will's unkindness. Ward thus handles the forgotten motif by weaving it into the narrative on the second repetition of the journey cycle. Like the rhapsodes of old, he skillfully stitches in this significant scene as he recalls it. The result is a paratactic performance that convincingly conveys the oral flavor of authentic folk composition.

During the third and final repetition of this journey to the king's palace, Jack carries sexually symbolic objects. But he has not picked up these objects accidentally; he has been instructed to do so by the hungry old beggar, with whom Jack has shared his meager lunch. It is this mysterious stranger who poses the real test of the quest hero. When Jack reveals his charity and brotherhood by breaking bread with the destitute traveler, he is rewarded with the secret needed to beat the princess in her verbal duel.

As Mikhail Bakhtin has noted in *Rabelais and His World* (1984, 296)—a work that draws deeply on folk traditions—food and drink have power to liberate human speech, "lending it a fearless and free tone." Accordingly, the old man's wisdom can only be revealed at table: his postprandial prophecy of Jack's victory awaits upon an invitation to dinner. The shared wine loosens the old man's tongue, and, in turn, his sage advice lifts Jack's spirits, alerting him how best to extemporize in his encounter with the princess. From this liberating atmosphere of the feast, Jack derives his frank refutation of the princess's three challenges. The episode represents a triumph of the tongue and the oral orifice, which interact with the world, biting, chewing, swallowing: ingesting the world and thereby making it a part of the body (Bakhtin 1984, 281).

Unlike Will and Tom, both of whom are disrespectful to their needy elder and consequently unlucky when faced with the princess's challenge, Jack is lucky, but his good fortune is contingent on his own virtue. Jack's generosity toward his fellow journeyman is the central theme of the riddle episode. The storyteller's implied moral and sense of ethics go a long way toward tempering the off-color elements in this traditional tale.

In Ward's telling, the princess's three questions are, in fact, declarative statements, a triple challenge: "Fär-me-oh. Fär-me-oh. Fär-me-oh." It is helpful to note that the Blue Ridge Mountain pronunciations of *fire* and *far* are often indistinguishable. The spelling I opted for in the transcription (*fär*) represents an attempt to convey Ward's pronunciation.[5] In answering the princess's plaint of "Fär-me-oh," Tom and Will guess that something has happened at a distance ("far" away), to which they are being asked to respond. They therefore answer incorrectly: "Which-a-way did he go?" Both Tom and Will misunderstand the princess's ambiguous audition and consequently lose their lives. This curious chant is only interpreted aright when Jack arrives on the scene and recognizes the words correctly as "*Fire*-me-oh."

Ward's princess is considerably more modest than the female riddler in Leonard Roberts's tale of "Quare Jack." In this Kentucky version, the rich man's daughter initiates the banter with the explicit exclamation: "*Fire* in my tail!" (Roberts 1969, 148). Similarly, in Vance Randolph's Ozark version, a big country boy comes courting the rich man's daughter and, in an attempt to make conversation, comments, "That fire sure is hot, ain't it?" to which the girl retorts, "My ass is a damn sight hotter" (Randolph 1976, 57). How the refined refrain of "Fär-me-oh" evolved in Ward's rendition is not clear. Perhaps the storytelling context subtly modified his performance at this critical narrative juncture—the life or death challenge charged with sexual innuendo. At any rate, the code-switching employed here, from the career teacher's customarily light regional dialect to his decidedly colloquial pronunciation of *fire*, serves to mask the carnal elements inherent in this confrontation between the female prize and her male competitors. Indeed, listeners who do not know related versions of this tale will likely remain as confused by the princess's phrase as do both Tom and Will. Thus, the storyteller builds suspense throughout this episode of his narrative as first Tom, then Will, journeys to the king's palace seeking a fortune but finding instead an untimely death. The mystery is not disclosed until Jack appears, laden with the articles necessary to best the princess in her verbal contest of wits.

The gathering of objects and presenting them to the princess is the most dramatized action yet related in the tale. Prior to this episode, Ward's gestures have been less illustrative of specific objects and events and more indicative of the storyteller's general animated involvement with the progression of the plot. At this point in the performance, however, Ward begins to show his audience, as well as to tell them, of Jack's exploits. For instance, Ward indicates with hands spread apart the length of Jack's crooked cane, which was "about that long." He suggests putting onto his head an imaginary cap, into which Jack has carefully placed eighteen pheasant eggs. Rubbing his hands together, Ward shows Jack peeling the "purtiest white nuts you ever saw" and putting them into his pocket. Earlier in the story the storyteller offers little or no vocal distinction between characters to suggest different ages or sexes. But as the narrative builds in tempo, Ward offers a slightly higher-pitched female voice that rises to the near-hysterical line, "DADDY, HE'S ANSWERED EVER' ONE OF THE QUESTIONS!" This Appalachian Atalanta now must marry Jack, the suitor who drops not golden apples but peeled hickory nuts and who thereby wins his quest. Ward finishes with the traditional narrative frame: "And they're getting along just fine the last time I heard tell of 'em."

This proves to be a false ending, however. The storyteller has momentarily forgotten the tale's second episode involving Jack's imprisonment in the lions' den, an essential element that gives the story its title. Yet the first half of this narrative is obviously a complete, self-contained story in its own right that could stand alone as a Jack Tale. For instance, during Jack's verbal sparring with the king's daughter, she taunts, "I bet you ain't got no nuts *to cap off this story with.*" Such a metafictional device signals the imminent conclusion of the tale. Moreover, Ward claims that when telling the story to children he modifies it. Perhaps his modification involves telling his young listeners only the riddle episode, deleting the lions' den episode altogether.

As the performer concludes the first half of his recitation, he begins to repeat the title: "And that's—." Then he catches his omission of the entire lions' den plot. After only a moment's pause and reflection, he recovers and segues back into the narrative that he had promised to tell "the way I learned it first. O-riginally." Ward is quickly able to recollect "the best part of this story." With little exposition, he introduces Jack's new adversary, the old rich man who will trick the young bridegroom out of his bride, and the tale begins anew.

The second episode concerns Jack's subsequent imprisonment in the lions' den. In performance, the seam shows where these two episodes are stitched together.[6] The storyteller brings the riddle episode to a false conclusion, having momentarily forgotten the lions' den episode that follows. Moreover, Jack himself undergoes a major transformation in character at this juncture. Throughout the initial riddle episode, Jack is an active character who is directly responsible for his own good luck. In the ensuing lions' den episode, however, Jack is a passive character, the victim of bad luck. The performer does not seem troubled by the contradictions of his Janus-faced Jack. His telling brings the clever trickster and his alter ego, the foolish numbskull, together in the same adventure.

While Ward's title might suggest Old Testament parallels, the second half of "Jack in the Lions' Den" is actually related to AT 559, the tale of the helpful dungbeetle (see n. 6). Having caught the princess with her own words, besting her in sexually suggestive repartee, Jack now makes an unlucky bargain with a rival for the young woman's hand in marriage. In exchange for a bag of gold, Jack takes a vow of silence to last for three successive days and nights. His new bride, angered by his silence, has him thrown into the lions' den, and the rival suitor takes Jack's place as bridegroom.

In Ward's telling Jack's rival is eventually driven off with barnyard waste brought in to befoul the wedding bed. Although Jack eventually emerges victoriously from this earthen womb or tomb, he has been, for the most part, neither especially lucky nor especially clever. In fact the plot is carried forward not by the pinioned protagonist but by his industrious animal helpers. Jack becomes what Victor Turner (1967, 99) calls a liminal figure, "that which is neither this nor that, and yet both," as he awaits completion of the rite of passage that will nudge him from boyhood into manhood. Similarly, the lions' den becomes a threshold, "a stage of reflection" (Turner 1967, 105), through which Jack must pass in order to come of age as a man and a husband.

At this juncture in the story, Bakhtin's topsy-turvy image of carnival becomes most enlightening. In *Rabelais and His World* he explores carnival's inversion of the normal political, religious, and socioeconomic orders and the consequent displacement of the highest by the lowest. This carnival inversion is duplicated in the physical body, where a scene of feasting is replaced by a scene of excrement, where the function of the mouth is replaced by the function of the anus, and where procreation and birth are replaced by death and burial. In accordance with Bakhtin's scheme, when celebration of the tongue ceases, when silence reigns or a lie is uttered, then both the hero's and the villain's worlds turn upside down. The regenerative act of procreation breeds only death and burial. The head is subverted by the buttocks. All speech is stilled by the inexplicable presence of waste and filth. Yet this scene of decay holds the promise of resurrection and rebirth, the restoration of the proper order of things both physical and emotional, and the full celebration of the liberating and regenerating energy of laughter.

In the present tale an inversion of the normal order of things is brought about because of Jack's vow of silence. The power of the tongue, which has just won the hero his prize, is now nullified. The bridegroom only smiles and laughs at his wife's entreaties. The consequence of his speechlessness is a downfall into the earthen lions' den, a symbolic womb or grave from which a regenerative birth will later occur. Such an inversion of high and low also appears in the bodily imagery in this episode of Ward's tale. No longer are men's heads chopped off and impaled on spikes for incorrect speech. Instead, comic emphasis shifts to the lower extremities of the human anatomy—the belly, the genitals, and the buttocks. But any act of copulation is prevented by defecation; the power of the phallus is thwarted by the workings of the bowels and the anus. The grotesque naturalism of the subsequent episodes convincingly demonstrates the authentic folk origin of Ward's tale about a lions' den, however much the storyteller's simple, candid recitation mitigates the grosser elements of his narrative.

Although Jack shows more traits of simpleton than trickster in his bet with the old rich man, while imprisoned in the lions' den he finally sees through his rival's machinations. Like Jack, the old rich man is given three successive nights during which to please the king's daughter. Jack's pet June bug, doodle bug, and mouse set out to insure that the old rich man will fail his wedding night test. The scatological emphasis in this tale precludes any suggestion of a sexual consummation of the princess's marriage with the old man. Instead, the hymeneal ritual is perverted. The bridal sheets are spotted not with a drop of blood but with barnyard dung. The bewildered old man encases himself twice in cocoonlike sacks and finally in a wooden box. These images suggest condoms and coffins. They connote not fertility but sterility and, prophetically, even death.

Ward's account of the rival's three successive nights with the princess is detailed and drawn out, with an almost poetic repetition of the several species of excrement hauled in to befoul the bed clothes: "barn manure, chicken manure, and ever'thing." Jack is largely inactive throughout these scenes, and consequently the storyteller's best-drawn portrait is of the unfortunate wife who wakes to discover filth in her bridal bower. Ward gives her character strong vocal distinction. Her voice, with its growing hysteria and indignation, can be heard not only in her own lines of dialogue but in Ward's third person descriptions as well. Thus, the emotional state of the distraught princess colors Ward's narrative. The eye that sees the work of Jack's industrious animals is the horrified one of the princess; the resulting lament is raised with her voice.

Ward brings his story to a neat conclusion as he blends back into the "Gold Kingdom" ending he has already told prematurely following the riddle episode. The performer then offers a brief apology for the mistake made earlier, explaining that he was somewhat unsure about this story because he "hadn't told it in a long time." "Jack in the Lions' Den" lasted over twenty-three minutes. An occasional slip notwithstanding, Ward told the tale with assurance, animation, vigor, and obvious delight.

Sexual symbolism, bawdy banter, a bigamous wife, wedding night sheets smeared with excrement, and a good deed performed for an old man: all combine to make "Jack in the Lions' Den" an unusual folklore find. Although the recorded Jack cycle as a whole is rich in earthy details and occasional amoral character motivation, the suggestive sexual innuendo and graphic scenes of bridal bower filth related in "Jack in the Lions' Den" set it apart from other accounts of the mountain hero who lends his name to this entire canon of tales. Yet Ward skillfully weaves his narrative-tapestry around the initial vignette of Jack sharing food with the needy beggar. This simple act of generosity demonstrates Jack's essential virtue and consequently shapes and colors all the events that follow.

The verb *give* is frequently used by traditional regional storytellers in reference to the act of sharing a tale with listeners. With characteristic generosity, Ward made a gift of "Jack in the Lions' Den" for the purpose of this study, just as, years before, he had given his stories to collector Richard Chase. The tales are given in trust, however. Marshall Ward instructed me to use the story and then to pass it on. It is my hope that this case study in some way repays my debt and passes on the narrative legacy that this gentle mountain man nurtured for a lifetime.

With Ward's death, this story, too, seems to have expired, vanishing from the oral tradition of Beech Mountain. The tale's narrative essence, however, lies preserved as in literary amber in this transcription of Ward's encore performance. The genetic code for its reproduction lies dormant in these pages. In a favorable environment this story's seed could again take root, sprout, and blossom into performance. The breath of a living voice could again resuscitate the story's perennial folk hero.

NOTES

1. It is interesting that Ward has conjectured that the Jack Tales came from Germany, although Harmon is generally held to have claimed that they came

from England. The Teutonic ancestry of "Jack in the Lions' Den" is supported by Stith Thompson (1946, 158), who traces the story's origins to a Middle High German poem.

2. Gutierrez (1978) describes the Wards' traditional storytelling context.

3. Chase ended up printing fifteen North Carolina tales and three Virginia tales, for a total of eighteen. The three tales that Chase collected in Wise County, Virginia, include "Jack and the Bull," "Jack and King Marock," and "Soldier Jack." In 1943, when *The Jack Tales* was published, Chase wrote that these three tales were "unknown" to his North Carolina informants (p. x).

4. For Chase's account of his meeting with Ward, see R. Chase 1939 and his preface to *The Jack Tales*.

5. Cf. *Webster's Ninth New Collegiate Dictionary*, 34.

6. Ward's full, two-part version is not as anomalous as it might at first seem. Although the tale, in other versions (and in Ward's presumed version for children), frequently ends with the first winning of the princess, a further episode or set of episodes, involving imprisonment of the hero, is an integral part of the story according to the Aarne-Thompson tale-type index. In the present case, however, what seems to have happened is that AT 853 has become crossed with another two-part story, AT 559, that regularly features escape from the lions' den and displacement of a rival from the bridal bed through the agency of helpful insects. The initial quests in the two stories are similar: outwit the princess in repartee (AT 853) or make her laugh (AT 559). The concluding test is practically identical: escape from confinement and re-win the princess. In this Beech Mountain tradition the second half of AT 559 has been grafted onto the first half of AT 853. Or perhaps the two tale types should more properly be viewed as subtypes of a single tale.

JACK IN THE LIONS' DEN

as told by Marshall Ward

Marshall Ward was the man who introduced Richard Chase to North Carolina Jack Tales. He did not, however, tell Chase about "Jack in the Lions' Den." He saved the full and unexpurgated version of this tale until a few months before his death, when he communicated it to folklore student Cheryl Oxford, as she relates in her essay.

*The story seems to be a cross between "Dungbeetle" (*AT* 559) and "The Hero Catches the Princess with her Own Words" (*AT* 853). Both stories involve rather similar tests to win the princess, and both stories lead up to an episode in which the hitherto successful hero is imprisoned but escapes to claim his bride. In this performance Ward almost forgot that he was going to tell the whole story. Apparently he customarily told only the first half, and that in a rather bowdlerized version.*

▼ ▼ ▼

[*The storyteller is seated, looking down and away from the camera as he begins.*]

I'm Marshall Ward from Banner Elk, North Carolina.
I live at
Banner Elk
and I was raised at Beech Creek.

I'm gonna tell a Jack Tale.
But I want to tell you 'bout these old stories.
I learned them from my dad, Miles Ward,
when I was a little boy.
I was born at Beech Creek, North Carolina,
December the tenth, nineteen-six.
And I learnt all these old Jack stories—
about twenty-five of them—
from my dad.
He told them to me when I was a little boy.

Now my dad,
he learnt these stories from Counce Harmon.
Counce Harmon was his great-
great-
uncle.
And Counce Harmon claims these stories came from England.

And Counce Harmon is my great-
great-
great-
grandfather.
He told these stories
over and over
to the children.
People way back yonder was very strict on people about
what they done
in religion.
They turned Counce Harmon outta the church two or three times
    'cause he told these stories. [*Laughs.*]
[*Smiling:*] They thought it was wrong telling stories like
Jack Tales and others.
Counce was a pretty lively old man.
He'd get the young people out, and—
they could play the fiddle and have a—
oh, a Virginia Reel
or a dance.
[*Smiling:*] And then they'd turn him out of the church for that.
They was pretty strict about what they was doing.

[*A tone of feigned repentance:*] But Old Man Counce
he'd go back and tell them he was sorry.
They'd take him back.
[*Smiling:*] But he just couldn't stay out of
being with the young people and having a good time,
and telling stories and
having a dance once in awhile.

[*The storyteller has begun to look up and around at his
environment, including the camera.*]

Well!
The story I'm going to tell
is, uh—
"Jack in the Lions' Den."
I'm gonna tell it the way I learnt it
first.
O-riginally.
I *have* modified it a little for the children [*i.e., when telling it in a school setting*].
And I'm gonna tell it just like Daddy told it to me
way back yonder.

[*Although the storyteller uses his hands fairly frequently throughout this opening section—rubbing them together, rubbing them on his knees or on the arms of his lawn chair—such gestures are largely nonspecific and nonillustrative of the narrative's unfolding drama. Instead, the storyteller seems somehow "charged" with his tale and eager to release it through performance.*]

One time there was a
old king,
now, lived in a kingdom.
And back—
well, if you know your European history,
they had a lot of kings and dukes and things,
lived in little kingdoms.
And they'd build
little walls around their castles and
they'd have drawbridges and things to keep the
enemies away.
Well, that's kindly the way it was when Jack lived.

The old king,
he had a beautiful daughter.
He wanted to do something great for his daughter.
And he was a pretty mean king.
And he put out a decree or law—
anybody
could answer three questions his daughter could ask,
he'd give them half his kingdom,

wealth,
and then
they'd get to marry his daughter
and 'come king after he died.

Well, you know, that enticed
old men, young men,
everybody's wanting to 'come
the king,
and everybody's wanting half the king's wealth.

[*Rapidly:*] But let me tell you—
they's more to it than that.

If anybody failed to answer them three questions,
they got their head cut off,
and the old king had a b-i-g garden out there,
and he had their heads stuck up on a sharp pole
out there.

He just mean, you see.

[*Smiling:*] He wanted to do something to see how many crazy people
    he had in his kingdom
would take a chance on
answering these three questions [*laughing*].
How many would do that for his daughter
or half his kingdom, wealth?

Well, the old king was pretty hard on the people,
and lot of people didn't care whether they lived or died,
they was having such a hard time
making a living.

Well, many, many people has went up to the old king's palace
and tried to answer the three questions the daughter asked.
And they'd all failed.
They's many, many heads had dried up on a pole
sticking up in the old king's garden out there.

And, you know,
Tom said
he wanted to go up and try it.

And Mother and Dad said,
"Son,
all these other people's tried it,
and," said, "you know they've lost their heads.
Do you want your head *chopped* off [*hitting fist into palm*], just cause
you want to try
to answer the three questions?"

"Yes, yes," said, "we going to try."
Said, "It's hard trying to make a living,
and," said, "just as soon to be dead as alive."

Well, nothing else would do Tom,
but he went up
to the king's palace.
    [*Sits back in his chair, assuming the pose of the king.*]
The king said,
"Young man, you know what you're asking for now?
You do understand everything?
Now, if you don't answer the *questions*
that my daughter *asks*,
the three *questions*—"
said, "your head is chopped off and [*pointing with right hand*] stuck
    up on a pole
with *all* these other people out here."

"Yes," said, "I understand that," said Tom.

And the king's daughter came out at ten o'clock,
and set in
her big palace—her big seat
in the king's palace.
    [*Indicates the girl's throne with both hands by a slow downward
    movement through the air, as if drawing its dimensions.*]
And she said, "*Fär-me-oh*:
Fär-me-oh, Fär-me-oh."

He said, "Which-a-way did he go?
Which-a-way did he go?"
   [*Leans forward in his chair after this line, as if to see whether his
   response as Tom had been correct.*]
She said, "That hain't right."
Said to the guards
[*pointing with right forefinger*], "Take him out.
Cut his head off.
Stick it up on a pole."

And that's what they did.

They took him out.
Cut his head off.
Stuck it up on a pole.

And, do you know,
it wasn't six months,
Will said, "Something must have happened to Tom."
He said, "I just got to go up there
and see about him."

Mother and Dad said, "Don't go, Will."
Said, "You'll end up just like Tom.
His head's up there
on a pole just like all them other people."
Said, "Stay at home with us, son."
Said, "We'd rather have you alive as dead."

"No, Mother."
Said, "I got to go up there and see what happened."

"Well, don't be so foolish as to try to answer the questions."

W-e-l-l, Will,
he went along the road,
and he traveled along.
Mother fixed him a good lunch as he went along.
   (And the same thing with Tom:

He went along.

Fixed him a good lunch.)

And he come to a g-r-e-a-t b-i-g sugar tree,

and a big spring a-running out of the bank of the road.

[*Rubs his hands together, as if washing them in the spring.*]

The water was good and cool,

and the water went down the hill saying,

"Ooo-gle, ooo-gle,

Boo-gle, boo-gle,"

as it went down the hill.

[*Makes sweeping, circular motions downward through the air with both hands.*]

And, you know,

Tom sat—

er, Will sat down there and eat.

(And Tom did the same thing.)

And there 'as an *old, old* man came out.

Said, "Hello there, son."

He said, "I'm an old, old man."

He had a long white beard [*bringing his hand up to his face and then dropping it down to his waist*]

plumb down to his waist.

Hair as white as snow.

Looked like he was a hundred years old.

Said, "Young man,

would you be so kind as to give an old man a bite or two of your lunch?"

He said, "I'm starved to death.

I ain't had anything to eat in a week."

"W-e-l-l,"

he said, "I'll tell you."

He said, "I've started up to the king's palace

to try to answer those three questions to get half the kingdom,

and," he said, "the king's daughter.

And if I get that,"

he said, "I'll come back and get you

and feed you good."

"Well, son," he said,
"I need it now."

He said [*shaking his head*], "I just b-a-r-e-l-y got enough for myself
   this time."
Well,
Will sat down and drank that good old cold water.
Eat his lunch.
And [*making a sweeping gesture with his right arm*] the old man just
   disappeared in the woods,
and Will didn't see him no more.

And he went on up there
[*looking up and pointing*], and sure enough, the first head he saw
a-sticking on a pole
was Tom's.

SCARED WILL ALMOST TO DEATH!

And he went in to the king's palace.
The king said, "Young man,
have you come to try to answer the questions?"

"Well," he said, "I don't know."
He said, "I been a-thinking about it."

"Well, now," he said, "you know
if you don't answer them right
your head comes off and stuck up on a pole
just like the rest of them."
   [*Looks from left to right, as if scanning the imaginary scene.*]
Looked like there was a thousand heads out there.

Will's knees was a-bumping together.
He was scared.
but he just couldn't back out now.
He had to try.

"Yeah," he said,
"I believe I'll try."

"Ten o'clock," he said, "in the morning,
here at the palace.
You be here
if you want to try."

Ten o'clock
Will was there.
Well, when ten o'clock come,
the king's daughter said,
"Här-me-oh,
Sir.
Här-me-oh, Här-me-oh.
Yes, sir."

[*Rapidly:*] "Which-a-way did she go?
Which-a-way did she go?"

"That's not right," she said.
"Take him out, guards.
Cut his head off."

Took him out,
and cut his head off and stuck it up beside of Tom's out there on a
    pole.

Well!

Went on for about six months,
and Jack,
he just couldn't stay home no longer.

He said, "Mother, I just got to go up,
—and Dad,—
to see what happened to Tom and Will."

Said, "Son, don't go."
Said, "You know their heads are sticking on a pole up there.
And we just don't want your head stuck on a pole up there.
And you're the only son we got left.

Please stay with us.
We're getting old.
We need you to stay here and help us.
Not your head up there at the king's garden
stuck on a pole."

"O-h-h," Jack said, "my head ain't gonna be stuck on a pole.
But," said, "I'm going up there and see if their heads's on a pole."

And Jack took off one morning.
And Mother fixed him a little lunch
—just like she did Tom and Will—
and he put it in a little bag and took off
right early one morning.

And about twelve o'clock he come to that big cool spring
and that big shade tree beside the road.
　　[*Repeats the sweeping, circular motions downward through the air
　　with both hands*.]
And that water was a-running down the hill and a-going down the
　　hill saying,
"Ooo-gle, ooo-gle, ooo-gle,
Boo-gle, boo-gle,"
as it went down the hill.

And, you know,
Jack was setting there, and he spread out his little lunch,
and out come that old man.

He said, "Hello there, son."
He said, "I see you're gonna have your lunch here."

"Yes, Grandpaw," he said.
"Set right down and
have some with me" [*indicating a place with a wave of his hand*].

"I don't care if I do," said the old man.

He set down
and Jack, he

began to break off a little piece of pone bread
to reach it to the old man.
He had a little bottle of wine.
He'd give the old man the first drink of the wine.
The old man, he'd drink and eat awhile.

"Well, son,"
he said, "I know what you're gonna do."
Said, "You're going up here to the king's palace
and try to answer them three questions."

"Now, son,
I want to tell you,"
he said, "it's gonna be a hard job but you can do it
if you be careful.
Now on your way to the king's palace,
from here on,"
said, "you take ever'thing that comes to your mind that you think
     you'll need to answer them questions.
Ever'thing you see that you think might be helpful to you,"
said, "you just take it.
And," said, "I'll guarantee you they'll be a help to you."

"Well, thank you, Grandpaw."

And Jack got in such a hurry he just left the rest of his lunch there.
He said, "Grandpaw,"
he said [pointing], "you have the rest of it."
Said, "I don't want it."
Said, "I want to get to the king's palace."

And he hadn't went
a hundred yards up the road above the old man
[pointing], looked off below the road and there
was a little crooked cane—
Well, it wasn't more than a foot long.
Prettiest little cane you ever saw
just a-growing there.
And Jack said, "I need that."

He went down there and took his knife and cut it.
He cut it about that long [*indicating with hands*],
and just stuck it in his hip pocket.

And he went on up the road,
and he got up there a piece,
and there was a pheasant flew out from under a log.
He run up there where that pheasant flew out,
and up there was *eighteen eggs*
in that nest.
And something said, "You'll need them eggs."
Said, "Take 'em.
Take 'em.
Put them in your cap lining."
  [*Mimes taking a cap from his head.*]
He took it out,
and his old cap was kinda ragged,
and he put them eighteen eggs in the lining of his cap,
and put it on his head right easy,
so they wouldn't break.
  [*Mimes replacing the cap on his head.*]

And he went on up the road.
And he come to a hickory nut tree,
and the ground was just covered with hickory nuts.
And something said to him, "Jack, you'll need a pocketful of them
    nuts."
And he went and peeled them nuts [*rubbing hands as if peeling*]—
purtiest white nuts you ever saw—
and he put his pocket full of hickory nuts [*bringing hand to hip
    pocket*].

In about a hour he come to the king's palace.

He went on in to the palace.
And the old king said, "Son, have you come
to try to answer the questions?"

"Yes," he said, "that's what I come for,
but I want to look around

and see whose heads's stuck out there in that garden" [*looking off to the right*].

First two heads he saw was Tom and Will's.
"Yeaup,"
said, "the boys has got their heads chopped off.
I ain't gonna get mine chopped off," said Jack.
"Something's gonna help me.
That old man said I'd be lucky.
I'm a-gonna be lucky," said Jack.

[*Pointing:*] "You be here at ten o'clock," the king said,
"at the palace,
and my daughter'll be out here with the questions."

And he was there at ten o'clock.
And the lady said,
"Fär-me-oh,
Jack;
fär-me-oh."

"Madam,
are you hot enough to roast these eggs?"

"Yes, sir, if you've got some eggs?"

"I've got some nice ones right here in the cap [*suggests removing cap*]—
in my cap here."
And he pulled off his cap.

She said, "I bet you hain't got a crooked stick to roll them out with."

"I bet you I have." [*Mimes pulling cane from hip pocket.*]
And he pulled out that crooked stick in his pocket,
and he took that old cap and held them out there to the queen's—
uh, the king's daughter's lap—
and he just rolled them eggs
one by one right out in her lap.

Eighteen of them.
[*With the imaginary cap in his left hand and the cane in his right,
mimes rolling first one egg, then a second, out of his cap and into the
princess's lap, using the cane as a paddle.*]

And her eyes was big as dinner plates.
[*Holds his curved hands apart in approximately the outline of a plate-
sized circle in front of his face.*]
She said, "I bet you hain't got no nuts to cap off this story with."
[*Mimes removing the nuts from his pants pocket and scattering a
handful on the ground in front of the princess.*]
"I bet you I have," said Jack.
"I bet you I've got a whole pocketful."
And he just put them—whole pocketful of them hickory nuts
and laid them out in her lap.

And [she] said [*fast and high-pitched*], "DADDY, HE'S
   ANSWERED EVER' ONE OF THE QUESTIONS!"

"Fine."
Said, "Take him in,
have him shaved,
give him a bath,
put on the king's best garments.
Make a prince out of him."

They took him in,
cleaned him up,
shaved him,
gave him a bath,
MADE HIM A PRINCE.
The prettiest man she'd ever seen in her life.
And she fell in love with Jack.
He was a *beauty*, she thought.

And he stayed there,
and they got to dating each other,
and, and she loved him ever' day better.

And after awhile they had a wedding—
it lasted a month.
Biggest one in that whole kingdom.

And they got married.
The old king lived for about ten years and died.
And Jack become king,
and he was the best king they ever had,
because Jack was a poor man.
And a-l-l them heads a-sticking in that yard out there,
Jack had them took down and buried in the garden,
Tom and Will with them.

And ever'body wants to come and join Jack's kingdom
because he found a gold mine
up in the mountains.
And he had the men
to mine that gold, and he give ever'body in his kingdom
a bag of gold.
And they called Jack's kingdom
"Gold Kingdom
Of the Earth."
And ever'body wanted to join Jack's kingdom.
And Jack just couldn't take ever'body in.
He just had to 'strict hisself,
and let ever'body that just had a house and land
and property
live in his kingdom.

[*Laughing:*] And they're getting along just fine the last time I heard
    tell of them.

[*Crosses his arms and sits back in his chair, as if finished.*]

That's "Jack's—"
[*The storyteller looks down, pausing for perhaps five seconds.*]

(Well, that ain't all of it.
I just got to a part of it.

Let me tell you a little more.
I left out the best part of this story.
Let me finish it.
This ain't all of it.)

Now there was an old *rich* man
lived there.
And he come around after Jack got married to the king's daughter
    (I left out the half of this story),
and he said,
"Jack," he said, "you ain't got no money
to go in," he said,
"and be *rich* like the king is."
    (This is 'fore the king died now.)
He said—
    (I left out a whole lot.)
He said, "I want to give you a *whole bag of gold*
if you won't talk to your
wife
for three days."

"All right."
He said, "I won't talk to her for three days."

Said, "You just be good to her and not talk to her for three days."

And the old king was—
If, if, if she wasn't satisfied with Jack
for three days
he'd be throwed in the lions' den.

[*Smiling:*] And Jack, he was with his wife,
and he just good to her
and he just smiled.
And she tried to get him to talk and he wouldn't talk.
She got mad.
She'd bite him.
She'd kick him.
And he'd just, he'd just laugh at her [*laughing*].
And she got so mad.

And the old king come down, said, "How you getting along?"

[*Fast:*] "Just fine, but Jack won't talk."

They took him to ever' doctor in their kingdom, and said wasn't a
thing wrong with him.

And, you know,
went right on the second night like that.

   [*Throws up both hands, as if the king is exasperated with Jack.*]
"One more night," said the old uh, king,
"we'll throw him in the lions' den."
And, you know, the third night
he wouldn't talk to her.
And they took and throwed him in the lions' den.

And the old rich man,
he got to marry the king's daughter
if
Jack didn't work out all right.
And that's what he was doing.

They throwed Jack in the lions' den.
And there was one old big lion,
mother lion,
with three little lions
down there.
And the old lion was asleep.
And Jack had a *big* last—
kind of like a muzzle—
in his pocket.
   [*Cups his hands together, as if to muzzle the lion's snout.*]
And he slipped that over the old big lion's nose
and tied it real tight.
Had some strings in his pocket and tied the big lion's feet together,
and she couldn't even get up.
Jack went to playing with the little lions,
and he was just having a good time with the little lions.

And they'd throw food down there to feed the old big lion and the
   little lions,
and Jack would eat what he wanted of it.

And that old big man—
mean man—
they had a wedding,
and she married that old man.

And Jack happened to have with him—
and he carried them in his pocket—
[*enumerating on his fingers*] a pet June bug,
and a doodle bug,
and a mouse.
He had them with him all the time.
And he carried this with him.

Well,
Jack sent his June bug out to see what was taking place.
And the June bug come back and told him they was having a
   wedding,
and that old man that give him that bag of gold
was a-marrying his wife.
And he could see through ever' bit of it now:
why he got throwed in the lions' den,
why he got him not to talk to his wife.
That's why he give him that bag of gold,
[that] wasn't gonna do him no good.

Well,
that night
they was going to sleep together,
that old big—uh, that old man
and the king's daughter.
And Jack sent his doodle bug,
and his June bug,
and the mouse.
And he told them
to carry *all kinds of filth*—

dirt and mud and stuff—
and put on that old man that night
in his bed,
but not put a bit on the woman:
"Don't get a bit on her side of the bed,
just put it on him."
And that's what the doodle bug done all night,
and the June bug.
They just smeared him good.

[*High-pitched:*] She got up the next morning, and boy, he was
    a-stinking.
She got out of the bed, a-crying
SHE DIDN'T WANT HIM!
SHE WISHED SHE HAD JACK BACK!

And the old king come down and said,
"How you doing?"

[*Loud, almost a chant:*] "O-h-h-h, I don't want this old dirty man."
Said, "He's got mud—
he's been out in the mud
and the dirt and ever'thing.
Look at him.
He just looks filthy.
Look at my bed.
Look what he done last night."

The old man was scared to death.
He knowed what would happen to him
if it happened anymore.
And you know what he done?
Next day he had him a bag made
out of leather—
just a leather bag
like, you know, almost like a sleeping bag,
put up,
and just let enought of his eyes and nose stick out to see so he
    wouldn't get out.

And Jack sent his June bug to see what was taking place that night.
And told him what the old man had done.
He was in that bag.
He sent his mouse and his mouse cut holes *all* in that bag.
And they packed it full of barn manure,
chicken manure,
and ever'thing,
and smeared the bed *all* over,
and the floor *all* over.
And it got to stinking, about midnight.
[*Smiling:*] She waked up,
and she got out of that bed and couldn't sleep no longer with him.
And she got the servants in there,
and got him out of there,
and drug him down in the basement and cleaned him up.
Boy, what a stinking mess he was!

She's setting out on the porch a-crying when the king come down
   next morning.

Said [*again loud, almost a chant*], "HE'S WORSER THIS TIME
   THAT HE WAS BEFORE!"
Said, "He got into a bag,
and," said, "*it* was plumb full of stuff.
Ever'thing—
barn manure,
chicken manure.
O-h-h-h, and," said, "it was a mess!"
Said, "I WANT JACK BACK!"

"*O-h-h-h*," the king said,
"the lions has eat him up."

"I don't believe it," she said.

"Well," he said, "he *was* clean."

Well,
one more time.

Said if he was—
One more night. . . .

And so,
this time
he had a—
this time
they had
two sacks made:
a silk one;
a leather one.
And put him in.
And then
they kindly made a *box* and put him in,
    [*Indicates the width of this box by spreading his hands apart.*]
just enough of air to get in so he wouldn't smother,
and set it inside the bed.
And they went back and told him [Jack] about it.

The mouse said he'd fix that.
He'd cut a hole into the box.
Said, "We'll fill that box full
of barn manure,
chicken manure.
And," said, "We'll put it all over the bed,
and we'll put all over
the girl this time."

And they worked all night,
and they just smeared ever'thing.

And, boy, she got out of there with such a-crying and a-hollering.
She sent for the king
and he got down there before daylight.
And that man was a mess.
Oh, it was a-running all over the floor and ever'thing else.
There, they, they done a good job that night.
And he said, "Take him to the lions' den."

She said, "HOLLER FOR JACK AND SEE IF HE'S DOWN
  THERE!"
Said, "I WANT
JACK
BACK!"

And, you know,
they went and hollered for Jack.
And he said [*as if from a great distance*], "*Hey, king,*"
he said, "I'm all right."
Said, "I'm a-having a good time down here with the little
lions."

Said [*as if calling down into lions' den*], "We want to get you out of
  there."

And when they got him out,
he went and untied the old mother lion.
Took the last—er, off her feet and legs [*moving hand in circular,
  untying motion*].
She pretty weak.
There's a lot of food down there.
And he [*suiting action to word*] put his hand under the muzzle and
  jerked it off.
They jerked him out.
And she went to eating that food.
[*Laughing:*] They throwed that old man in.
She eat him up before he hit the ground,
she was so hungry.

And then Jack told them
what he'd done, and said he thought just three nights
being not talking
wouldn't be nothing—
and get that big bag of gold.
That's why he done that.
And, *oh-h-h,* she was so happy and Jack was so happy.

[*Rapid chant:*] *Then,* that's when Jack—
the old king died about ten years later,

and Jack become king,
found a gold mine and give ever'body gold,
and that made it the "Gold Kingdom."
And *now* he's a-getting along just fine and getting along happy.

  (I'm sorry I about left out a part of the story—
  one of the best parts in it.
  You know, I hadn't told it in a long time
  but that—
  that was supposed to go in it.)

And Jack's made a good king.
[*Laughing:*] You may go to see him some of these days,
if you ever find where he lives.
    [*The storyteller sits back in his chair to signal the finish of this tale.*]

CHAPTER 4

THE
GENTRY-LONG
TRADITION
AND ROOTS OF
REVIVALISM

▼ ▼ ▼ ▼ ▼

MAUD GENTRY LONG

▼ ▼ ▼ ▼ ▼

Bill Ellis

"It would be on a long winter evening," Maud Long recalled, re-creating the context of her family's Jack Tales during her 1947 Library of Congress recordings,

> when, after supper, all of us were gathered before the big open fire, my mother taking care of the baby or else the baby was in the cradle very near to Mother and she would be sewing or carding. . . . The older girls were helping with the carding or the sewing, and all of us little ones would either have a lap full or a basket full of wool out of which we must pick all the burrs and the Spanish needles and the bits of briars and dirt against the next day's carding; for my mother wove all of this wool that had been shorn from the backs of our own sheep raised there on the farm. . . . And so she needed every bit of

the wool that she could get ready, and to keep our eyes open and our fingers busy and our hearts merry, my mother would tell these marvelous tales, the Jack, Will and Tom Tales. (M. Long 1955a, A1)

Rae Korson, director of the library's Archive of Folksong, called Long's description "quite colorful, solid Americana." Korson, at the time, was working on an LP release of Long's Jack Tale recordings. "Very quotable also, as far as reviewers go," she added, recommending that they be quoted in full on the recording's jacket. In a later note, she stressed, "We should try to get the jackets printed in time for Christmas as we need a new release to stimulate sales" (Korson to Dr. Harold Spivacke, 7 November 1955, MLF).[1]

Long's loving but realistic perception of the tales' place in hardscrabble subsistence farming contrasts sharply with Korson's perception of them as Americana to be hyped as Christmas presents. But in this contrast we see in capsule the cultural changes that Maud Long (1893–1984) and her mother Jane Hicks Gentry (1863–1925) lived through in Appalachia. "The Heifer Hide," repeatedly mentioned as one of Long's favorite tales, is one tale that survived this change. The Gentry-Long version was collected four times. First, in the summer of 1923 Gentry told this and other tales to Isabel Gordon Carter (1925, 343–46). Then, sometime in 1937 Richard Chase, seeking variants of tales he had found in the Ward family, visited Long and used her as the major source for his *Jack Tales* version of "The Heifer Hide" (R. Chase 1943, 161–71). In 1941 Long recorded "Jack and the Calf Hide" on a borrowed disk cutter for private collector Artus Moser (Botkin 1949, 519–25), and early in 1947 she recorded it again for the Archive of American Folk Song at the Library of Congress. In 1954, as Duncan Emrich prepared to release two LPs based on these recordings, Long was asked if she had any preferences. She named three tales: two were included in the set, while the third, "The Heifer Hide," remained unissued. None of these collectors placed this or other tales into the context of Hot Springs community life or asked what they meant for those who preserved them. As a result, we need to rediscover the tradition Maud Long received from her mother and committed to posterity, to see what images and messages she intended to build out of this material.

Long's mother, Jane Hicks Gentry, the daughter of Ransom and Emily Harmon Hicks, was born on 18 December 1863 in Watauga

County, North Carolina. Jane Gentry recalled hearing the tales from her grandfather, the legendary Council Harmon, ultimate source of the Ward family tradition recorded by Richard Chase and the Hicks family tradition documented by Barbara McDermitt (1983 and 1986), among others (see Chapter 5, figs. 1 and 2). She told Carter only that the stories had always been told "to amuse children," recalling that she and others would "hire" Council to tell them (Carter 1925, 340). Miles Ward likewise recalled running to meet Council whenever he came to visit and immediately asking him to tell a tale (R. Chase 1943, ix–x). From Gentry and Ward, then, derives an image of the tales as part rustic leisure-time entertainment.

In the Blue Ridge as in the European contexts described by Dégh (1969), however, tedious handiwork, not leisure, originally called forth the märchen. The wife of R. M. Ward recalled the tales' original function as "keeping the kids on the job": "We would all get down around a sheet full of dry beans and start in to shellin' 'em. Mon-roe [one of Chase's primary informants] would tell the kids one of them tales and they'd work for life!" (R. Chase 1943, viii). The colorful description Long gave of Jane Gentry and her family preparing wool is corroborated by others from the same area who recalled cloth making as a dirty, wearisome chore. The worst part—picking trash out of the raw wool—was routinely passed to the children. Between picking, washing, dying, carding, spinning, and winding the wool and, finally, warping the loom, one local weaver estimated that twenty hours of preparation were required for every hour of weaving (Painter 1987, 202). What became Americana in the next generation would have been torture for the Gentry children without some kind of compensating entertainment.

Such a work-intensive context was not confined to subsistence farming in the stereotypical isolated Appalachian farm. Beginning in 1895 Julia Phillips, recently appointed principal at the Dorland Institute in Hot Springs, had made trips into the countryside around the resort town of Hot Springs, trying to convince farming families to send their children to the newly established settlement school. Partly because of uncertain northern funding sources and partly because families rarely could pay tuition in cash, the new institution required that students (and their parents) pay for their education by becoming part of a strict work routine. All students began the day with an hour's mandatory work, followed by a chapel program, Bible study, and

intensive instruction in the "three R's." Following book learning, students then spent an afternoon doing graded "industrial training":
sewing, cooking, cleaning, washing, and—for the boys—farm work
on a nearby model farm. "Industry, economy, and perfection" were
the three traits emphasized in nearly every aspect of life at this school.
Even the teachers were obliged to stay long past spring graduation,
processing and canning the produce brought in by supporting families for use during the fall and winter to come (Painter 1987).

The school succeeded due to Julia Phillips's shrewdness and to a
work ethic that matched the area's mores. Jane Gentry was an early
convert despite the hardship caused by the loss of a hand about the
farm and the need to set aside produce and handcrafts to barter for
tuition and clothing costs. One early tack the Gentrys took was to pay
part of the tuition with hand-woven coverlets. Hence by the time
Maud Long was old enough to become involved in the process, the
family's cloth—woven equally of child-picked wool and Jack Tales—
already went to pay for an education that would transform domestic,
rough-edged traditions into polite, civilizing influences.

The Gentry family moved to Hot Springs in 1905 so the children
would not need to travel so far to school, and they managed to purchase Sunnybank, an old inn that sat next to Dorland. Jane Gentry
brought her industry to a new job, maintaining boarding quarters
and preparing famous meals for tourists and residents. In 1988 Peggie Dotterer recalled her as fascinating but demanding:

> She was the busiest handyperson I've ever known. And if you went
> over there and they were peeling apples, you always got in on the
> deal—I mean she never let people just sit around and do nothing.
> She'd hand you a knife, and you'd better start peeling apples. . . .
> Her way of keeping everybody happy was to tell you a tale of some
> kind or to sing you a ballad. . . . You were peeling apples for her and
> you didn't realize you were doing it because she was entertaining
> you all the time. (Dotterer 1988)

In this way Gentry came to the institute's attention. Unable to force
children to stay at Dorland, teachers looked for ways to keep their
pupils from defecting. To forestall homesickness or to provide pleasure, Jane Gentry began to present her folksongs and tales as part of
the school's chapel program. The results were sometimes awkward.
Gentry was no illiterate—in fact, she was proud of her ability to spell

in the old syllabic "Blue Back Speller" style (Painter 1987, 153). But she was self-conscious about speaking the mountaineer dialect that the school tried to eliminate from their students, and she often apologized for the roughness of her material. Even so, Pat Gentry recalled having to "scrooch down" in his seat for embarrassment when his grandmother performed (Painter 1987, 198).

As Jane Gentry became more and more involved in the school, the administrators relied increasingly on her social skills when important out-of-town visitors were due. She became a celebrity after Cecil Sharp recorded sixty-four ballads and folksongs from her in 1916, and she even spent a month in New York City as the guest of journalist Irving Batcheller. Although she overcame her self-consciousness, she still preferred the ballads as a public art form. When Carter asked for her tales, "at first Mrs. Gentry could not take seriously the writer's request. . . . No one [before] had asked for the stories" (Carter 1925, 340). Carter also notes that Gentry was still trying to emend their style toward the Dorland accent: "The stories are taken down exactly as Mrs. Gentry told them. Speech is rapidly changing in the Blue Ridge and there is little consistency in the use of such words as 'clomb' for 'climb', 'uz' for 'was', etc.—the two forms may appear in the same sentence" (Carter 1925, 340). But Carter's versions preserve many old characteristics: the "run," or rapidly spoken refrain, in "Old Bluebeard" is a Scotch-Irish narrative technique absent in most other Appalachian texts. If her version of "The Rabbit Herd" ("The Enchanted Lady") is not as explicit as some (see Chapter 1 discussion of "Fill, Bowl, Fill"), it does show Gentry aware of a rougher version: her Jack offers to hand over the magic drill to the king's daughters and wife "If you'll hug me and kiss me right good" (Carter 1925, 350). Richard Chase (1943, 94) softens this detail to an offer of money. Taking the tales by dictation may have hampered Gentry's performing style, but Carter's texts remain our earliest and most authentic documents of the nineteenth-century Harmon family tradition.

Jane's daughter Maud graduated from the Dorland Institute in 1908, one of twelve Gentry children or grandchildren to attend (Painter 1987, 263). Receiving a degree from the Asheville Normal Teachers' College, Maud Gentry returned in 1918 to teach at her old school. In that same year Dorland united with the nearby Bell Institute to become Dorland-Bell School. In 1920 her husband, Grover

Cleveland Long, was transferred to Greeneville, Tennessee, but they returned to Hot Springs in 1931. Taking over "the old home place" and continuing its business, Long went back to work at the newly established public elementary school and gave piano lessons, both public and private. But Long also maintained her links with Dorland-Bell, and between chapel programs there and at the public school, she was in continual demand for ballads or folk tales. Emergencies might lead to a command performance before groups of fractious grade-schoolers. Peggie Dotterer recalled:

> She could hold a whole group of unruly children spellbound. So [laughing] whenever we had a problem: "Come on and tell the Jack Tales!" I can remember one time, it was rainy weather, we couldn't go out on the school grounds, we got all the—I don't know why there was such a crisis, something happened—and we got them all in the lunch room and had her telling them to all the grammar school children, right up to the eighth grade. They were all sitting there—they loved them. (Dotterer 1988)

During his efforts to reestablish folk dancing in the Appalachians, Richard Chase had visited Dorland-Bell in the early 1930s (Painter 1987, 200), staying at Sunnybank. Just how Chase collected tales from Maud Long is unclear: Marshall Ward's memories and the correspondence located by Charles Perdue (1987) establish that Chase preferred to have a secretary take down Ward's stories in shorthand or have written texts sent to him. In any case, he credited Long as a source for his "Hardy Hardhead" and "The Heifer Hide," adding that she "tells them delightfully." Chase and Long became friends, the collector returning often to enjoy the sumptuous meals that were a regular feature at Sunnybank. When *The Jack Tales* was published, he sent Long a presentation copy and continued to stop by for years afterward.

Long also came to the attention of Artus Moser, a former student of ballad scholar Edwin Kirkland at the University of Tennessee. Moser had borrowed a portable disk cutter from a wealthy Knoxville doctor and made several field trips of his own, recording fiddle tunes and ballads. In 1941 Moser made the recording of Long narrating "Jack and the Calf Hide" already mentioned. In the fall of 1944 Moser became principal of the Hot Springs school and used his close connection with Long for more recording sessions. In October and

November she sang "Barbara Allen," "The Broken Token," and "Jackie's Gone A-Sailing" for Moser and got her seventh-grade class to contribute "The Tree in the Woods," a cumulative children's song.

The next summer, Moser gave a presentation at the University of North Carolina at Chapel Hill, illustrating his talk with his home recordings. The talk was successful, and Moser offered his collection, now over 100 records, to the Archive of American Folk Song (Moser to Library of Congress, 4 August 1945, AMF).[2] Duncan Emrich, the archive's director, hoped to expand its modest catalog of 78-rpm recordings, drawn from field recordings, to subsidize its equally modest budget. Moser's field disks, however, were too worn to serve as masters, so Emrich loaned him one of the archive's disk recorders to rerecord some of Long's selections (Emrich to Moser, 8 November and 21 December 1945, and Moser to Emrich, 30 December 1945, AMF).

Moser evidently indicated to Maud Long that the archive would pay her for these ballads. Before she was rerecorded, she wrote directly to the archive on 4 April, asking, "Could you tell me, without first hearing the record, the amount paid for the release of a song that you do not have in your files[?]" Perhaps recalling her 1941 tale recording, she added, "Do you take records of Folk Stories such as 'Jack, Will, and Tom Tales?' " Emrich explained that the archive did not pay informants simply for adding songs to their archives, but they did give $15 per side if they issued the numbers in one of their albums. In fact, Long received payment for two of Moser's rerecordings within the month.

By August, Moser, near the end of his collecting tour, proposed adding Jack Tales to his agenda, a suggestion that delighted Emrich and his superiors (Emrich to Moser, 13 August 1946, AMF). Presumably it was at this time that he sent the library the transcription of the 1941 recording as a teaser; this, rather than Long's later recording of "Jack and the Heifer Hide," was used by Benjamin A. Botkin in his 1949 popular collection, *A Treasury of Southern Folklore* (519–25). With the library interested, Moser contacted Long and soon reported that she "was eager to record them all for the Archive (She knows a dozen or so)" (Moser to Emrich, 17 September 1946, AMF). Moser's plan to record the tales at Hot Springs fell through, though, and he was forced to return the disk recorder to Washington before collecting them.

But circumstances led Long to arrive at the Library of Congress in person. In 1946 her husband died after a long illness, and she received a message from Caroline Pond, her former English teacher at Dorland, who had retired to Washington, D.C. In failing health, Pond asked Long if she would come as a live-in nurse, offering room and board in exchange. Long resigned her teaching position and moved to Washington, and Moser probably arranged a direct meeting with Emrich. On 20 January 1947, Emrich submitted a formal proposal for funds to "make perfect studio recordings" of Long's repertoire, emphasizing the value of her tales:

> The collection of tales is an extremely rare one. Richard Chase of Virginia has collected in writing some of the "Jack Tales" told by Mrs. Long and published them in his book of the same title. They have not been recorded nor has Chase acquired the full collection from Mrs. Long. . . . As part of the developing work of the Folklore Section it would be most valuable to have these tales added to our collections. They contain material valuable for an album, for reference for publishing by Chase and other folklorists, for use by motion picture firms such as Disney, for books for the blind, etc. (Emrich to Spivacke, 20 January 1947, AMF)

Long remained in Washington for three years and was able to arrange regular visits to the archive. By 10 March 1947, Emrich could write Moser that Long "is almost a weekly visitor and we are trying to pry loose everything in her memory." In addition to ballads and a large collection of children's songs, rhymes, and riddles, she recorded eleven Jack Tales. The records show her perfectionist attitude: while her first take of "Hardy Hard Back" sounds satisfactory, something evidently dissatisfied her about it. When one of her sisters visited her in Washington, Long took her to the archive one day for a retake of the tale's conclusion: she "wanted to change some, to get it just right" (Jacqueline Burgin Painter to Joseph Hickerson, 30 October 1984, MLF).

The archive saw Long's tales as valuable properties beyond their importance as oral documents. Richard Chase's book and its sequel, *Grandfather Tales* (1948), proved that there was a broad, educated audience for Appalachian folktales, and Botkin's collections tapped this same market. Walt Disney's Mickey Mouse versions of "The Brave Little Tailor" and "Jack and the Beanstalk" suggested further possibilities for exploiting the material, to both the archive's and Long's advantage. Regrettably, Disney chose to go the way of fakelore, preferring Pecos Bill to Jack, while Chase moved from publishing tales toward performing and reviving folk dancing.

The archive did produce two LPs of Long's tales in 1955, but Emrich passed over the "Heifer Hide" that she had singled out as a favorite. Perhaps Emrich believed that the tale was no longer new since both Chase and Botkin had published texts crediting Long as the source. But the "new" tales that the Library of Congress released were actually learned from or modeled after Chase's literary versions. Long's recording of "Jack and the Giants' New Ground" differs from Jane Gentry's "Jack the Giant Killer" in many ways, while it agrees closely with Chase's "Jack in the Giants' Newground," even reproducing dialogue word for word. Likewise, her "Jack and the Varmints" clearly departs from the bawdy Gentry tradition, in which the hero wears a belt labeled "Stiff Dick killed seven at a lick." Chase obviously had encountered this version of the tale, as he admits that his hero's rhyme ("Strong man Jack killed seven at a whack") was his invention. The original, "given by all our informants," Chase says, "had to be altered for printing" (R. Chase 1943, 192). Long also bowdlerizes the line. More tellingly, in his "Fill, Bowl! Fill!" Chase admits to altering the king's final challenge from "sing the bowl full" to "sing this bowl full *of lies*"—a suggestion from Stith Thompson himself (R. Chase 1943, 94, 193). "The point of singing the bowl full of lies," Chase admits, "seems to have been lost in the Ward-Harmon tradition." Long, following Chase, has Jack "sing the bowl full of lies."

Long felt there was nothing wrong with her use of Chase's versions. Those who knew her well all spoke for her modesty. She did not publicize her connection with Chase or her recordings at the Library of Congress, choosing rather to stress her role as an educator and as an elder in the Presbyterian church, where she took an unusually active role for a woman in her day. Her community achievements in this area were, in fact, so significant that Jacqueline Painter was well into a project of compiling her biography before she learned that Maud Long had even made recordings for the Archive of Folk Music. Peggie Dotterer, one of her closest associates at her school, recalls that when Long returned from Washington, she frequently spoke of having met Peter Marshall, former chaplain for Congress, but never once alluded to her archive recordings. Dotterer also recalled that when she would appear at folk festivals in nearby Asheville, she preferred not to mention her work to people who knew her back home.

Nevertheless, Long was keenly aware of the value of her ballads and tales, both as sources of much-needed supplemental income and as positive expressions of Appalachian lore. There was not much money to be made teaching school in Hot Springs, whose economy suffered a steady, irreversible decline after its major tourist hotels closed and the Presbyterian church merged the Dorland-Bell Institute with Wilson College. Joan Moser told me that when one of Long's workshops was recorded on an early videotape recorder, she requested that the tape not be shown publicly, commenting, "This is my bread and butter."

What are we to say, then, about the connection between the Library of Congress recordings and the Richard Chase book? When Chase contacted Long in the late 1930s, she was certainly telling some of her mother's tales in private and informally at her school. But Long recognized and admired the way in which Chase was adapting the tales to make them entertaining to wider audiences. She certainly entertained him royally several times, greeting him with a king's banquet that might have formed the basis, as her daughter has commented, for the several groaning tables described in his *Jack Tales*. When the book was published, the recognition it gained her meant that she was called upon more and more often to present her tales. Like a successful rural musician who has found a good songbook, she found Chase's versions invaluable in broadening her repertory: later she claimed to be able to tell any story in *The Jack Tales* and *Grandfather Tales*. The closeness of many of the archive recordings to Chase indicates that Long brought her copy of the book with her to Washington and used it to prepare for her sessions. But apparently she regarded Chase's book as a resource, not a bible. What we know of Long's personality makes it clear that she felt no compulsion to follow a printed text verbatim. Joan Moser recalled:

> When I went to piano lesson . . . I remember her putting up on the piano, was quite interested that she put the Sharp book [*English Folksongs from the Southern Mountains*] up on the piano, and she had her own copy . . . and she took *our* copy and she . . . penciled in notes, corrected the transcriptions. She said, "My mother sang it this way; Sharp didn't quite get it." And she would make corrections. . . .

So I always was intrigued by that because at that point, being just a child, it didn't occur to me that somebody could take a pencil and change the music in a book. And this is what she was doing. . . . She was much like a craftsperson who is not satisfied with just producing a wood carving or a basket, but they want it to be a certain way, for it to represent the quality of work that they can be proud of. (J. Moser 1988)

The irony, however, is that the two archive recordings that differ most substantially from Chase are precisely the two for which Chase gave her primary credit: "Hardy Hard Back" and "The Heifer Hide." Probably Long was familiar enough with these two that she did not need to consult the printed versions. In many of the places in which Long parts company from Chase, she agrees more closely with her mother; in others, she takes a line independent of both. In "Hardy Hard Back," for instance, Long employs a "run" or repeated formulaic phrase not found in either her mother's or Chase's version: "From the other side of the woods, there came a little old gray man with a long gray beard and a high-pointed hat and a little stick in his hand." While Long does not speak her run very rapidly, as her mother had done in "Old Bluebeard," she uses the phrase to divide the narrative into oral stages in a way effaced by Chase's literary version.

Long's "The Heifer Hide" shows a similar mix of conservatism and innovation. Long retains the term *passenger* that her mother had used to refer to the adulterous woman's lover, a detail elided by Chase. But Gentry and Chase agree in having Jack initially act foolishly and set out to travel randomly with his calf skin, while Long, in both the 1941 and 1947 versions, inserts foreshadowing that Jack is not such a fool after all. When the brothers predict that he will return "about *nighttime, starved* to death," Jack replies simply, "No, bedads . . . I'll not be coming back *that*-away." Indeed, Jack's return, carefully crafted to form an ironic mirror image of this parting scene, shows that there is wisdom behind the fool's nonchalant mask.

Jack's apparent carefree attitude reflects traditional Appalachian performing styles. When I asked how Maud Long performed her tales, her daughter, Jane Douglas, corrected me: Long never performed; she *told* the stories, not setting herself apart from or above her audiences. Dotterer agreed, adding that what she called the mountaineer sense of narrating was almost completely nondramatic. While an outsider would add dramatics and hand gestures to a funny story, the mountaineer remained deadpan: "They never crack a smile or say it in a way that would say, 'Well, I'm telling you a joke.'" *Performing* a story, in this sense, meant forcing listeners' attention. *Telling* the story meant allowing listeners to decide if they liked the story; if they did, extra dramatics were unnecessary. The mountaineer "acts like he doesn't care," Dotterer concluded; "in fact he *does* care" (Dotterer 1988).

If we recognize this dynamic in Long's tale telling, we can see the shrewd irony in Jack's apparently unconcerned reactions to the abuse he takes from his brothers. In fact, Jack *does* care about being imposed on, but Long uses his silence to highlight the other characters' ridiculousness. When she clearly shifts voices in a more performative style, she is enacting characters who are obviously lying, such as the adulterous woman who feigns "the rheumatiz," or the husband anxious to bargain for the "magic" heifer hide:

> "Why, I, I'll just give you *any*-thing for that, Jack,
> I'm b-o-u-n-d to *have* it."
> Said, "It'll talk to me just-like-it-talked-to-you, won't it?"
>
> "S-u-r-e!" Jack says,
> "It'll talk *just* the same to you as it talked to me."
>
> So the old man said, "Then bedads I'm just *bound* to have it.
> Now, what'll-you-take-for-it!"

Thus Jack, in his dry irony, contrasts delightfully with his greedy foils.

Maud Long, herself a direct link with the underlying oral tradition, accepted Chase's literary re-creations as valid versions of the tales for new situations and contexts. Her archive recordings represent not so much her memories of what she heard her mother say to the room of fretful children as what she wanted people to remember about her mother's storytelling. She took pride in the letters she received from Japan, England, and Alaska after Chase's *Jack Tales* were published, saying that "children of these lands are as captivated [by them] as were the American children" (Long to Rae Korson, 15 June 1957, MLF). To this extent, then, she had already chosen not to be one of the last "authentic" tellers of Jack Tales, for this would have limited her and her art to the painful contexts that brought them forth, contexts that she had left behind. Rather, she chose to be one of the first—and most successful—of the revivalists.

As such, she was no passive tradition-bearer, nor a passive imitator of Chase. She actively interpreted the tales and their significance for new audiences. Even tales essentially modeled after Chase's versions contain characteristic additions and ornamentations. Tradition, for Long, though, was not a thing to be cherished in itself but, rather, a means to an end. Her aim was to satisfy audiences looking to the Appalachians not only for the raw material for their own desire to entertain but also for positive models of the past. In the end, Maud Long did care deeply about the work ethic and family values that her mother represented. Both Douglas and her niece Jane Gentry commented that Long "wanted to be an exact copy of her mother." Other Gentry children and grandchildren chose careers that took them away from Appalachia, but she retained the "old home place" and alone of the children kept the ballads in her active repertory. Being an educator, however, she was anxious for her students and her daughter to move beyond the restricted life of Hot Springs. She saw the Dorland Institute as "like the Master Himself in that it is come that we might have life and have it more abundantly" (Painter 1987, 195). She was well aware of the changes in context between the endless nights of picking dirt out of wool and the present audiences of children undergoing a thorough cultural scrubbing before heading for a world where "hillbillies" were still stereotyped as rough, amoral, and dirty. The restraint of most ballads made them immediately attractive to cultured audiences, in spite of their frequently violent content. The tales, often rife with amoral violence and thinly disguised sex, were harder to present; she could no more have told these rough versions before audiences of educators than she could have offered the archive dirty jokes.

By making Jack a "simple boy" who breezes through adversities, Long created an ironic persona that by his very lack of concern for hard work showed up the greed and duplicity of the world around him. In taletelling, as in life, self-important gestures were not necessary. Joan Moser recalled:

> What I remember so clearly about Maud Long . . . was that I never missed the histrionic gestures of the dramatic, stage-like presentations that I see now. I remember very clearly that she often sat

simply like we're sitting with her hands folded in her lap, but her vocal projection, which was never strained or anything—I remember a very sweet voice, very clear. But she had a way, as Daddy says, of bringing all these characters to life. . . . It was always so wonderful that I was only aware of her voice, of the characters in the story and I—what little gestures she may have used never detracted and was not something that I remembered. And yet I remember the stories very, very clearly. (J. Moser 1988)

That was what Maud Long cared most deeply to accomplish.

NOTES

1. Correspondence is from the Maud Long files in the American Folklife Center, Library of Congress (abbreviated MLF in citations), and is published with the library's permission and that of Jane Douglas, Maud Long's daughter.

2. Correspondence is from the Artus Moser files in the American Folklife Center, Library of Congress (abbreviated AMF in citations), and is published with the library's permission and that of Artus Moser.

JACK AND THE HEIFER HIDE

as told by Maud Gentry Long

"Jack and the Heifer Hide" (AT 1535) is a variant of a widespread tale (perhaps most familiar to readers in Hans Christian Andersen's retelling, "Big Claus and Little Claus"). Maud Long of Hot Springs, North Carolina, received the tale from her mother, Jane Hicks Gentry, the granddaughter of legendary storyteller Council Harmon. It was repeatedly listed as a favorite by Long, her family, and her friends. In the spring of 1947 she temporarily relocated to Washington, D.C., to care for an elderly woman who had been her English teacher at the Hot Springs settlement school. While there, she paid weekly visits to the Library of Congress's Archive of Folk Music, to record her entire repertoire of folksongs and stories, including eleven Jack Tales.

▼ ▼ ▼

The name of this story
is "The Heifer Hide."

Once upon a time there was a man who had three sons:
Jack, Will, and Tom.
Will and Tom, the two older boys, were great big, fine, strapping
    fellows,
and the father knew *they'd* be able to take care of *their* farm
when he was gone,
with all the horses and cattle and sheep that he could leave them.
But p-o-o-r little-old Jack!
He just wondered what in the world would *become* of that boy!
For he never—had—seemed—quite—right.
So he just left to him
one little-old heifer calf.

Jack said that 'as all right, bedads,
if that 'as what his father wanted him to have,
that's what he *wanted.*

The two older boys were to take *care* of Jack
and look *after* him.
But soon after the father's death,
they begun to mistreat him, and they *imposed* upon him—
they made him do all the housework—
all the cooking—
and just *everything*.
And they were out in the fields, in the woods,
and, as Jack thought, having a real—good—time.

One day when they'd come home to the noon meal, Will said,
"Jack, when you finish up these dishes, I guess you better go down
    yonder by the wood lot
and skin your little-old calf.
I done cut a tree down on her and *killed* her."

"Well, bedads, I *will*, then."

And so after he'd finished his—dishes,
down to the wood lot he went, and sure enough, there laid his little-
    old-heifer-calf—dead.

He skinned her hide,
brought it back up to the barn,
tacked it up to the barn to dry.

In about two weeks he went down and that hide was just as bo—dry
    as a *bone*.
He took it down,
got him a little piece of rawhide and a peg 'n awl,
n' sewed that hi—calf hide up,
stuffed it with chips and straw,
took it by the tail and went dragging it up to the house.

[*Deep voice:*] Thumpety-bump, bumpety-thump.

Will and Tom said, "Jack, what in the *world* are you going to do with
    that little-old calf hide?"

"Oh, bedads, this is my *fortune*.
I'm going out into the *world* in the morning.
And when *I* come back,
I'll come back with pockets of gold!"

"Humph.
You'd better—stay—*here*!
You'll be coming back about *nighttime, starved* to death, and not a
    bite of food cooked in the house."

"No, bedads," Jack said, "I'll not be coming back *that*-away."

So morning came.
Took his little-old calf hide and started off down the road.

Thumpety-bump, bumpety-thump.

Walked a-l-l day
dragging that thing behind him.
And about night he begun to get hungry—and—tired.
He wished he could find a place to spend the night.

And along then he saw a nice-looking little house by the side of the
    road and one light shining out of the window—
Walked up to the door, knocked, and when a nice-looking lady
    came, he said,
"Kind lady, would you let a little-old boy named Jack spend the
    night here with you?"

[*Brisk:*] "Oh, no, son!
I can't be bothered with you!
Why, my husband isn't home and uh—
no, I can't be bothered with you, just run on down the road."

"Oh," he says, "kind lady, I'm just *so* tired.
Uh—I won't be a *mite* of trouble.
Please take me in.
Just give me a place to *sleep*, that's all I want."

"Oh, well, Jack, come on *in* then.
Go on upstairs to that room right at the head of the steps
and you'll find a bed there, and go on to sleep."

Jack thanked her and went on up the steps—
and when he got into that room,
he saw coming right up through the middle of the floor,
through a knot hole,
a beam of light.
Went over and put his eye down to that light
and saw—down—below
that he was looking right into a dining room.

And there—was—a—*nice-looking*—table
spread with *all*—the—good—things—you can *think* of to eat,
And a nice-looking young man sitting on one side of the table,
and a nice-looking lady on the *other*.
And they were just having the—*best*—time.

Oh, there was *chicken* and *ham* and *pie* and *cake* and *preserves* and
   honey,
just everything you could *think* of that a person wanted to *eat.*
And they were having *such* a good time.
Jack—just—looked,
and his mouth watered.

And about that time,
out in the yard they heard a *great* commotion:
"W-H-O-A! W-H-O-A! WHOA THERE!"

"O-h, o-h, quick-quick-quick," she said,
"that's-my-husband-he's-come-home.
Hurry, hurry, get-into-something, right-quick, here.
Here, jump into this great old big case!"

Jumped over there into a great—old—big—chest.
She let the lid down all but just a little bit and begun pushing those
   things off of the table as fast as she could into a little cupboard
   over there.

And about that time somebody was *knock*-ing on the door:
"OLD WOMAN, OLD WOMAN,
LET ME IN HERE.
Here I am come home *early*."

She just whisked the things all off the table and folded up the nice
    linen tablecloth and finally got to the door and he said,
"Well, what makes you so long in coming to the door!"

[*Feebly:*] "O-h," she says,
"my *rheumatiz* hurts me tonight."

"Well," he says,"rheumatiz or no rheumatiz,
get me something to eat;
I'm *starved—to—death*."

"Well," she says, "there's not a thing in the world in this house but
    just bread and milk."

[*Jauntily:*] "Oh, well, cornbread and milk is just good enough for
    anybody.
Bring it *out* here!"

And she brought out a great—big—bowl,
and a big pitcher of cold milk,
and a great big platter of cornbread.

And Jack a-l-l the time had his eye glued right to that knothole,
just watching it, every bit.

He waited until the man had eaten one big bowl of milk and bread,
    and he just couldn't stand it any longer.
Reached round, took hold of the tail of that calf hide, and gave him a
    great shake over the floor—

Old man looked up, said,
"Old woman, what *is* that?"

"O-h, a poor little-old simple boy
that I let go upstairs to sleep,
dragging a little-old calf hide or *something* behind him."

"Yeah, and," he said,
"And I *bet* you didn't—even—offer him any supper."
Stepped out into the hall. He said, "Jack? Jack!
Don't you want to come down here, son, and have some bread and
    milk?"

"Well, bedads, I don't care if *I do*!"

And so Jack took his calf hide by the tail
and came *dragging* him down the steps,
bumpety-thump, thumpety-bump,
r-i-g-h-t up by-the-side of his chair, and sat down.

The lady had brought out another big bowl of, of, uh—
porridge, bread, and milk,
and brought in another pitcher of milk, and
oh, didn't Jack have a *good* time with that first bowl!

He'd eaten that and started on the second one,
reached down and took that calf hide by the tail and gave him a
    good—thumping—rattle
right on the floor.

"No," he said, "you hush up!
Don't you say another word to me, sir!
Now, shut—your—mouth and don't let me hear you open it again!
Now, you just be quiet!"

The old man says, "Jack?
Well, what did he *say*?"

"O-h, n-o, *s-i-r*!" Jack said,
"I'm sorry, I can't tell you!
O-h, no, no.
This bread and milk sure—is—good!"

Finished up the *second* bowl.
Reached down and he gave that calf hide *another* good rattle.
"Now," he said, "didn't I tell you to keep your mouth shut?
You—just—*shut that up* right now and don't let me hear you speak
   again!
Now you under-*stand* me, don't you?"

The old man said, "Now, listen, Jack;
why, I want to know
what is that he's saying to you?"

"O-h, no," Jack said,
"it, it might hurt the nice lady's feelings,
and she's been *aw*-ful *good* to me.
No, sir!
I'm sorry. I just can't tell you."

The old man said, "Now, listen, Jack,
you *can* tell me *too*, sir."
He said, "Y-o-u come on and tell me!
Won't hurt your feelings, would it, old lady?"

[*Falsetto:*] "O-h, no,
I guess not," she said.

"Oh, w-e-l-l, then," Jack said,
"if it won't hurt her feelings,
I'll just *tell* you what he said.
Over in that—corner—cupboard
there's a-l-l *kinds* of good things to eat.
There's chicken,
there's pie,
there's ham,
there's cake,
there's jelly
and preserves
and honey—"

The old man said, "Old woman, is that so?"

"O-h, *well,* there's just a *few* little things over there that I had for me
and my poor kin folks."

"Well, bedads, me and Jack's your poor kin folks.
Get that *out* here!"

And she spread the tablecloth,
and brought out *a-l-l* of those good things to eat,
and Jack and the old man just began a-l-l *over* again.

Oh *my,* but Jack had *one*—good—meal.

The old man said, "Now, I tell you, Jack,
I want to *buy* that hide from you."

[*Chuckling:*] "O-h n-o, *sir!*" Jack said.
"I'm sorry! that's my fortune!
N-o, *sir,* I—can't—part with *that.*"

"Oh," he says, "Now, come, Jack, you can!"   .
Said, "Listen!
I'll give you anything in the world you want.
Just name your price, uh—
look around you—
just anything you see.
Why, I, I'll just give you *any*-thing for that, Jack,
I'm b-o-u-n-d to *have* it."
Said, "It'll talk to me just-like-it-talked-to-you, won't it?"

"S-u-r-e!" Jack says,
"It'll talk *just* the same to you as it talked to me."

So the old man said, "Then bedads I'm just *bound* to have it.
Now, what'll-you-take-for-it!"

"W-e-l-l," Jack said, "you've been awfully good to me.
I'll-tell-you-what-I'll-do. I'll take that-big-old-chest-over-there.
I'll swap even with you for it."

"Oh, Law, yes," the man said.
"Just *take* the old chest, Jack,
and give me that hide!"

He gave the old man over the hide,
picked up that big chest, swung it on his shoulder, and walked out
    the door.

Walked on down the road,
and [*sighing*] uhhh, begun talking to himself.
And he said,
"Now, I've played it!
Here—I've—sold—my—fortune
for this old—empty—chest!
I'm going to throw the *thing* into the well
just as soon as I come on down the road a little piece."

And inside the chest there was a great knocking:
"NO! NO! JACK! JACK!
JACK!
Don't *throw* this into the well.
Don't you know I'm in here?"

[*Falsetto:*] "O-h, *Law*," Jack says, "Bedads, that's right,
I was about to forget,
you *are* in there!
Well, what'll you *take* for me not throwing you in the well?"

[*Normal voice:*] "O-h," the passenger said, "why, I'll just give you
    a-l-l the gold you want, Jack."

[*Deeper voice:*] "Bedads, that's just what I'm a-looking for!
I'll e-a-s-e you right down here off my shoulder—
and you just begin handing me out the gold!"
And the passenger handed out gold
till Jack had his pockets full.
Tied the pants legs,

and filled the pants legs just as full of gold as he could walk with,
and started back home.

Now, he got home j-u-s-t as the—Will and Tom were finishing up
   breakfast one morning.

Walked in,
and they said, "Why! What are *you* doing back here?"

Well, Jack says, "Bedads, I've made my fortune.
That's what I'm a-doing back here."
And he begun pulling out hands—full—of—gold and putting them
   on that table,
and Jack—Will's—and—Tom's—eyes just liked to popped out of their
   head.
They said, "Where—did—you—get—all—that—gold, Jack?"

"Humph!
Told you.
I sold my calf hide for it.
That's where I got it."

They looked at each other right quick.
Said, "Come on!
Let's go to the barn and kill the *finest* horse that we have.
You know good and well,
if Jack could get all of *that* gold for a little-old measly *heifer* hide,
what—will—we—get for one of our big-old fine horses? Come on
   right quick!"

And before you could say Jack Robinson,
down they went,
and had killed the finest horse that each of them had.

Now, they couldn't wait for it to d-r-y! O-h, *no!*
They sewed it up *right then,*
stuffed them full of straw and chips,
and started off to the nearest village.

And they got there,
went up and *d-o-w-n* the streets, calling [*deep chant going falsetto on*
    "sale"]:

"Horse h-i-d-e-s f'r sale!
Horse h-i-d-e-s f'r sale!"

Just up and down the streets,
and the people looked at them like they thought they must be *crazy*
    men.

And they just *kept* doing that,
day—after—day.

Now, you know it was *summer*-time.
And o-h m-y,
those old horse hides were *g-r-e-e-n*.
And the first thing you know it begun to leave a *terrible* smell!
And the people had just stood it as long as they were going to.
And they came out with *sticks* and *stones*,
and they told those two men to get out of their town, and get in a
    hurry,
with those old smelly horse hides.

And they started back home.
Mad?
Every step they took, they got madder.

When they come to the house, they said, "Now, look here, Jack, you
    just *plain lied* to us.
Why, those people even *drove* us out of the c—out of the town.
And here you said you sold your little-old-calf-hide for it!"

"Well," Jack says, "I've been telling you just exactly what I done."

"Well, now," they said, "listen. You *didn't* either, and *we're* going to
    throw *you* in the river!
T-h-a-t's what's going to become of *you*!
So *just* come right *on*, we've got the sheet *here* to tie you up in!"

They took Jack by the hand,
and the sheet,
and started to the river bridge.

O-h,
but they forgot to take a *rope* to tie it with.
And when they got there they begun to fuss which one was to go
    back and get the rope.
Will said, "Now, Tom,
you ought to go 'cause you're the *oldest*."

"No," Tom says. "Will, you ought to go
because you're *not* the oldest—
now you just go on back and get the rope."

Well, they fussed and they quarreled and Jack just stood there.

Said, "Get down here, Jack.
Lay down in this sheet, we're going to roll you up,
and we going to *leave* you laying right on this bridge.
And now, believe me,
you'd better *be* there when we come back,
and we'll go *together* back and get that rope."

They rolled Jack up in the big-old sheet.
Left him laying there on the side of the bridge.
And went back to the house.

Well, Jack kind of w-o-r-m-e-d his way along out to the edge of the—
    of the big-old sheet and was laying there with his head sticking
    out, just about like a terrapin.
And he saw coming on the other end of the bridge
o-h—the—
prettiest—flock—of—sheep—you've—ever—seen!
And a little-old bit of a man with a l-o-n-g gray beard, uh—
kind of shooing them on
[*in an animal-calling voice*]: "Sheep!
Sheep!
Sheep!"

—getting them up onto the bridge,
'cause they saw something kind of *strange* lying out there on the
     middle of the bridge, ·
but Jack just stayed as still as could be and the sheep came right—
     on—by him. ˋ

And when the little man got alongside of him, he said,
"Son,
what in the *world* are you—doing—in—that—sheet?"

[*Sighing:*] "Well," Jack says, "Father, I'm going to heaven.
That's *just* what I'm a-doing."

"Oh," the old man said,
"Jack,
I've wanted to go to heaven for *so* long!
Listen, son,
why you're *just* a boy!
Get *out* of there, won't you please,
and let me get in your place,
and let *me* go to heaven?"

[*Sighing again:*] "Well," Jack says,
"my father always did tell me to be *nice* to old people.
Yes,
I'll get out,
and you lay down here on this sheet and I'll roll you up and you stay
     j-u-s-t as still as you can be.
After a while they'll come back two fellows,
and they'll *tie* you up
and send you off to heaven."

Says, "Now, Jack, all those sheep are yours.
Just take 'em, son."

Jack took those sheep and he got them back off of that bridge just as
     hard as he could and round the great big old rock cliff—
And he stayed just as still as could be.
He kept peeping around the rock every once in a while and after a
     while he saw Will and Tom turn around and go back home.

Well, he waited until they'd had a little time to
about get there
and he started his sheep across the bridge again.

[*As before:*] "Sheep!
Sheep!"

And—
the sheep just obeyed him just like he'd *always* driven them.
Right across that bridge they went without a bit of trouble,
Jack just having the *best* time.
Drove those sheep right—on—up to his gate.

He said, "Will! Tom!
Come on out here, can't you, and help me get—these—sheep in!"

W-e-l-l,
when they bounced onto the door—
onto the porch,
and *saw* Jack with all—of—those—sheep,
they just came flying down and opened the bars and they said, "Jack,
    where—in—this—*world* did you get those sheep?"

"In the river;
where do you *think* I got them?"
Says, "Come on, though, and open those bars a little better and help
    me get 'em in."

"Listen, Jack, listen," Will said.
"Will you throw me in the river if I, i-, i-, if, if *I* get my sheet?"

"Why sure," Jack said.
"I'll throw you in the river if you'll get your sheet."

"But"—uh—"Well," Tom says, "then if you're going to throw *him*,
you'll just simply have to throw me too."

"Sure.
Sure, I'll throw you in too.

That's all right, you just go on and get your—sheet, Will.
But now, listen, both of you get you a rope.
You understand?
I'm not going to carry nobody's rope for him."

"Oh, sure, we'll get us a sheet and a rope, too."
And away they went, just as hard as they could go,
to get them a sheet and a rope.
And down to the river bridge they went.

And a-l-l the way down there
they were fussing which one was going to be thrown in first.
Tom said that he ought to be
'cause he was the oldest,
and Will said, "No, sir, I ought to be because I'm the youngest. Now,
     you just
let him throw me in first."

"Oh," Jack says, "let's just hush.
I'm going to throw you *both* in and there's plenty of sheep for *both* of
     you."

And so they finally worked it out,
Tom was to go first.
Got down and got into his sheet and Jack tied a great—big-old—
     hard—knot,
picked that sheet up and gave it a swing,
back—and—forth,
back—and—forth,
and ka-*bang*!
out into the river it went.

     [*Very fast:*]
'Course, he begun kind of kicking around.
Will says, "What's-he-doing-Jack-what's-he-doing?"
"W-h-y," Jack says,
"I—just—know—he's gathering in sheep."

"Oh," he said, "hurry, hurry, quick, tie me in a hurry,
Throw me in there before he *gets* them all!"

[*Resume normal speed:*]
Jack gave him a good old swing and a hard tie and
out into the river he went—
Turned on around and went back home—
And do you know when I left there,
Jack was just one of the richest men there was in that country.

CHAPTER 5

THE
TELLER AND
THE TALE

▼　▼　▼　▼　▼

STORYTELLING ON
BEECH MOUNTAIN

▼　▼　▼　▼　▼

W. F. H. Nicolaisen

At superficial glance, tradition seems to defy creativity and to exclude individuality. So it is not surprising that concepts of anonymous origin and of communal reception, adaptation, and transmission long dominated the product-oriented study of items of folk culture. Even the investigation of the complex relationships between types and variants did little to derail approaches in which the group was central and individuals were on the periphery, if they were recognized at all. Types, after all, are abstractions, as are motifs. Consequently, neither of Stith Thompson's great working tools pertaining to the classification and structural analysis of folktales contains any reference to named individual storytellers who, from this perspective, are only purveyors of those variants from which ultimately the type can be distilled.

Yet, during the period when this view prevailed, folklore field-workers were aware of, indeed worked with and collected from, individual tradition bearers. Somehow, though, they failed to account for these encounters in their theoretical assessments of what folklore and tradition were and how they functioned—a failure that baffles us today (see Nicolaisen 1984). It is puzzling—to say the least—to imagine how those who insisted on communality and anonymity as fundamental factors in movement of stories envisioned, let us say, the transmission of märchen from generation to generation. Perhaps they never really seriously considered the dynamics of such transmission, focused as they were on the product of that transmission, that is, on the story (the song, the sampler, the quilt, the decoy duck, etc.). But as scholars began to place greater stress on the process by which that product was created or re-created (a process, in the case of stories, in which performance is central), the vital role of the individual as teller and as listener in the process of transmission became apparent. Folklorists began to see how, by participating in the process of transmission, individuals appropriated and shaped such stories (songs, samplers, quilts, decoy ducks, etc.). Clearly they turned them into their stories (their songs, their samplers, their quilts, their decoy ducks) by transforming them into personal versions within the limits of personal creativity that tradition permits despite its commitment to continuity and its resistance to change. Once folklorists acknowledged the central part that individuals, both encouraged and hampered by tension between creativity and tradition, play in shaping folklore—or to put it somewhat differently, once they "discovered" the individual tradition bearer—research into a storyteller's or a singer's repertoire and into his or her attitudes toward the stories he or she tells and the songs he or she sings became an exciting possibility. Folklorists could provide synchronic descriptions of such repertoires and ask diachronic questions about the source of the art and the sources of the individual items.

If any justification for the earlier view can be adduced, it is the well-known observation that, historically speaking, many of the items folklorists collect through fieldwork are indeed anonymous in origin and in channels of transmission. But anonymity must not be confused with nonidentity. Rather, individuals hear stories from individuals and, if they feel so inclined, tell them again to other individuals (either alone or in groups). This view has become an accepted fact of life for the folklorist in general and the student of folk narrative in particular. Nevertheless, it is still far from easy to trace individual artists in the historical process of transmission and to pinpoint with some accuracy their specific personal influences on that process. Their shaping hands and minds are seldom seen in action, their voices are seldom heard, and it is typical of all folk tradition that it is hard to get back beyond the generation or two of tradition bearers behind the current teller (or singer, embroiderer, quilter, carver). For that reason, although not for that reason alone, the Jack Tale tradition within several generations of the Hicks-Harmon family and of identifiable individual members of that family, mostly in the Beech Mountain area of North Carolina, offers an unusual, almost unique, opportunity. Here it is possible to examine how related, nameable, and knowable storytellers have shaped that tradition through their individual, personal performances. At the same time, this very special situation might allow us to investigate possible links between the biological family tree of the storytellers and the genealogy of the stories they tell.

As a first step in that direction, it is, of course, necessary to establish the genealogy of the family of storytellers in question. Fortunately, James W. Thompson has already done much of the spade work in this respect, and the results can be briefly summarized here. It has been known for several decades that the group of tellers of Jack Tales that features so centrally in many contributions to this volume consists of members of one large family sharing traditional narratives that go back to a common ancestor. Richard Chase, who was one of the first to note these family connections, put it this way in the subtitle of his published collection of Jack Tales: "Told by R. M. Ward and his kindred in the Beech Mountain section of western North Carolina and by other descendants of Council Harmon (1803–1896) elsewhere in the Southern Mountains: with three tales from Wise County, Virginia." It is Old Counce Harmon, therefore, who is the common biological ancestor of all those who tell Jack Tales in the Beech Mountain area, although the surname Harmon is no longer found among them. Instead we encounter names like Ward, Presnell, Hicks, and Proffitt. The genealogy is complicated by two connected factors: first, Council Harmon had fifteen children from two marriages (seven by his first wife and eight by his second), and second, there has been considerable intermarriage among his descendants in later generations. For these reasons, the folk-narrative family tree is also anything but simple, and purely linear lines of dissemination are not to be expected. Thompson has done an admirable job in disentangling the genealogical lines of descent, mostly on the basis of census and vital statistics records of Watauga County. The resulting genealogical chart (fig. 1), which has been augmented and modified by information from a more recent genealogy (Hicks et al. 1991) is far superior to and much more comprehensive than the one that I attempted on the basis of fieldwork several years ago (Nicolaisen 1980, 99–106). Thompson's chart includes only family members who have had some bearing on the taletelling tradition within the family, either as active storytellers or as parents or spouses. Considering the size of Council Harmon's family, the complete family tree would undoubtedly display many more branches, some of them intertwining, and perhaps we should be grateful that, not unexpectedly, not every member of the family was an active tradition bearer.

One of Thompson's achievements (confirmed in Hicks et al. 1991) is that he has succeeded in tracing the genealogy for a further two, possibly three, generations beyond Council Harmon. This historical extension has enabled him to argue persuasively that Council learned his stories from his mother and his maternal grandfather, Samuel Hicks I or "Big Sammy." This Samuel Hicks, in his turn, is likely to have learned them from his own father, David Hicks, Sr., who is supposed to have emigrated to America from England, possibly London, when his son Samuel was four years old (around 1760). Since thus the family originated in England, there can be little doubt that their rich song and tale repertoire, including the Jack Tales, is ultimately also of English provenance and that the Jack of Beech Mountain, North Carolina, spent his early life in an English cradle.

Unfortunately, there appears to be no certain way of knowing where exactly in England, or Britain, that cradle once stood, for the only related item that Katharine M. Briggs, after an exhaustive search, includes in her *Dictionary of British Folk-Tales in the English Language* summarizes only the last episode of the story that is the pivot of this chapter, "The Heifer Hide," under the title "Sheep for the Asking." This abbreviated story that features "a young man, Jack, whose two elder brothers wanted to get rid of him as he was supposed to be a simpleton, was originally told to T. W. Thompson by a gypsy, Durham Lees, at Oxenholme, near Kendal in the English Lake District on September 7, 1914" (K. Briggs 1970, 2:263). It would be rash, however, to draw any conclusions, on the basis of a summary of one connectionless performance by a gypsy in the English northwest, almost a century and a half after David Hicks, Sr., emigrated from the south of England, about the precise geographical origins of the Hicks family and associated taletelling tradition. A comprehensive survey of the whole corpus of tales told in the Beech Mountain area and of their British analogues might have a better chance of success. There has been speculation that the Hicks family may have been from Somerset (Warner 1984, 212), but there is no definite proof for this hunch. While this genealogical obscurity is disappointing, it is even more disappointing, and not a little troublesome, that there is so little surviving evidence of the "Heifer Hide" story being told in England. In fact, if it were not for the one summary of a partial telling of the tale noted by one fieldworker, one might quite easily and legitimately have reached the conclusion that this story was not known in England and that, in this particular case, there might be a closer link with the Grimms' "Little Peasant" (AT 1737) and therefore with the German Harmons rather than the English Hickses. Fortunately, that entry in a fieldworker's notebook has saved us from a misleading conclusion.

Leaving the unexplored and perhaps unexplorable "prehistory" of this whole matter aside, this study, in order to explore the potential links between biological and folk-narrative genealogies, concentrates on three of Council Harmon's descendants: Marshall Ward, Hattie Presnell, and Ray Hicks, cousins more or less in the same age group, all of whom I recorded in May 1978. It is based on selected portions of their versions of "The Heifer Hide" (or "The Old Man in the Chest"). Since a full version, as told by Maud Long (1893–1984), another descendant of Council Harmon's, forms the basis of Chapter 4, I confine myself to indicating its relationship to the versions discussed here. Long, in addition to being a great-granddaughter of Council Harmon's (one of her grandmothers was his daughter Emoline), is also related to Council's grandfather Samuel Hicks I through her maternal grandfather, Ransom M. Hicks, who was one of his great-grandsons and therefore Council's second cousin. Her family tree, linking her with the Beech Mountain group of storytellers, appears in figure 2. As this genealogical chart implies, not only does her biological descent have a double link with Samuel Hicks I, but her folk-narrative traditions also merge two strands that come from the

Figure 1. Genealogy of the Beech Mountain Storytellers

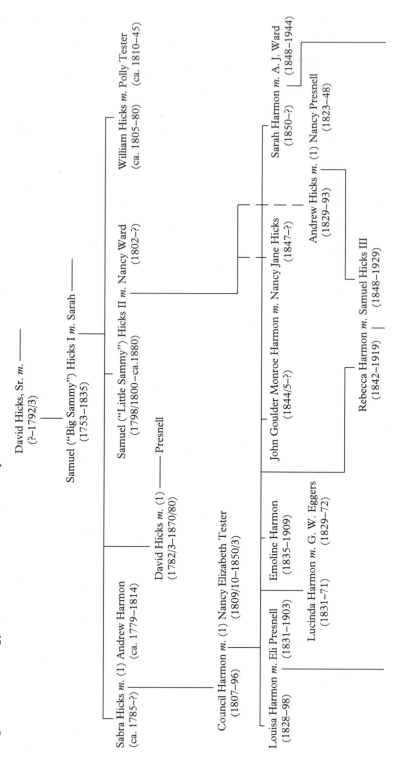

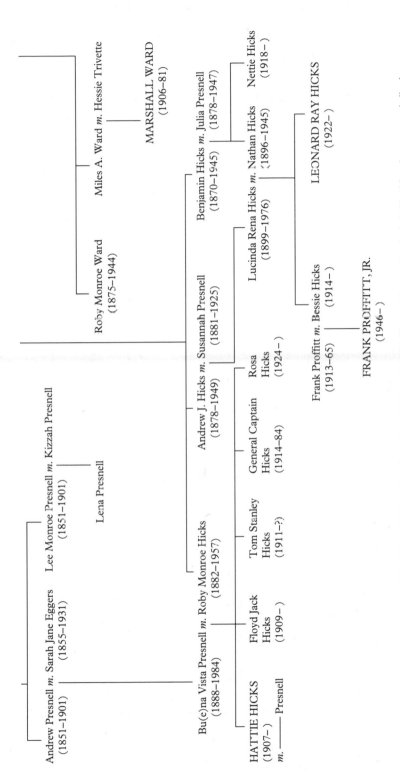

Andrew Presnell *m.* Sarah Jane Eggers
(1851–1901)   (1855–1931)

Lee Monroe Presnell *m.* Kizzah Presnell
(1851–1901)

Lena Presnell

Roby Monroe Ward
(1875–1944)

Miles A. Ward *m.* Hessie Trivette

MARSHALL WARD
(1906–81)

Benjamin Hicks *m.* Julia Presnell
(1870–1945)   (1878–1947)

Lucinda Rena Hicks *m.* Nathan Hicks   Nettie Hicks
(1899–1976)   (1896–1945)   (1918–   )

LEONARD RAY HICKS
(1922–   )

Andrew J. Hicks *m.* Susannah Presnell
(1878–1949)   (1881–1925)

Bu(e)na Vista Presnell *m.* Roby Monroe Hicks
(1888–1984)   (1882–1957?)

Floyd Jack   Tom Stanley   General Captain   Rosa
Hicks   Hicks   Hicks   Hicks
(1909–   )   (1911–?)   (1914–84)   (1924–   )

HATTIE HICKS
(1907–   )
m. ——— Presnell

Frank Proffitt *m.* Bessie Hicks
(1913–65)   (1914–   )

FRANK PROFFITT, JR.
(1946–   )

Source: Adapted from Thompson 1987, with additional information drawn from Hicks et al. 1991. Names of storytellers included in this volume are capitalized.

Figure 2. Genealogy of Maud Gentry Long

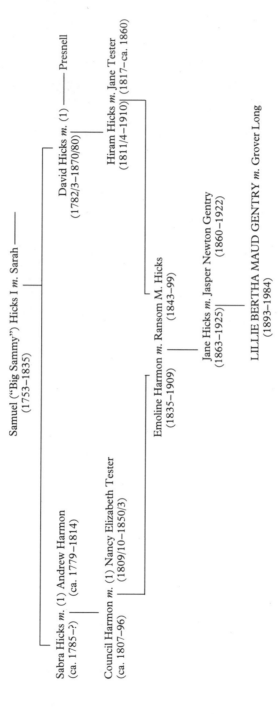

same source. Her version of "The Heifer Hide" has come down to her through her mother Jane Gentry (1863–1925) (see Carter 1925), Cecil Sharp's celebrated ballad singer, who appears to have learned it, together with her other stories, from Council Harmon himself. Though somewhat removed from the Beech Mountain tradition, it is of special value because it may possibly contain elements that, via Ransom H., Hiram, and David Hicks, are traceable to Samuel Hicks I but that his grandson Council did not pass on to his descendants.

Jane Gentry and Maud Long are not the only members of the Hicks-Harmon family to whom a multiple legacy of storytelling may have been transmitted. Not one of the three storytellers on whom this discussion concentrates is the recipient of a single-stranded tradition; whether this has meant reinforcement or confusion is difficult to say, especially when the intermixing (as the result of intermarrying) happened in earlier generations for whom no storytelling record exists. We do know, however, from the authoritative testimony of the late Marshall Ward (1906–1981) that he learned his stories not only from his father, Miles A. Ward, but also from his uncle Roby Monroe Ward (Richard Chase's R. M. Ward) and his aunt Mary Ward (not listed in James Thompson's family tree). Although Hattie Presnell professes to have learned her stories from her father, Roby Monroe Hicks, it is more than likely that she, as well as her brother Stanley, also occasionally heard her uncle Ben Hicks (Ray Hicks's grandfather) tell the same stories. Ben Hicks is the main source of the Jack Tales in Ray Hicks's repertoire, for Ray learned his stories from his grandfather rather than his father, Nathan (who was the transmitter of other kinds of traditional lore). Another factor that this kind of study has to take into account, therefore, is the ever-present possibility of stories (as well as other items) skipping a generation, passing from grandparents to grandchildren. Only in exceptional cases will it be possible to disentangle all these strands.

On the other hand, an important element, already referred to, in the transmission and particularly in the reception of stories in the folk-cultural register is sometimes recognizable in information from the storytellers themselves; this is the question of how conscious they—the storytellers—are of the ways in which they retain or innovate, re-create or create, in the course of their personal appropriations, especially within such a tightly knit family structure. For that reason, after they had first performed for me their own versions of

"The Heifer Hide," I asked the three Hicks-Harmon descendants whom I recorded in May 1978 about their respective attitudes and strategies on this issue. Their comments were at that point still performance-oriented and hence did not smack of distanced reflection or scholarly abstraction.

When I asked Hattie Presnell, who had earlier told me that she had learned her stories from her father, Roby Hicks, "Is that the way your father told it?" or if she had altered anything, she replied, "No, I never changed anything. I just tell it like he used to tell it." To the best of my knowledge there is no recording extant of Roby Hicks's version of AT 1535 or of any of his other stories, although he is listed as one of Richard Chase's informants (R. Chase 1943, 199). It is, therefore, impossible to put Presnell's assertion, nay conviction, to the test. However, this is perhaps not a very serious loss, for what matters here is her perception of what she is doing insofar as it conditions her basic stance as a self-conscious transmitter of stories, as a guardian of a personal family heritage, and as heir of a narrative tradition. In addition, her statement and denial appear to characterize her as fundamentally re-creative rather than creative, to the extent of ruling out, in her perception anyhow, any kind of innovation. It would be misleading, however, to infer from her statement that there was any sense of mission in her voice, any reverberation of zeal or inflexible determination, for her answer was offered quietly and conversationally, with no suggestion of responsibility for the integrity and fidelity of the text as text, or hint of its unalterability bordering on definitiveness, as if it had been engraved in her mind. Illuminating in this respect was her later claim that it did not matter to her to whom, to how many, and under what circumstances she told her stories (she had just performed for an audience of one—me). "I pay no attention to that," she said, citing as contrasting examples a folk festival on one hand and two visiting students on the other. Quite clearly, her father's voice, her father's words, and her father's authority are in her ears and mind when she tells her stories, eliminating, as far as she is concerned, the need or desire for creative alteration. A text is a text, especially when it is a paternal one.

In contrast, her cousin Ray Hicks, perhaps the best known of the trio, deliberately adds small touches of his own to the stories he learned from his grandfather Ben Hicks. Before our recording session started, he had confided to me that he does this so that the stories become his own. But when I asked him again, after he had told me a version of "The Heifer Hide," whether he ever changed anything, he eased into a version of "Jack and the Firedragon" (as he calls it) in order to demonstrate that he had made the firedragon puff his pipe like the blowers of a steam engine, explaining that this particular reference was to "the blowers in a steam-engine sawmill." "I worked in a sawmill," he said, "that's why I put it there." The additional simile he had chosen had therefore been triggered by his own working experience and could not have been easily provided by any other storyteller—or so it seemed. When I asked him what his grandfather had said at this point in the story, he said, "Oh, he just had it that he lit his pipe." Again, this may be perception rather than fact, for in Richard Chase's published composite version for which Ben Hicks had been one of several sources, the relevant passage reads, "that old pipe a-sendin' up smoke like a steam engine" (R. Chase 1943, 107). We do not know, of course, whether this particular portion came from Ben Hicks or not, but the steam-engine simile existed before Ray Hicks used it. Even if Ray's memory is inaccurate in this instance, however, the elaboration is his insofar as he translated the simile into the setting of his own working life, an internal appropriation, so to speak. Whatever the extent or exact significance, moreover, there is no doubt about Ray's introduction of creative additions (see below). While in principle a preserver of tradition, like Hattie Presnell, rather than a changer, Ray Hicks does not regard his deliberate, conscious, personal innovations as violations of the text he has inherited; nor does he appear to think of them as improvements per se. They merely—if *merely* is the right word here—function like a proprietary branding iron stamping the stories he tells as his own.

The third of the cousins, the late Marshall Ward, was the best educated of the three and also the eldest. As already mentioned, he learned his stories from his father, Miles Ward, as well as from an aunt and an uncle, and he was one of Richard Chase's chief guides and informants when he was collecting materials for his Jack Tales volume more than fifty years ago (R. Chase 1943, vii–viii). Ward claims that he started telling stories even before he went to school, and he remained, until his death on 11 July 1981, a much sought-after storyteller who enjoyed performing his tales before students of all ages, such as Cheryl Oxford, for whom he performed "Jack in the Lions' Den" just weeks before his death (see Chapter 3). When I followed his lively telling of "The Heifer Hide" not only with genuine praise but also with the usual query concerning the degree of innovativeness in his telling of the Jack Tales, he stressed repeatedly, "I am telling them my way," deriving his justification from Chase's treatment in his published versions. "My way is different than Richard's book. Richard told them his way."[1] In general, he thinks, "My way is a lot longer than the others," but he is also aware of the various changes he introduces in each performance. "Every time a little is added to, a little may be taken from, the way my dad told them." Although he acknowledges three main sources for his stories and is therefore perhaps more aware than his cousins of variations within the previous generation, Marshall Ward measures the character and quality of his own tellings by the yardstick of his father's versions. Nevertheless, there is nothing sacrosanct about these parental texts, and he enacts an endless series of appropriations. In particular, he regards the stories' endings as his own hallmark: "I end them the way I want. . . . I always get Jack married." These hallmark endings sometimes got him into trouble with puzzled schoolchildren who wanted to know how it was that Jack got married each time. Discarding the notion of a Jack cycle, Marshall Ward explained to them that each Jack was a different Jack and that, in fact, there were different Jacks in different generations. That seemed to satisfy them. In Marshall Ward, therefore, we have a storyteller who is quite ready to make changes according to circumstances, response to his audience being one of them. Knowing about variability, indeed expecting it because of his genealogical background as a storyteller and his close association with Chase in his younger years, he is not bothered by textual changes, as long as they are within reasonable bounds. His own personal thumbprint is his regularized happy ending, symbolized by marriage.

Thus we find attitudes ranging from Hattie Presnell's responsible conservatism via Ray Hicks's limited personal creativeness to Marshall Ward's greater flexibility but also greater personal stylization. Even the most audacious of them, however, Marshall Ward, only nibbles at the texts he has inherited. Tradition, especially family tradition, is a powerful force for him too, a force that he cannot, and has no desire to, escape.

How do these "authorial" perceptions work in practice? Quite clearly, such professed attitudes or perspectives can only be verified, or at least tested, by an overall assessment of actual tellings and performances of a tale. A transcribed text on a page, whether verbatim, faithful, or edited, will never permit more than a glimpse of the essential, creative, individual, personal, but oh so elusive performance. Nevertheless, we will have to be content with something less ideal and, one would hope, not completely misleading, in the little comparative exploration that follows—with transcribed texts of actual performances. By their very presence on the printed page the transcriptions take on an apparent quality of definitiveness and invariability they do not rightfully possess, and they only hint at such essential audible characteristics of a performance as timbre, accent (a factor that, for instance, clearly sets Ray Hicks apart), tone, and variation in speed and emphasis, as well as the whole range of supporting visual and paralinguistic features (see Note on the Texts). As presented here, the texts reflect no more than one telling on one particular occasion and under one particular set of circumstances. They are therefore to be understood in their fundamental uniqueness, and any generalizing argument advanced on their basis must take this fact into account by leaving room for creative variability in other performances of the same tale by the narrator on other occasions. Any stylistic or other comparison is to be interpreted with these limitations in mind.

Any comparison involves the recognition of both similarities and differences. Let us dispose of some of the major similarities first, since these point to the stories' origin and dissemination within the same family tradition. All three storytellers (like Maud Long and her mother, Jane Gentry, before her) tell a tale consisting of the same final three episodes of tale type AT 1535 as presented by Aarne and Thompson: III. Magic Cow-hide; IV. Fatal Imitation; V. Fatal Deception. Their choice and sequence of motifs within these episodes is also identical. (It is worth noting that the motif index associates these motifs primarily or exclusively with AT 1535.)

The scene-setting events leading up to these three episodes (the "orientational" opening almost amounting to an introductory episode) are also similar since they depend on the same personnel, a boy called Jack and his envious and jealous older brothers, Will and Tom. The only difference is that while for Marshall Ward and Hattie Presnell (and for Maud Long) Tom is the elder of the two, Ray makes Will the oldest. For all of them, Jack, as the youngest, is the bright fool, the unpromising hero who, in the role of persuasive trickster, outwits everybody. The remaining personnel—three women whose husbands are absent, especially the third adulterous woman, her lover, her cuckolded husband, and an eminently dupeable but also likable aging shepherd—also show no difference.

When the general structure and the personnel of the story as well as their specific manifestations demonstrate such a remarkable degree of sameness, stemming from their common origin (ancestor), like physical build or facial features displayed by the descendants of the same great-grandfather, any evidence for personal individuality is bound to be found in the handling of detail, the treatment of little things, whether these be linguistic or extralinguistic. Accordingly, three brief passages in these stories are closely compared to identify differences in detail. The passages are (1) Jack's observation of the surreptitious meal, (2) Jack's acquisition of the chest, and (3) Jack's conversation with the shepherd. When appropriate, reference is made to Maud Long's and Jane Gentry's versions, which share all these features but treat some of them a little differently.

JACK'S OBSERVATION OF THE SURREPTITIOUS MEAL

Marshall Ward
And she hadn't more than got down in the kitchen
—she had on that table an old oil cloth,
and the corners were wiped,
and she had on old dirty clothes.
And you know, she began to, she put a white linen cloth on the table
    over that old oil cloth
and she began to set place for two.
And she begin to—in the cupboard she brought out some boiled
    ham.
She brought out some roast beef set on the table,
some mashed potatoes and beans,
and she went and set out a bottle a brandy
and a bottle of whiskey,
and then she went an set out some pie and cake.
And Jack's mouth was just a-watering.
Oh, my!
And where Jack was layin' on that straw

there was a hole in a crack in the floor
and he could see down through there good
and he was watchin' everything,
and it wasn't ten minutes she come out of the bedroom in the finest
    clothes it looked like anybody had in those days.
Dressed up.
And it wasn't but a minute in come a middle-aged man about her
    age.
And he never saw so much huggin' and kissin' in all his life.
And he said, "That cain't be the old drunk."
He said, "There's somethin' goin' on here."
And d'you know,
he watched them and they set down and went to eatin',
and they was having a good time,
a-laughin' and a-talkin' and a-eatin', you know.

Hattie Presnell
And he peeped down through this knothole.
There's an ole parson come in,
and this ole woman, she'd baked cakes and she'd baked pies and she
    fixed meat,
roasted a pig and fixed it all up
for him and her eat a whole lot.

Ray Hicks
And he 'gin to hunt over in there and found a rat hole.
And when he looked down there through it,
one eye wanderin',
directly he looked in there,
and there was the eating table—old time eating table.
And imagine, down there was a man with a big suit o' clothes on
and a black high topped hat—ten-gallon hat—
and was a suitable lookin' man, young ma—middle-aged man.
And he says, "Man, I'm gonna watch."
And he kept watchin',
and directly they took hands, went and danced around the table.
She went to the cupboard
and got out hog meat
and beef and chicken meat.

Eat some of that.
Then him and her took hands and danced around the table agin.
She went and got old timey fruitcake and punkin pie.
Then eat some of it,
and took hands and danced around the table.
And she went to the cupboard
and brought out pure corn whiskey and wine—
it was aged: it had turned brown.
And one glass was all you'd a needed to make you kick a, runnin'
—of that wine, one drinkin' glass full.
And so, he said, when they drunk, got whiskey and wine,
they took hands and, said, boys they did dance a buck dance around
    that table.

Jack's triple request for overnight accommodations, which Ward, Presnell, and Hicks include in their versions (in contrast to Gentry and Long, whose versions have only one such request), is answered by three prospective female hosts who modestly claim that they cannot allow a young man to enter the house while their husbands are away. Jack is finally admitted at the third house, given scant food, and taken upstairs to sleep, his heifer hide bumping up the steps behind him. From his vantage point the still-starving lad observes—through "a hole in a crack in the floor" (Ward); "through this knothole" (Presnell); through "a rat hole" (Hicks)—a veritable culinary feast being prepared. It consists of "boiled ham . . . roast beef . . . mashed potatoes and beans . . . brandy . . . whiskey . . . pie and cake" (Ward); "cakes . . . pies . . . meat . . . roast pig" (Presnell); "hog meat and beef and chicken meat . . . old timey fruitcake and punkin pie . . . pure corn whiskey and wine" (Hicks). Long has "*chicken* and *ham* and *pie* and *cake* and *preserves* and *honey*," and her mother provides "baked pig and stuffed goose and roast chicken and pies and cakes." The feast is for the woman herself and her clandestine visitor—"a middle-aged man about her age" (Ward); "an ole parson" (Presnell); "a man with a big suit o' clothes on and a black high topped hat—ten-gallon hat—and was a suitable lookin' man, young ma—middle-aged man" (Hicks). Compare with Long's "nice-looking young man" and Gentry's "old man" called "Mr. Passenger." This visitor is destined to be bundled into an old chest when the woman's husband is heard arriving home unexpectedly. One cannot help thinking that a narrative statement like "and through a (knot) hole in the floor Jack saw a table set with the most delicious homemade food" has here permitted, or even encouraged, creative storytellers to indulge in fancies of their own when imagining that food in their own minds, a meal that, in addition to making Jack's mouth water, would also have the same effect on narrator and audience even without any exotic, nontraditional ingredients. In fact, Ray Hicks goes out of his way to call the fruitcake "old timey," and Maud Long's "preserves" is probably intended to convey a similar notion of wholesome, rich, tasty, homemade, traditional fare. In passing, it is interesting to note that whereas the male storytellers add alcoholic beverages to the feast, the women do not include them in their vision of feasting.

In a corresponding vein, the male visitor is usually made to look an attractive or at least acceptable alternative to the woman's (drunk) husband, except by Hattie Presnell, who describes him as "an ole parson," a characterization that looks like an innovation but has several well-attested parallels in the international distribution of the tale. Jane Gentry's use of the peculiar name "Mr. Passenger" may indicate that she or someone in her ancestry had heard the man identified as a parson or even a paramour. (Her daughter Maud Long calls him a passenger when he is being transported in the chest.)

The goings-on in conjunction with the sumptuous meal have also provided much scope for personal embellishment. While Maud Long's "nice-looking" man and woman are concentrating on the food and are "having the—*best*—time" without moving from opposite sides of the table, and Hattie Presnell's couple simply "eat a whole lot," the two male storytellers are not satisfied with such limited entertainment. Marshall Ward assures us that the woman was "dressed up" and his Jack is sure "he never saw so much huggin' and kissin' in all his life," while Ray Hicks tells us that the man in his sartorial splendor and the woman "directly . . . took hands . . . and danced around the table" immediately on his arrival, repeating the performance after each course and ending up with a "buck dance" after consuming both whiskey and wine. Rather than ascribing these differences to differing inherited traditions, it seems feasible that they indicate gender-related perceptions as to what it means to be having a good time behind your husband's back, or at least contrasting views as to what can be properly told to a mixed audience, since the men clearly hint at an adulterous relationship. It would be interesting to know how Hattie Presnell's father, whom she faithfully follows, handled this situation as a male narrator.

It is also worth noting that Richard Chase, in shaping his own version of a composite "Heifer Hide," is content with letting "a man . . . dressed up awful fine, necktie stickin' out, and a pretty little moustache" stuff himself on "all kinds of good somethin' to eat" and conduct the kind of conversation that made Jack finally decide that "that feller wasn't the man of the house" (R. Chase 1943, 163). Probably conscious of the audience for whom his collection of Jack Tales appears to have been mainly intended—young people—he must have omitted more suggestive or boisterous depictions of this scene as he is likely to have heard them from storytellers in previous generations, such as Roby Monroe Ward, Miles A. Ward, and Ben Hicks, whom he lists among his sources and who were also the people from whom Marshall Ward and Ray Hicks learned versions of "The Heifer Hide."[2] It is, one would think, unlikely for the more daring portions of the meal scene to have been added simultaneously but independently to the culinary delights by both Ray Hicks and Marshall Ward; there must have been hints in earlier renderings. One also suspects Hattie Presnell's "ole parson" was not just calling in the hope of a better meal than he was accustomed to getting in the parsonage. Because of the basic incongruity implied, the lecherous minister is, of course, a well-known figure of ridicule and contempt in humorous folk narrative, especially in the genre that in German is called Schwank.

JACK'S ACQUISITION OF THE CHEST

Marshall Ward

"Well," Jack said, "that's fine,
but 'fore you can have my heifer hide
I want that old wooden chest a-settin' over there in the corner
for a boot—a bargain—to close the deal."
Said, "I want that old chest."
"Well, you can have that danged old chest. It ain't worth nuthin'."
    Said, "It just settin in the way."
And the old woman jumped up: "He can't have that chest, My
    great-great-grandpa give it to my great-great-grandma. My great-
    grandma give it to my grandmother—"

"Shut up, old woman."
Knocked her back on the floor. Said, "Take the blame thing."

Hattie Presnell

He said, "If ya give me that chest over there and a thousand guineas,
   I will trade."
"Boy, you won't be selling that chest. My grandpa give it—my great-
   grandpa give it ta my grandpa, my grandpa give it ta my uncle,
   my uncle give it ta my cousin, my cousin give it ta me and you're
   not selling that chest," she says.
"Doggone your uncles' cousins," he said,
"Jack shall have the chest."

Ray Hicks

He said, "I'll take the hundred guineas and that old chest that you
   got over thar in the corner.
"And," Jack says, now,
"yeah," he said, "the trades broke,
the trades broke:
smokes went up the chimney."
And 'bout that time, out come the woman, the lady,
and said [*very fast, and unclear*], "No, no, no, the table. I cain't let
   you have the chest. My grandfather give it to my half sister, my
   half sister give it to my first cousin, and my first cousin give it to
   me. You ain't gone give that away."
He said, "Your first cousin's grandpa's half sister's uncle's, great-
   uncle's, whatever they be, that's Jack's chest."

The little scene described here ends the drawn-out haggling over
the heifer hide that the woman's husband wants to buy at all cost
because Jack, through deception, has tricked him into thinking that it
has prophetic gifts. Again, the three Beech Mountain cousins differ
markedly from Maud Long and Jane Gentry in their treatment of this
episode. In the latter accounts the chest is the only payment for the
hide (with promise of money to come from the man hidden inside it),
the deceitful wife offering no resistance or objections to the deal. In
The Types of the Folktale, Aarne and Thompson list the purchase of
the pseudo-magical cow hide and the exchange of a chest for it as
alternative sub-episodes, but Marshall Ward, Hattie Presnell, and

Ray Hicks all employ both exchanges together in a cumulative bargain—Jack receives both money and the chest (and, of course, more
money from the man hidden in the chest who, as Jack had antici-
pated, is bargaining for his release). The fact that Richard Chase has
Jack selling his hide for both a hundred guineas and the chest is a clear
indication that Jack also succeeded in gaining both in previous generations, at least as far back as Ben Hicks but possibly right back to
Council Harmon himself.

The use of guineas as currency is the most persuasive pointer to
the English origins of the story. Only Marshall Ward (or, less likely,
one of his sources), who often told the story to young schoolchildren,
translates the purchase price arbitrarily into $3,000, while Hattie
Presnell has 1,000 guineas. Richard Chase's 100 guineas seems to
have been derived from Ben Hicks, since his grandson Ray also men-
tions this sum, feeling the need for an explanatory aside: "Now a
hundred guineas, back at that time they called it, what I mean, in my
time a-growin' up, bout like twenty dollar bill or fifteen dollar (a ten
and a five), the way they called a hundred guineas." (In another
performance Hicks expanded this aside considerably; see Oxford
1987, 247–48). The guineas seem inherited from David Hicks, Sr.,
and Samuel Hicks I, or their forebears, as the currency valid at the
time they told this story. But the implication by the more recent
American tellers is not that the events happened in England or when
America was still in British hands. Rather, the designation guineas
has become a convenient indicator for the considerable age, perhaps
even the ahistoricity, of the tale. Hicks, for instance, also refers to
guineas in "Hardy Hard-Ass," the story included in full in this collection. In the temporal setting of these stories in the Beech Mountain
tradition, therefore, "once upon a time" seems to be synonymous
with "at a time when important purchases were made in guineas."

The woman's objections, if Richard Chase's inclusion of them and
the fact that they are shared by all three cousins are anything to go by,
are also part of an older, inherited stratum. To increase the humorous
effect, these heirloom sequences are usually spoken at a much faster
pace in the excited, high-pitched tones of the nagging wife, in contrast to the much slower, because exceedingly slow-witted, speech of
the henpecked husband.

JACK'S CONVERSATION WITH THE SHEPHERD

Marshall Ward
And while they was a-fightin' that,
along come an old man with three thousand sheep,
and a dog that could take care of them sheep,
and he had a fine horse,
and a fine saddle and bridle on it all decorated up with gold.
Shinin', it was,
with little bells on it a-jinglin' like jingle bells.
He said, "Hey mister, what're you doin' in that sack there aside the
    fence?"
He said, "Don't talk to me, be quiet".
He said, "I'm fixin' to go to heaven."
He said, "You talk like a young man."
"I am a young man. I'm only twenty-one years old."
"Well," he said, "I'm ninety-nine years old
and I just ready to die,
and," he said, "I'd like t' go t' heaven."
He said, "I got three thousand sheep,
I got a fine horse,
and I got a dog can take care of every one of these sheep. I tell you
    what I'll do.
I'll swap places with you and give you all this."
"Well," Jack says, "on one condition:
when the angels come to get you,
if you won't talk to 'em—"
Said, "They might not take you if you talk to 'em—"
Said, "I'll swap with you."

Hattie Presnell
Well, a man come along with a big bunch o' sheep,
and he says, "Ho, what you doin' in that sack?"
Jack says, "It's me, Jack."
"Well," he says, "what're ya doin in there?"
He says, "I'm goin' ta heaven."
"Goin' ta heaven?"
"Well," he says, "there's two angels comin' directly, ta take me ta
    heaven."

"Well," he said, "let me in, I'm old";
said, "How old are ya?"
"Well," he said, "I ain't very old."
"Well," he said, "let me in";
said, " I'm real old!"
"No," he said, "I mean, I started, I better go on."
"Well," he said, "I have a thousand head o' sheep out here:
you let me get ta heaven."
"Well," he said, "untie the sack,
the dadjuket sack."
He untied the sack and Jack put him in, tied it back.
"Now," he says, "before you go,
two angels come talking along:
don't you open your mouth."
Said, "They find out it ain't me, they won't take ya."

Ray Hicks
But while he was doin' that there was an old feller,
sheepherder,
had come up on the rise,
and up on top of the hill,
and was a-herding a hundred head o' sheep.
And he had seed Jack down thar,
and, thinking it was a ghost
or somethin'—he didn't know what it might be.
And he got on his all fours.
Crawled down that rise.
And he'd stop and he'd look, peepin',
and crawl a little more, and he'd peep,
and directly he got clost enough.
And he seed
a little bit that it might be somebody in the sack.
He said, "Hello,
or who are ya,
or what are ya doin' in thar,
or where ye goin'?"
Jack said, "Goin' to heaven."
He said, "Goin' to heaven!"
Jack said, "Yeah, goin' to heaven."

Said, "The gabriels is come after me,
two gabriel angels is come after me a while ago."
He says, "How old are you."
He says, "I'm twenty-one."
He says, "Oh, son,"
he says, "Gosh, you've got a lotta good things in your life to get yet,
    to live fer."
Said, "Gosh, your life is just started."
Said, "You goin' to heaven yet, that young?"
He said, "I'm ninety-three. Been awful wicked."
Said, "I been a wicked man."
He said, "Now,
it wouldn't be any chance for me to buy your way would it?"
Jack says, "Now, I might live on old and get mean,
like you said you was,
and lose heaven."
He says, "I better take it now, if I am young,
while I'm fit to go."
"Well," he says, "I'll tell you what I'll do."
He said, "If you can trust my word,"
he said, "I've got a hundred head o' sheep up there on the rise that's
    got the wool on 'em,
and they's gonna lamb pretty soon."
And Jack says, "Hell."
He says, "Yeah, if you can believe me, I'll give you the sheep, to go in
    your place."
And Jack held out a while,
to hold, to keep him from maybe catchin' on,
he held out. And directly he says, "Augh! It ain't but a few minutes
    till them gabriels, two gabriels be back."
He says, "I believe I'll trade."
Said, "Roll the log off that, quick."
Rolled it off, and Jack got out and he got in it.

In order to appreciate fully the narrative skills of our three story-tellers, as well as of Maud Long and her mother, in the realization of this dialogue, it may be helpful to quote the equivalent passage from the summary of the English tale: "A man passing, asked him what he was doing in a sack and hearing that he was going to Heaven was envious; so Jack exchanged places with him." A bland outline like this offers storytellers the opportunity to do their very best in fleshing it out, and as the creation of lively and entertaining dialogue is one of the special strengths of the Beech Mountain group, they do not spurn this chance, especially since Jack as trickster is essentially a bamboozling talker, a scheming and charming verbalizer. It is in a vignette like this that the twin forces of tradition and creativity, with the aid of the welcome device of permitted, indeed encouraged, variability, are best seen in action. This observation is not meant to suggest that our storytellers had nothing but the outline quoted above to work with; quite the contrary. Although conversational language may differ according to the linguistic register and usage of each narrator, the inherited traits are clearly discernible, including the large size of the flock of sheep, the shepherd's curiosity (particularly exploited by Ray Hicks), Jack's claim to be going to heaven, the contrast in age that almost gives Jack's trickery the veneer of a good deed, and Jack's admonition to the shepherd not to give the game away by talking to the supposed angels. The pull of tradition and the re-creative, imitative nature of storytelling within that tradition are obvious for all to see, and it is intriguing to speculate whether it was Old Counce or one of his forebears who injected some of the specific qualities just noted into that powerful tradition. What about personal creativity in such a situation? Here is just one sentence, the old man's curious inquiry, to illustrate the way it works:

> Ward: "Hey, mister, what're you doin' in that sack there aside the fence?"
>
> Presnell: "Ho, what you doin' in that sack?"
>
> Hicks: "Hello, or who are ya, or what are ya doin' in thar, or where ye goin'?"
>
> Long: "Son, what in the *world* are you—doing—in—that—sheet?"
>
> Gentry: "Stranger, what are you doin' here?"

There can be little doubt that "What are you doin' in the sack (sheet)?" is the inherited basic interrogative sentence, as it is the right kind of question to ask. All five storytellers, however, appropriate this simple question and, through rephrasing, filter into it, in their own fashion, the sense of disbelieving surprise the old man must have felt at discovering Jack in this peculiar predicament. Hattie Presnell is the most sparing in that respect, but her initial "Ho" is much more than just the means of hailing and starting a conversation with a stranger. Marshall Ward's "Hey, mister" fulfills the same function with similar effect. Ray Hicks has a number of alternatives to offer that demonstrate unmistakably the old man's bafflement—he does not know what to say. Maud Long's "What in the world" also seeks to express this feeling of utter incredulity. Her mother's question lacks this phrase, and she addresses Jack as "stranger," which her daughter replaces with "son," emphasizing the age difference. None of these questions is simply asking for information, and where the words in the text may fail to make this clear, the voices of the narrators and their raised eyebrows do.

Where does all this leave us in our quest for a genealogy of narratives to match, or at least resemble, the known genealogy of narrators? As envisaged, the main problem attending such a search is that, whereas there are census and vital statistical records available in courthouses for the latter, no such reports exist for the former. Whatever evidence we employ, therefore, has to be quite circumstantial until we come to the point at which we can scrutinize, analyze, and evaluate actual texts. Even then, a comparative examination of different storytellers' versions of the same tale would require a scale of operations beyond the scope of a chapter in a book. Our less ideal substitutes have been three short but telling passages from such versions. A close reading of them has suggested certain lines of inquiry well worth following.

Through judicious assessment of these passages it appears to be possible to identify several features that have been inherited, and to distinguish them from some others that the individual storytellers themselves have contributed. These inherited features include not only constituent elements such as plot, personnel, and motifs, but also syntactic features and even such fine details as the tone of surprise in the old shepherd's question. Contrary to what one might have expected, however, a distinction between imitative and innovative narrators does not seem to hold in the Beech Mountain case. Within the small sample studied, and bearing in mind that we are dealing here with a recognized, perhaps even self-conscious, family structure, there is very little noticeable difference in the degree of willingness to adopt the whole inherited general framework for the story, including the sequence of episodes and motifs but also some more specific ingredients such as syntactic models and the characterization of subordinate figures. My questions put to Marshall Ward, Hattie Presnell, and Ray Hicks in May 1978 seem, therefore, to have been misleadingly phrased and to have failed to elicit the ways in which the storytellers are distinct one from another. More applicable than the storytellers' own perceptions of the role they are playing in the transmission process might well be a set of distinctions that D. A. MacDonald (1978) and Alan Bruford (1978) utilize in connection with studies of Hebridean storytellers in Scotland. In the course of their studies these researchers examined different kinds of memories—conceptual or structural memory (as exemplified by ability to remember plots), verbal memory, and visual memory. All our storytellers, so it seems to me, are exemplary in the first category; Marshall Ward and Ray Hicks are also strong in the second; and Ray Hicks particularly excels in the third. What differentiates these storytellers, then, is not what they add to what they have inherited. What differentiates them is the way in which they appropriate and express what they have inherited. The hallmark of personal acquisition and creative impact does not lie, therefore, in the degree to which what has been adopted has been adapted but, rather, in the way in which the adopted (inherited) patterns are given verbal and presentational substance without losing their evident identity. This is where the choices lie for Marshall Ward, Hattie Presnell, and Ray Hicks, but also for Jane Gentry and her daughter. This is where stylistic features distinguish one storyteller from another. This is where the personal branding iron is applied (Marshall Ward's endings, for example, and Ray Hicks's asides). A further factor that comes into play appears to be gender, but even this contrast, where it can be reliably detected, leaves the overall pattern intact and ready to be re-realized by the next generation of storytellers. One of the ways in which this kind of personal acquisition achieves creative impact, and by no means an insignificant way, is that Marshall Ward's story is more than 7,000 words long (see his statement above); Ray Hicks requires over 5,000 words to tell the same story; Maud Long requires about 3,500 words; and for Hattie Presnell just over 2,000 words are sufficient. Whatever their professed attitudes to the process of transmission, these storytellers (making ample use of the opportunity to diversify) do make the story their own, whether deliberately or unintentionally, but never overstep the bounds within which tradition obliges them to operate. Council Harmon speaks through all of them, but the voices we hear are authentically those of Marshall Ward, Hattie Presnell, Ray Hicks, and, of course, Jane Gentry and Maud Long—guardians and innovators all.

NOTES

1. Hattie Presnell and Ray Hicks, like Marshall Ward (and Maud Long and Frank Proffitt as well), are/were aware of Chase's book and read it. While doubtless they were not able to escape the authority of the printed word completely, and while Chase's publication of the composite versions is likely to have rekindled an interest in the Jack Tales and in the narrators who tell them, it would, in my view, be erroneous to put too much stress on the book's distorting influence. Marshall Ward probably speaks for all three storytellers recorded: "My way is different than Richard's book." It may be of tangential interest in this connection that Hasan el-Shamy, commenting on a very different culture, comes to a conclusion that may be equally valid for the Beech Mountain area: "The literary text is largely confined to the fixed (printed) 'book' format with little oral circulation" (el-Shamy 1990, 100).

2. The question of the sources for Chase's version of "The Heifer Hide" is not easily answered. Chase indicated that Maud Long was his principal source, but his version is substantially different from hers (see Chapter 4). Marshall Ward obviously considered himself a source. His recollections, quoted in Oxford's essay in Chapter 3, indicate that he performed sixteen stories for Chase, and he seems to suggest that all the stories in The Jack Tales, with the exception of the Virginia stories, were stories he had shared with Chase.

JACK IN THE
STORYTELLING
REVIVAL

CHAPTER 6

THE
TELLERS AND
THE TALES

▼ ▼ ▼ ▼ ▼

REVIVALIST
STORYTELLING

▼ ▼ ▼ ▼ ▼

Ruth Stotter and
William Bernard
McCarthy

A quiet revival in storytelling has been going on in the United States for at least half a century, but during the 1980s the revival produced an explosion of professional storytellers and storytelling festivals. In 1989, for example, over 4,000 people attended the National Association for the Preservation and Perpetuation of Storytelling (NAPPS) festival in the tiny town of Jonesborough, Tennessee; 16,000 attended the Corn Island Festival in Lexington, Kentucky; and throughout the United States there were dozens of smaller storytelling festivals and conferences. These new festivals both spread Jack Tales beyond the southern mountain homeland and alter them in performance. The NAPPS festival, for example, held in the heart of Jack country, has invited Ray Hicks, a traditional Jack Tale raconteur, to every festival since its 1973 inception. But, as Kay Stone points out in a yet-to-be-published manuscript, when professional and traditional tellers listen to and watch one another, this interaction can affect subsequent delivery and choice of material.

Storytellers come to the festivals seeking new stories to add to their repertoires. (Of course, the Jack Tales are also found on recordings and in published form: Richard Chase's collection, for instance, is available in libraries and bookstores.) It almost seems that for tellers hearing Jack Tales even for the first time, there is an immediate sense of recognition and connection. As Massachusetts storyteller Doris Smith related, "I find that when I tell these tales at places like old age retirement homes and at shelters for abused young women, it is the Jack Tales that they remember the most, maybe because of the subtle trickery—and some not so subtle trickery." Storyteller and folklorist Joyce Hancock, in discussing the popularity of these tales, notes that Jack Tales are about how one remains human while exercising survival skills (Hancock 1987).

Joseph Sobol, likewise a storyteller as well as a folklorist, points out that the name Jack, with all its associations, works as a keyword introducing a hypnotic, story-receptive trance state (Sobol 1987, 82). Indeed the name—and the word—has strong cultural associations for most Americans. Jack and the Beanstalk is a well-known children's story; preschoolers are introduced to Jack and Jill, Jack-be-nimble, Jack Sprat, and Jack Frost. Children play with jack-in-the-box, bounce a ball and pick up jacks, carve jack-o-lanterns, and at a slightly older age, play blackjack. We use a jack to change a tire, a lifting jack, and a jackknife, and refer to a handyman as a jack-of-all-trades. There is a lumberjack, the distinctive flower jack-in-the-pulpit, and in the animal world, a jackrabbit and a jackass (who sometimes loans his name to humans). We eat Monterey Jack cheese, Cracker Jacks, and flapjacks. There is the strange juxtaposition, jacking off and the Union Jack. We exercise with jumping jacks and, if we are lucky, hit the jackpot. Perhaps part of the mystique of the Kennedys was their names—Jack and Jackie. Jack, according to the dictionary, is a generic name for any representative of the people. Jack is one of the folk, an everyman figure. Thus, it should not be surprising that in recent years the Jack Tales have been emigrating north, east, and west. Over half the tellers asked in a 1988 survey (by Stotter) at the NAPPS festival answered that they have told at least one Jack Tale.

Folklorists, seeking to record authentic performances, focus on traditional stories told in traditional settings to traditional audiences. Cultural relevance and studies of past performances are used as criteria in establishing authenticity. But when a revivalist, nontraditional storyteller provides a Jack Tale, there is no way of knowing, unless the storyteller offers an explanation, whether the story was obtained from a book, from a recording, or from live performance, whether by professional, amateur, or traditional teller. Even on recordings produced by professional tellers, Jack Tales are rarely identified as stories associated with, or collected from, a specific geographic region or population. Furthermore, professional and nontraditional tellers assume complete autonomy in story selection and delivery style, limited only by their experiences, imagination, and availability of audiences willing to provide performance opportunities.

Similarly, there is no certification or set of criteria that grants a person the title "professional storyteller." Storytellers develop a repertoire and are invited to perform, or seek out performance opportunities. Among revivalist tellers, just as among traditional tellers, there is great variety in performance style, interpretation, digression, texture, and performance-audience attitude. A teller may use a lot of body movement and space or may remain seated. A teller may alter the story—content, style, structure—for a specific performance context (radio, theater, storytelling festival) or may adapt it for an adult audience or for very young children. The same story retold by different tellers may be humorous or scary. Despite changes, however, it does seem that in a revivalist storytelling context as in a traditional context the storytelling event, the experience of an audience listening to a narrator, remains remarkably consistent.

But does this consistency mean that oral narratives from the folk tradition are available for retelling by anyone who wants to use them? To what extent do professional revivalist storytellers have the right to adapt traditional tales? (Although many traditional tellers are also paid for their services, this discussion restricts the term *professional storyteller* to paid nontraditional revivalist performers.)

To consider this question fairly, we need some idea of how revivalist storytellers do in fact change traditional tales. How much of the traditional color do they retain? What embellishments do they add?

Most important, to what extent are changes merely accidental, and to what extent do they affect the substance of the story? Chapter 5 demonstrates the range of variation in traditional narrators within a single family tradition by focusing on the tale usually called "Jack and the Heifer Hide" (AT 1535). In this chapter we concentrate on performances of two familiar and popular tales, "Jack and the Animals" (AT 130) and "Soldier Jack" (AT 330/332) to show the range of variation among professional and revivalist storytellers.

The first story, "Jack and the Animals," tells how Jack, with the help of four or five cast-off domestic animals, scares a gang of robbers away from the deserted house they have been using as a hideout and gets rich off the abandoned loot. In the Grimms' better-known version of this story, "The Bremen Town Musicians," there is no human protagonist, and the animals frighten the robbers away with their singing. In the Appalachian variant, the animals cleverly stage an offensive attack. The performances of this story by Richard Chase, Donald Davis, and Ed Stivender cover the same plot matter but display dramatic differences in the appropriation of that matter for performance.

The first teller, Richard Chase, collected from Appalachian informants many of the most frequently told Jack Tales and was one of the earliest revivalist professional storytellers visiting schools and libraries. Though Chase's popular collection *The Jack Tales* contains versions of this and other stories that he had honed in public performance, we here refer to a commercial recording of Chase performing the tale before a young audience. (For more on Chase, see the Introduction and Chapter 4.) Chase has the most elaborate opening of the three:

Now one time Jack forgot to split his kindling.
That was his job and his daddy had told him what he'd do next
    time he forgot.
So, sure enough, Jack's daddy come in one day
and there wasn't a stick of kindling there for his mommy to make
    the morning fires.
Well, Jack's daddy took him by the ear
and he took him right out to the smoke house
and he took a little paddle
and he laid it on him.

I'll just tell you he smoked Jack's britches.
And Jack was getting to be a pretty big boy.
He thought he didn't like that being whipped, you know,
for forgetting about his kindling,
so the next morning early
before anybody else was up,
Jack slipped out of the bed
and he lit out from there.
He thought he'd run away from home because he was mad.
Well Jack traveled on and traveled on.
The sun came up and he kept on going,
and he got lonesome.
So Jack got to looking over the country
and he finally looked and there in the pasture field ahead of him
    was an old ox. (R. Chase n.d.)

The second teller, Donald Davis, an ordained minister as well as a professional performer, grew up in North Carolina hearing Jack Tales in a traditional context (see Chapter 8). "Jack and the Animals" is one of the stories Davis has internalized through repeated listenings. In a personal interview at the NAPPS congress in St. Louis in 1987 he reminisced about listening as he worked on chores: "I grew up with people who told stories—not to make a living—storytelling was a way of interpreting all of human life." Of his storytelling technique he said, "I don't even think about it. It just sort of comes out." Davis's repertoire has changed as he has become an increasingly popular revivalist storyteller, frequently featured at the NAPPS storytelling festival as well as other festivals throughout North America. He still tells traditional tales, although he has lately become better known for original stories based on his own life experiences. The opening of "Jack and the Animals" demonstrates the "down home" delivery with which Davis presents all his stories, original as well as traditional.

You've heard about old Jack and his beanstalk.
Let me tell you another story about old Jack.
One time Jack was going out to seek his fortune.
He was just going along through the world trying to decide what he
    was going to do,

maybe get a job somewhere,
or maybe he'll live somewhere,
and as he was just walking along one day,
thinking about where he might go next,
he heard a funny, funny noise. (Davis 1983b)

Davis's story is very different from the self-consciously created
stories of Ed Stivender, our urban, Pennsylvania teller, who has studied dance, mime, and clowning and holds a master of arts degree in
theology from Notre Dame University. Stivender, like Davis, has
been featured at the NAPPS festival and other national storytelling
conferences and festivals. We quote from a performance recorded at
the University of Connecticut.

Hi! My name's Jack and I'd like to tell you a story about one time
    when I went out to seek my fortune.
I said to my momma, "Momma, I'm going out to seek my fortune."
She said to me, "You be careful, Jack.
Don't talk to no strangers on the road,
and you take good care of yourself."
I said, "Don't worry about me, momma, I'll be all right."

And so, I started down that road to seek my fortune. (Stivender
    1983)

Stivender's rapid-paced delivery is for college students, while
Davis and Chase are telling the tale to children. Chase and Davis
both have a conversational, folksy, rural style, but Davis's is native,
while Chase's is acquired. Finally, Chase is more expansive than
Davis. Already it is clear that these are going to be three very different
performances.

One of the most interesting and perhaps controversial aspects of
Stivender's performance is his direct appropriation of the role of Jack
as he turns the story into a first-person monologue. But, as W. F. H.
Nicolaisen (1978, 27–36) has pointed out, tellers characteristically
project their own personal Jack (see also the quotation at the end of
the Chapter 2 essay). While Donald Davis does not go so far as
Stivender, he too identifies with Jack. In the interview, when asked
what Jack looks like, he answered after a long silence, "I don't know. I

can see Will and Tom and the king, but I never had a feeling of
looking at Jack. Jack comes from inside me. I'm Jack [pause]: Jack
looks like me." Davis later commented that Jack is the only three-
dimensional character in the telling. "He's amoral as the story opens,
but he is capable of surprise, growth and change." Similarly, Bill
Harley, a professional teller from Rhode Island, has confided that
after listening to his tales children often ask, "You're Jack, aren't
you?" Even Chase personalizes the story by incorporating a scene
that reflects his personal life as a storyteller and folklorist. After Jack
and the animals have eaten, Jack sits outside with the animals gathered around, the dog's head on his knee, and they start "telling old
tales, singing old songs, telling riddles too." Each Jack, not just Stivender's Jack, is indeed a reflection of the performer.

The middle of the story is taken up with the business of gathering
the animals. Here the differences among narrators are not so striking,
though Chase evokes rural values more than Stivender does, and he
remains slightly more expansive than Davis, as in the following excerpt from Chase:

> And they got down to where in the old man's yard was an old, flea-
> bitten hound dog.
> He had his head all tucked down, you know.
> They got down there and Jack saw that old dog;
> old dog kinda looked up at him, sorta sad like,
> and Jack said, "Hi!"
> and the old dog said,
> "Whooooooooooooooo,
> good mooooorning!
> Whooooooo, whooooooooooooooooooo!"
> Says, "Now, what's troubling you?"
> Said, "Ohhhh, Lord, I'm getting too oooold to hunt coons any-
> more,
> ain't got but one tooth left.
> That old man says he's going to kill me and shoot me with a shot-
> gun
> 'cause I ain't no good to hunt cooooooooons no mooooore.
> Whoooooooooo!"
> Jack says, "Well, why don't you come go with us?
> There's no use in you just standing around here and letting the old
> man shoot you.

So, why don't you take off?
You can come go with us,
as you don't want to stay, do you?
Come on, let's leave."
The old hound dog says, "Yes,
well you know, I was just studying about that myself."

Davis is still characteristically laconic:

Well, they're going along a little bit and they pass a house. As
they're passing this house, they hear something strange. . . .
They hear something going "Whooo, whooooooooo,
whooooooooooooo."
[*Children in audience:* A dog.]
Yep. A happy dog?
[*Children:* No.]
A sad dog. A dog just crying.
And they go over there,
and Jack looks under this porch
and back under there he sees this old dog,
and Jack says, "What is the matter?"
And he says, "Well, I'll tell ya, I'm so old that I can't bark and be a
watchdog at the right time anymore,
and my master says that he's going to get rid of me and get a new
dog,
and I'm so scared,
what am I going to do?"
Jack says, "Come go with us."
They get out there on the road and start off.
And now let's see, here's Jack, a cow, a donkey and a dog, all going
down the road.

Whereas Stivender has turned the story into a first-person monologue, Davis has turned the story into a cumulative tale with audience
participation.

In this central part of the story we begin to see how Stivender
reimagines his monologue in contemporary terms.

I said, "Howdy, Mr. Dog.
What seems to be the problem with you this morning?"

Mr. Dog looked up at me with his sad brown eyes and said,
"Hhhooo, Jack,
my master says I'm too old to be of any use to him.
So tomorrow he's going to take me to the Humane Society,
and there ain't nothin' humane about that.
Hhhhhoooo, hhhooo, hhhooo."

These stories were recorded with live audiences; recordings cut in a studio lack the social interaction that distinguishes genuine storytelling events. However, with a live audience unpredictable things can occur. On Davis's tape, for example, when he says, "And that robber can't see, because the light had blown out," a child interjects, "He can't see 'cause he got a stockin' on his face." Davis, courteous and unflappable, responds, "He might, he might have some stocking on his face and that's partly why he can't see," and without breaking rhythm, continues the story. All three recordings include audience laughter when the robbers are fooled by the animals, a peak point in the story's plot. Elsewhere, however, the tellers elicit laughter in distinctly personal ways. Chase uses repetition to build mounting laughter as the dog languidly persists in commenting, "I was just studying about that." Stivender's dog comments, "He's going to take me to the Humane Society and there's nothing humane about that." Stivender regularly connects with his student audience by using contemporary language, incorporating the name of local geographical landmarks and in this story having the thieves threaten to steal bikes (a very real threat to college students).

More dramatic differences in appropriating the story for personal delivery can be seen in the following extracts from Davis's and Stivender's performances. Davis describes the robbers den:

So they look in the window,
and inside they see that this house is full of chests of gold and
    money and jewels,
and the table is all covered with food,
but it's a little old house, and Jack says,
"My goodness, all this treasure in this little old house,
it must be a robber's den.
And if it's a robber's den,
then that food in there is not theirs.

They must have stole it from somebody else.
And if it's not theirs,
then we wouldn't be stealing it from them if we went in and ate
some."

Here Davis, who retired from his ministry in 1989 to become a full-time professional storyteller, has gently moralized taking the robber's loot. Stivender's exaggerations contrast sharply with Davis's quiet style:

Well, we had that money about half-counted
when all of a sudden, we heard another mournful sound.
It went like this:
"Hhhrrrfffttt, hhrrfftt, hhrrfftt, hhrrfftt,
WE ARE THE ROBBERS. WE'RE VERY, VERY MEAN.
WE'RE THE MEANEST ROBBERS YOU EVER SEEN.
WHEN WE FIND SOMEONE THAT WE DON'T LIKE,
WE KICK THEM IN THE STOMACH AND WE STEAL
THEIR BIKE."
I looked out the window
and there I saw coming up the path
ten of the meanest, ugliest looking robbers I've ever seen in my life.
The shortest one of them was eight-foot-eight.
The tallest one was thirteen-foot three-and-a-quarter inches.
He was so mean and ugly he looked like hamburger.

At the end of the story, while Davis gently moralizes and Stivender relates the tale to the experience of his audience, Chase adds a link with the geographic area where the story was collected:

Jack got to thinking how good his momma's biscuits and gravy
would be
—and so he took all those animals home.

Though not a mountaineer himself, Chase regularly tries to keep his revisions in line with his conception of the story's rural mountain setting (but see comments on Chase's revisions in the Introduction and in Chapter 4).

In these three retellings, the story line is consistent but details change. Even in the denouement, Chase has the robbers think a man with a pitchfork has attacked them, Davis has the robbers think the attacking animals are witches with long fingernails and broomsticks, and Stivender has the robbers run away from an unknown horror. While respecting the basic plot, individual performers make their own decisions about the embellishments that bring "Jack and the Animals" to life.

"Soldier Jack," the second story we will consider, likewise demonstrates embellishments and performance decisions. But in addition, in performances by traditional mountain teller Ray Hicks and professional tellers Jackie Torrence and Jim May we can trace the migration of our hero from Beech Mountain fireside to urban folktale scene, noting differences in style of embellishment and basis of performance decision in each case.

Hicks, a traditional Appalachian mountain teller, has achieved notoriety from featured appearances at the NAPPS festival (see Chapter 1 essay). Though Hicks's mountain dialect can be hard for an outlander to understand, especially when he chooses to remove his teeth before performing, he currently tells stories "to tourists who seek him out, to neighbors, to anyone who has a few hours to spare." In "Soldier Jack," the hero has agreed to stay in a haunted house overnight. Here is Hicks's description of what is haunting the house:

Well, hadn't laid there but just a few minutes
till he heard something coming down the steps.
And they come on down,
and it was six little black de'ils [devils]. (Hicks 1963)

Hicks is a wholly traditional performer, though his style has certainly been affected by his festival experience (see Chapter 1 essay and Chapter 5). At this point in the story he uses the traditional Appalachian motif of little black devils also used by James Kilgore, a Wise County, Virginia, storyteller (Perdue 1987, 72).

Jackie Torrence is a transitional performer. Torrence heard Jack Tales as a child while visiting her grandparents in North Carolina. While employed as a library aide, she was asked to read books to children. One day, when she decided to put the book down, she discovered the children loved to hear her tell the stories. She told a 1985 NAPPS festival audience, "The Jack Tales are still the hardest

for me to learn." Since then she has cut two records of Jack Tales.
This is how she describes what Jack sees in the haunted house:

> And all at once this awful sound came roaring down the chimney
> and there a great big round green ball fell right at Jack's feet,
> and out of the middle of that green ball popped a little green haint.
> And all Jack could say was, "Howdy do?" (Torrence 1984)

A little green haint smacks more of popular culture than do six little
black devils.

Illinois resident Jim May derives his version of "Soldier Jack" from
that of Jackie Torrence, though he has heard Ray Hicks tell the story
too. May seeks to adjust his style to suit the type of story he is telling.
In Jack Tales he adopts a folksy rural rhythm and incorporates southern expressions. He tells us this story took place "in the southern
mountains," adds a "magnolia tree," tells us "Jack stayed in a roomin'
house because there weren't any fancy hotels," and has Jack whittling
and eating biscuits and gravy or a basket of fried chicken. But he also
imposes contemporary language and themes. Jack programs himself
not to be a wimp and to "speak with authority." Instead of the haints
or devils who usually haunt the house Jack spends the night in, May
introduces a . . . but let him speak for himself:

> Jack, he's watching
> and he's swaying back and forth,
> back and forth,
> and then he saw soot dribbling out of that chimney into the fire-
>   place,
> and then a purple ball of flame,
> and out of that purple ball of flame stepped a purple boogie. (May
>   1986)

May's imagery and diction—a purple boogie with yellow arms and
red fingernails who later boogies out of there—is blatantly contemporary. Less obviously, his visualization of the boogie's manifestation
amid billows of purple smoke is likewise contemporary, influenced as
it is by movies and Saturday morning cartoons. Ironically, in his
effort to suggest a rural setting, he has Jack stay in "a roomin' house
because there weren't any fancy hotels," although Ray Hicks, the
traditional rural teller, says Jack stayed in a hotel.

As in the case of "Jack and the Animals," the story line in these tellings is consistent, while details vary. Hicks brings six little black devils from the chimney, Torrence describes a total of seven green haints, and May elaborates his purple boogie. Torrence says that Jack receives a new suit (like a man released from prison) when he leaves the army. A magic sack catches "seven great big fat wild turkeys" in Torrence's version, twelve in Hicks's, and five in May's. Torrence adds a rural touch by having Jack smoke a corncob pipe, which, because it's new, is hard to start. Another teller of this story, Bill Harley, who confided he never wanted to tell this story until he heard of Jim May's purple boogies, inserts pacifist views: Jack leaves the army when he figures out that he would be fighting people he does not know, about issues he knows even less about, just because the king does not get along with someone. At the end of the story in May's and Torrence's tellings, Jack meets an old man who cannot die because Jack has captured the death angel. In Hicks's story, it is just "death" that has been captured, and a woman who tells Jack she cannot die. But in all three stories, Jack frees death and is the first to die.

Obviously, within a traditional culture tellers of a story vary among themselves and from performance to performance. Unlike published stories frozen in books, stories in oral tradition remain fluid. Paul Radin (1915, 35) notes that one traditional teller may be noted for artistic individuality and verbal remodeling, another for humor, another for memory and historical information, and another for characterizations. Eleanor Long, speaking of narrative song, notes that folk artists are not required to be alike. Differences are valued by a performer's peers and serve both to maintain and to revitalize folk tradition (E. Long 1986, 106). But in a traditional culture certain conservative restraints on the storyteller's freedom are operative (see Chapter 5). Within the particular culture the item of folklore (in this case a story) functions to encode and inculcate cultural values and to promote psychological well-being as well as to entertain. The so-called law of self-correction ensures that radical changes do not normally occur: audience-performance interaction inhibits them.

Nontraditional performers, however, do not operate under the same conservative cultural restraints. They claim autonomy in choosing and adapting material. Artistry is innovative and dynamic, and for revivalist storytellers the entertaining story is the thing. Adler (1980,

147) points out that for the revivalist storyteller there is no single right or wrong way to tell a story: texts are not sacrosanct. Further, Ben-Amos (1972, 3) notes that any divorce of tales from their indigenous locale and society inevitably produces change. Accordingly, urban and urbane teller Stivender adds contemporary language ("Miz Cat," "hamburger," and a comic marching chant), and May has Jack caution himself not to be a wimp.

Nevertheless, at first blush it appears that a traditional tale in a professional teller's repertoire, whether or not that teller shares the cultural or geographic roots of the story, undergoes a metamorphosis analogous to that it undergoes within it's own geographic/cultural area. Plot, characters, and motivation remain consistent, while performance style, embellishments, and performer-audience interactions vary with the individual artist. In his essay "English Jack and American Jack" (1978), Nicolaisen has suggested that the academic's obsession with group traditions limits appreciation of the appropriate role of the individual teller in preserving and transmitting as well as in performing within tradition. Might not that multiple role be acceptably appropriated by urban revivalist storytellers as well? It is noteworthy that in the examples cited, despite the intensely personal adaptations and performance styles, the story line and structure of core episodes remain consistent. The spirit of Jack—his optimism, compassion for the animals, foolish bravery, innocence, and trickster qualities—remains intact. Even when the revivalist tellers add embellishments that are idiosyncratic or hokey, the tales remain, at the core, Jack Tales, preserving the essence of the Jack archetype.

So it would seem, at first blush. To assume responsibility for the way a story is told, however, assumes a standard or judgment against which the performance can be evaluated, but the revivalist teller's autonomy in story selection and performance style precludes responsibility to the people who created, tell, and retell the story. At stake here, more than the preservation of cultural roots, are ethics and cultural understanding. If audience members hear a story identified with a particular region or people, they generally trust the teller to provide an "authentic" experience from that culture. If the teller, willfully or unconsciously, misconstrues the plot, characters, or core episodes, this can be both offensive and a potential source of prejudice ("simple story—but then, they're simple people").

Are these innovations, then, offensive, or do they insure the performance and transmission of the Jack Tales? Folklorists may have both professional and personal responses in evaluating the tastefulness and the level of courtesy to the folk from whom the tale was taken, as they evaluate a performer's choices in relation to tradition. It is irritating to find a core episode altered or major characters such as little devils becoming a purple boogie with red fingernails. But it is hard not to be amused by a Miz Cat in the company of Mr. Dog, or by robbers who threaten to steal your bike.

So far, it appears that Jack usually succeeds in smuggling in his Appalachian roots, even when the teller has no connection to or interest in the place of the story's origin. Published texts further help preserve the cultural rootedness of the Jack Tales collected from the folk. Yet, Jack Tales transported to a modern urban setting by revivalist professional tellers frequently lose much of the richness of their southern mountain savor. Of course, before Jack became an Appalachian folk hero, he had to immigrate from Europe to America. *Jack and the Beanstalk* became *Jack and the Bean Tree*, with a slingshot, a rifle, and a quilt replacing the gold coins, the harp, and the hen with golden eggs. But, as Carl Lindahl points out in the introduction to this volume, Jack Tales did acquire a particular identity when their hero moved into the hills. It may be only a matter of time before a revivalist performer has Jack climb a skyscraper and run off with a computer and cellular phone. But will it really be Jack? Will he be true to his Appalachian roots? More importantly, will revivalist performers who tell these stories be making new and permanently meaningful connections?

At this point it is hard to judge whether these storytellers will in the long run preserve—and even enhance—the essence of the Jack archetype in our present world, or whether the Jack Tales are in danger of becoming saccharine generic entertainments. Americans today are encouraged to cherish our cultural diversity. Certainly many contemporary storytellers see themselves as cherishing that diversity when they tell tales such as the Jack Tales from a region and culture not their own. We would like to hope that these nontraditional storytellers play a vital role in maintaining the integrity as well as the popularity of these traditional tales, preserving both the essence of the Jack archetype and the individuality of all the little Jacks that Carl Lindahl speaks of in his introduction. Jack can add a lot of zest to our cultural salad bowl. Sometimes, though, he seems destined for the melting pot.

CHAPTER 7

WHAT JACK
LEARNED AT
SCHOOL

▼ ▼ ▼ ▼ ▼

LEONARD ROBERTS

▼ ▼ ▼ ▼ ▼

William Bernard
McCarthy

When we read a tale or even when we listen to a
performance, it is often hard to tell how much of what we are reading
or hearing is tradition and how much is the individual talent of the
taleteller. From time to time, though, we can compare an individual's
performance with the source from which that person learned the tale.
Henry Glassie describes such a case in the notes at the end of his *Irish
Folktales* (1985). Hugh Nolan learned a favorite tale, "Huddon and
Duddon and Donald O'Leary" (an Irish version of the heifer-hide
story, AT 1535), from a chapbook text reprinted by Yeats and thence
reprinted by a local newspaper, where Nolan remembers having read
it. Nolan's text is much longer than the chapbook version and is en-
riched in several ways. Glassie suggests that Nolan's use of a printed
text "provides us a good means for examining the creativity of the
storyteller who must, Mr. Nolan said, repeat the tale accurately while

using words of his own." Glassie urges his readers to look up the chapbook version in Yeats and make their own comparison: "You would find it fascinating to read Mr. Nolan's oral performance against the entire written text from which he learned the tale" (1985, 352).

Leonard Roberts seems to provide us with another such case. When he tells "Raglif Jaglif Tetartlif Pole," he expands considerably on the text he received. It will be worthwhile to consider his oral performance against the entire text from which he learned the tale. The text in question came from an aunt on his father's side, Columbia Roberts. Leonard's mother and Columbia Roberts were contemporaries, and both as children had heard Aunt Columbia's mother (Leonard's paternal grandmother) tell the tale. Neither Leonard's mother nor his father, however, passed the tale on to him. He did not hear it until 1950, when he collected it from his aunt. When Aunt Columbia began talking to Leonard about Old Raglif Jaglif, she seems not to have remembered much of the tale. But, as he describes it, "[daughter] Rachel and [Rachel's] younger sister Olga went over the tale with their mother until she was able to do it fairly well for my tapes. Now it is my favorite one for telling" (Roberts 1969, 186). Roberts first printed Aunt Columbia's text in *Mountain Life and Work*, in 1952, and most recently in *Old Greasybeard* (Roberts 1969, 65–68). I first heard him tell the tale to a group of teachers in my folklore class at Pikeville College, in the summer of 1980. This is the performance transcribed here.

"Raglif Jaglif Tetartlif Pole" is a remarkably full version of "The Girl as Helper in the Hero's Flight" (AT 313), containing all six elements of the tale as outlined in *The Types of the Folktale* (Aarne and Thompson 1961), though sometimes with a unique twist. The basic elements of the story are as follows:

1. *Hero comes into ogre's power.* In Roberts's version the hero comes to the home of the ogre (magician) not to fulfill a gambling debt but to claim a gambling debt from the ogre, who has lost to Jack and has promised his daughter in payment of the debt.
2. *The ogre's tasks.* Unlike the hero in many versions of this tale, Jack must perform the magic tasks himself, though he can do so only by following the girl's seemingly nonsensical advice. Finally he must recognize the girl by her missing finger, but his own carelessness is the cause of the missing finger.

3. *The flight.* There are only two escapes, not the usual three in the magic flight (see below).

4. *The forgotten fiancé.* This element is conventional. When his dog jumps up and kisses (licks) his face, Jack forgets all that has happened.

5. *Waking from magical forgetfulness.* Using magic she has learned from the magician, the girl makes magic boxes from which the talking birds (here a hen and a rooster) emerge to remind Jack of what has happened.

6. *The old bride chosen.* The final element is handled rather economically, and the tale ends with Jack and the girl riding off together on Raglif Jaglif Tetartlif Pole and getting married.

This is the tale Roberts tells. As teller of the tale, Roberts presents us with several paradoxes. First, Roberts is not only from one of the most remote regions of the United States, namely the mountain fastness of eastern Kentucky. He even had the good sense to be born in a log cabin at the head of a holler. Nevertheless, second, he did not grow up with this tale despite the fact that his mother had heard it, for she did not tell it to him. Moreover, his aunt's version is not the only source of his version, nor does he make any pretense that it is. Clearly, he has read many versions of AT 313C, including the American text of Richard Chase, the Irish texts of Jeremiah Curtin, and the German texts of the Grimms. This is not a version uninfluenced by print. Third, Roberts was an educated person who read, taught, and enjoyed literature. Ultimately he obtained a Ph.D. in English from the University of Kentucky. Fourth, both Roberts's version that I collected and Aunt Columbia's that he collected were obtained by folklorists eliciting them. Roberts narrated his tale in a situation fairly typical for him, an invited presentation before an adult audience with sincere interest in mountain culture. But Aunt Columbia's text would never have come together if Roberts had not intervened to convince his aunt to recall her tale, and to convince her daughters to help her reconstruct it. Even then, what Roberts obtained seems to be a report of content only, without any true breakthrough into performance. Finally, the text we have printed comes from a narrator whose local reputation was as a folktale narrator but whose professional reputation was as a folktale specialist. Roberts was a folklorist as well as a folk performer.

The case, then, is complex. But I think I can throw a fair amount of light on it simply by analyzing what happened to Aunt Columbia's tale as Roberts told it again and again over a thirty-year period.

Though telling essentially the same tale, Roberts's text is different in a number of ways from Aunt Columbia's. The two noble gamblers of her text, for example, have become Jack and a wicked magician. Jack himself, not the girl, must perform the magical tasks. Most significant of all, Roberts's text is almost exactly four times as long as his aunt's (5,592 words versus 1,392).

When I look at Roberts's text, I can identify five layers: core, elaborations, embellishments, personal additions, and overall concept. Roberts had three principal resources to draw on as he operated on these levels. These resources are the tradition he grew up in, his own personality, and his scholarship. The core, the essence of the tale, is purely traditional, although paradoxically he, a legitimate heir of that tradition, did not inherit it until he stepped out of the tradition to act as a scholar-collector. The outermost layer, the overall concept or gestalt, he brought to the tale from his wider scholarship as a märchen specialist. The intermediate layers, successively less integral to the tale and successively more concerned with style, combine traditional, personal, and scholarly elements. On all layers, aesthetics is a major consideration.

The first layer, the core, consists of the basic plot. Clearly the plot has been much elaborated, but it is still AT 313C, as received from Aunt Columbia, who got it from Roberts's grandmother, who got it who knows where. Roberts has elaborated and embellished the plot, but he has not altered it in any basic way, whether by adding new plot elements, suppressing elements, or substituting elements. In this regard he treated the tale quite differently from the way Richard Chase treated Nancy Shores's version in *The Jack Tales* (R. Chase 1943, 135–50; Perdue 1987, 28–38). Chase entirely suppressed certain sexual elements in Shores's version (Jack sleeps with the girl after her father gives her to him to be his wife, and he attempts to seduce her during the period he is magically forgetful of her help). For two of Nancy Shores's tasks Chase substituted chores from a different southern mountain version of the tale. For the remaining task of cleaning the manure out of the stable, Chase substituted a more savory task of cutting thorns, a traditional motif he seems to have drawn from his reading in the European tradition. Roberts has made no such changes. If we can trust the text as reprinted in *Old Greasy-beard* and elsewhere, he has retained the tale, in every essential element, as he received it.

Roberts has not scrupled to elaborate on the tale, however. This elaboration constitutes the second layer. It consists of the motifs, elements, and details that Roberts seems to have picked up from his wide knowledge of folktales to expand the tale as he received it. I call it elaboration because something simple in Aunt Columbia's version becomes longer and more complex and often acquires greater motific depth. Roberts seems to have acquired the elaborative elements as much through reading as through immersion in Kentucky oral tradition. Whatever his particular sources, however, such use of elaboration is highly traditional, and not only in taletelling. In *The Singer of Tales*, Lord (1960, 86–89) describes how Avdo Međedović, the Yugoslav oral poet, elaborated as he recomposed epic tales that he had heard. Avdo called this elaboration making the piece more beautiful.

The first significantly elaborated plot element is the quest for the gambler's daughter. In Aunt Columbia's version the boy seems to know the gambler, and when the girl is not forthcoming, he simply goes to the man's house and asks for her. In Roberts's version this element is elaborated into the traditional magical quest, including the motifs of the journey to a far country, the fruitless search that succeeds only when the hero gives up, and the benighted refuge in the house of an ogre. Jack has no idea whom he is up against. He sets out for the end of the world, if necessary, to find the girl. Only when he is about to give up and return home does he stumble on the magician's house. This sort of elaboration clearly gives the episode greater motific depth. Roberts has enlarged the family, too: the two daughters have become a whole passel of daughters, or perhaps captive maidens, seated around a table twenty feet long.

Most of the traditional elaborations with which Roberts develops the first two tasks were already in his aunt's version. The magical horse, uniquely named and uniquely important in this family's tradition, identifies the tale for Roberts and his family. The third task, gathering magic eggs, is expanded in more detail, with Roberts specifying the height of the tree, changing the crane to an eagle, and having the girl give Jack her fingers and him forget one.

The missing finger is important to Jack's next task, distinguishing the helpful girl from her sisters. In Aunt Columbia's tale there are only two girls, but they are twins. In Roberts's version there is a whole tableful of the most a-pretty girls, but they are not identified as multi-tuplets or even as sisters. In many versions these girls pass some of their time in bird or animal form, and the hero must distinguish the true helper when all are in their swan skins or, in Shores's version, greyhound skins. Roberts presents an adaptation of this motif: the girls are at a costume ball or mummery and are wearing identical costumes. The true girl identifies herself by holding the hand with the missing finger out from under her costume. In Aunt Columbia's version the motif of identification of the true love by a missing finger had been reduced to its most rudimentary form. Roberts treats the motif rather more elaborately.

The next important plot element, the magic flight motif, is already amplified in a rather interesting way in Aunt Columbia's text. The magic horse, old Raglif Jaglif Tetartlif Pole, is a double instrument of escape. Only he is fast enough to succeed, and even he could not succeed if he did not have the magic stick in one ear and the magic drop of water in the other. Usually there are three obstacles in a magic flight tale, but this particular elaboration, in which the magical objects are found in the horse's ears, permits only two. This part of the tale is a little confusing in the text received by Roberts. Aunt Columbia seems to put the hero on the wrong horse: "She went out and caught old Raglif Jaglif Tetartlif Pole and got on him and he got on the other one" (Roberts 1969, 67). It would be awkward for Jack, seated on the back of the other horse, to reach over and extract objects from the magic horse's ears. Roberts solves the problem by putting both hero and heroine on Raglif Jaglif.

The final elaboration of a plot feature concerns the magic boxes. Roberts tells us how the girl came to be able to make those boxes, but his greatest contribution is a purely oral one, impossible to set down in a transcription. He imitates the clucking of a hen as he repeats the messages. The first message sounds so much like chicken squawks that it is completely unintelligible. But he makes the messages of the hens successively clearer by softening the imitation. The third message is perfectly intelligible, though Roberts now sounds rather like a talking hen in a cartoon. Thus the listener, like Jack, gradually comes to understand the magic messages and so participates in a special way in the enchantment of the tale.

In addition to plot elaboration, Roberts likes the form of verbal elaboration called run. In a run a conventional narrative unit is transformed into a verbal formula suitable for rapid-fire recitation. This device appears at the very beginning of the tale. Roberts is not satisfied to start a tale the way Aunt Columbia—and most of his other Kentucky informants—do, with a simple "Once" or "Once upon a time." He expands "Once" in the extravagant Irish style: "Once upon a time, not my time, not your time, but once upon a time." The incorporation of runs is traditional in the Kentucky folktale performance style, as it is in many other regional and national styles. There is a brief run near the beginning of Aunt Columbia's text:

> Well, days passed and nights passed,
> weeks passed and months passed.

The messages of the chickens are also runs. Roberts has retained these runs at approximately the same places in the tale and has embellished the narrative with others. Some of the runs are short and simple:

> Ay, he played and he played,
> and he played rather skillfully.

But the description of riding old Raglif Jaglif is fuller:

> But then when he turned to the front,
> the r-o-a-d stretched out like a highway.
> And they just r-o-d-e on like the wind
> on old Raglif Jaglif Tetartlif Pole.
> All through the night and *way* up the next day
> before they slowed that horse down.

Like an epic theme (in the oral-formulaic sense of that word), this run is composed of formulas that can be used separately. Thus, when Jack and the heroine begin the magic flight, we are told that they rode "through the night and *way* up the next day before they slowed down." When they run away from Jack's wedding,

> they just r-o-d-e away from there,
> on through two or three county seats,
> before they slowed down.

One run, the description of the music and dancing at the masquerade, was so rapid-fire it quite defeated this transcriber.

Elaborations, then, are traditional tropes and motifs, both minor and major, that function to expand the tale in length and in motific depth. Expanding the narrative, they simultaneously beautify the tale by extending its imaginative horizon.

The third layer, embellishment, is also largely stylistic and aesthetic. Roberts was steeped in the Kentucky mountain narrative tradition, a tradition of tall tale and legend as well as wonder tale. His generally quiet and laconic style reflects that tradition. In addition there are specific elements that I think can be traced back to that tradition. These elements, derived directly from the narrative tradition in which he was steeped, are what I mean by embellishments.

Embellishments differ from elaborations in that they are not international motifs or narrative units used to expand the tale. Rather, they are incorporated into the telling of the several narrative units of the tale. When Jack sets out on his adventure like a good international wonder tale hero, he puts a budget on his back, like the good eastern Kentuckian he is. When he is benighted and must seek shelter in a strange and ominous dwelling, as international wonder tale heroes always must, he is put to sleep on a pallet on the floor because that particular dwelling is at the end of the eastern Kentucky world. The next morning he and his evil host converse on a proper eastern Kentucky front porch. Similarly, when he is to marry, it is in a typical mountain church, and when he runs away with the true bride, two or three counties away is far enough. The presence of such details in a wide variety of narratives from the region demonstrates their traditionality. In addition to characteristic elements of time, place, and action, embellishment includes certain formulaic, understated bits of diction and conversation. Children jump up and marry, Jack bumps the girl up behind him, the old man's table is covered all around with the most a-pretty girls, and variations of the following conversation occur three times:

"What are you doing down here, Jack?"
"Oh, wouldn't do any good to tell you."
"Go ahead and tell me. Won't do any harm."

The humor of the love story is likewise an eastern Kentucky embellishment, based as it is on the persona of the country boy as lover that is traditional in this and adjacent regions, or was until recently. Like Jack, who "feels right at home," the country boy believes he is a great hand with the girls. But he proves awkward and shy when actually confronted with a girl in a one-to-one situation. Roberts's audience for this performance, mostly eastern Kentucky schoolteachers, laughed appreciatively at the jokes about what a hand Jack was for sparking—walking, for instance, on the other side of the road from his new sweetheart.

The fourth layer is the most distinctive. This consists of the narrator's more personal additions, suggested by his own vivid reimagining of the events in the tale and by his intimate knowledge of the region in which the tale is imagined as taking place. The tale is full of such elements, beginning with the large family, of which Jack is the only one left home. The description of the shovels is what we would expect from someone who has probably bought and worn out more than one shovel. The Sunday afternoon gambling, the particular games, the family table, the sunny mornings, the worn halter, the hilly pasture, the staubs to climb the tree, eggs in his bosom, and the officiousness of the minister at Jack's interrupted wedding are other examples of accurately observed local color.

Though incorporating traditional humor, the careful development of the love story, too, seems to be largely Roberts's contribution. I have encountered no Appalachian wonder tale with a parallel presentation of a developing human relationship. Interspersed among the traditional motifs of the tale are the moments of shy glances, conversation, handholding, confidences, first endearments, and first quarrel, which chart the course of the love story and give the lovers distinctive personalities.

A certain rationalizing tendency in Roberts's version seems likewise to be his own contribution. He provides the old man with an excuse for not giving up the girl—a claim that Jack cheated and is continuing to cheat. Further, the old man tries to kill Jack each night. That is not part of the bargain, but it is certainly human nature. Even the magic is not too magical. Once Jack gets the right shovel, he still has to clean out those fifty stalls one at a time, and he, not the girl, does this dirty work. These rationalized additions and developments give the tale a realistic, novelistic quality marking it as Roberts's own and distinguishing it from the tales of even such expansive Appalachian storytellers as Ray Hicks and Marshall Ward.

The fifth aspect of the tale is its overall concept. Roberts's tale is obviously longer, more expansive, and more leisurely than the original. This is easily explained if the original is not a true performance.

Roberts's version, however, is also longer, more expansive, and more leisurely, by a good margin, than any tale in any of his Kentucky collections.[1] If, by and large, those texts represent the wonder tale as actually told in Kentucky, and they seem to, then there is an important way in which Roberts, though steeped in the tradition, does not represent it. The plot, the language, and many of the details come from Kentucky, but the expansive leisureliness, the overall concept, is alien to the Kentucky tradition.

This is not to say that longer narratives are unknown in Appalachia. Indeed, Beech Mountain, North Carolina, storytellers Ray Hicks, Frank Proffitt, Jr., and Marshall Ward sometimes tell tales approximately the length of "Raglif Jaglif Tetartlif Pole," as the examples in this book show. This particular tale may be a special case anyway: the version of Nancy Shores, from Wise County, Virginia, is the longest Jack Tale collected by the Virginia Writers' Project (4,300 words as compared with Roberts's 5,600).[2] Despite the similarity in length, however, there is a distinct difference between the longer Appalachian wonder tales from Beech Mountain (and from Granny Shores) and the present tale. Roberts's leisurely style dwells on incidents for their own sake, dramatizing them with a wealth of lifelike detail. Consider, for instance, the initial gambling scenario, the first dinner at the old man's house, or the entire narrative of the first task, with the discussion about shovels, the description of the girl, Jack's efforts, the sparking, and the walk back up to the big house. Where did Roberts learn to tell a tale in this expansive and personal way? Here I can only speak impressionistically, but I think he gives us a hint in his very first words. His opening formula is the opening formula of the Irish and Scots storytellers, especially the English-speaking tinkers. Roberts's story, though far longer than Kentucky tales, is about the length of many Irish and Scots tales. We can see in those tales the same dwelling on the details of narrative for their own sake that we can see in Roberts's long tale. In the following selection from "Jack and the Witch's Bellows," Scots traveler Duncan Williamson uses a similar leisurely style:

> The North Wind's sitting with this big long beard, long hair and a big long coat, and his feet stretched out—sitting in the chair.

> The old witch gave him a cup of tea sitting next to Jack in the chair, so she told him, "It's Jack from the village up sorting my bellows for me."

The North Wind's sitting (it could speak to the witch), "Oh aye," he said, "ah, those bellows I gave you years ago."

She says, "You never gave them to me years ago, North Wind. You gave them to my great-great-great-great-Granny years ago."

He said to her, "But I see they're still working."

"Aye, they're still working. Well anyway," she said, "Jack, it's getting late and the North Wind and I have got a lot of things to talk about. It's time you were getting away home."

"Aye," he said, "I'll soon have to go home." (Williamson 1983, 117)

Oney Power, Irish tinker, is similarly expansive in this episode from "The Master Thief" (AT 1525):

So, off he started to the town, an' he bought a pair o' top boots that raeched up to his knees. I suppose he gev a pound or two for them. An' he bought two half pints o' whiskey, an' he stuck wan in aech boot. He came an an' he hid; an' he watched for the fellas wit' the sheep. An' he dhropped out wan o' the boots before the fella wit' the ram. He gev it a kick. "Bedad, that's a t'undherin' boot," he says. "Some poor fella that was dhrunk lost that. If I had the comrade o' that, wouldn't I be landed. They'd do me for years." So, he wint an about a mile, an' wasn't t'other wan lyin' before him. "God," he says, "there's t'other wan," givin' it a kick down in the dhrain. "I beg y'ur pardon min, I won't delay ye a minnit. I'll be afther ye in five minnits." So, he tied the ram to a bush an' back he goes for t'other boot. The minnit he goes, out pops Jack: an' away wit' him wit' the ram. So, whin the man came back, he had no ram, only the pair o' boots an' the two half pints o' whiskey. So, what does he do, only tear his clothes; an', whin he ca'ght up wit' t'others, tould thim the ram murdhert him an' got away an him; an' Jack havin' the ram at home at his mother's house. (Gmelch and Krout, 1978, 57)

It seems to me that in overall feel and expansiveness Roberts has more in common with blarney spinners such as these than with Appalachian masters of concision. Reading the tales of the tinkers seems to have shown him the possibility of another kind of story, quite outside the aesthetic of his Kentucky family and friends.

My point is not that Roberts is a better storyteller than his Kentucky informants such as Jane Muncie, to cite just one example of a brilliant storyteller. I am saying, rather, that the informing aesthetic or concept of his tales is different. The Kentucky tales are economical and concise; the tinker tales are expansive and richly embroidered. In this particular respect Roberts's tale is more like the Scots and Irish than like the Kentucky tales, despite the fact that it incorporates Appalachian elements and traditions on other levels.

In sum, then, "Raglif Jaglif Tetartlif Pole" exists as it does because Roberts was a folklorist and a performer as well as an eastern Kentuckian. In it we can identify five levels. He learned the core from his aunt while doing fieldwork. His knowledge of other versions and other wonder tales enabled him to fill out and elaborate the narrative. His rich experience of the Kentucky narrative tradition supplied him with a voice and a language to embellish the story. His own creative genius enabled him to reimagine the story personally in great richness of detail. His reading of the Irish and Scots storytellers showed him how to combine all of this in a new overall gestalt. Roberts's own favorite story, "Raglif Jaglif Tetartlif Pole," is thus an expression of Appalachian narrative tradition and an expression, as well, of the personality, experience, and expertise of this master folklorist and storyteller.

NOTES

1. The tales in Marie Campbell's eastern Kentucky collection *Tales from the Cloud Walking Country* (1958) are likewise short.

2. Though Roberts had read Chase's adaptation, he could not have known the Shores text directly. It was lost until Charles Perdue rescued and published it in the late 1980s, after Roberts's death. Nevertheless, there may well be some connection, now untraceable, between Granny Shores's version and Aunt Columbia's version. After all, Wise County is only about fifty miles east and south of Harold, Kentucky, where Aunt Columbia lived. Granny Shores's text has more incidents than Aunt Columbia's, but in the common incidents the motifs are the same. Granny Shores, for instance, includes the same three tasks as Aunt Columbia, though other sets of tasks were known in Wise County at the time (see Perdue 1987, 39–50).

RAGLIF JAGLIF TETARTLIF POLE

as told by Leonard Roberts

Leonard Roberts, the teller of this tale, was a native eastern Kentuckian who became a noted folktale scholar, frequently cited in the essays in this volume. In his late years he was much in demand as a storyteller at folk schools, museums, and other venues throughout the Southeast. A typical performance consisted of an informal talk on Appalachian culture, some tall tales, and "Raglif Jaglif Tetartlif Pole."

Roberts told this story as part of a lecture he had been invited to give to a folklore class at Pikeville College in the summer of 1980. Roberts's favorite story, it is a remarkably full version of "The Girl as Helper in the Hero's Flight" (AT 313). The storyteller sat quietly throughout the generally understated performance, but his voice was remarkably expressive in quality, pitch, and pace. He used a number of runs or near-runs, here indented. The few lines lost during changing of the tape have been reconstructed and inserted in brackets at the appropriate place.

▼ ▼ ▼

And so once upon a time,
not my time, not your time, but once upon a time,
there's an old man and a woman who lived back in the mountains,
a-n-d they had a pretty good family,
but most of 'em had jumped up and married and left,
and had only Jack at home.
Old Jack was a pretty fine good little old boy when he was growing
   up.

By the time he was age thirteen,
he was going down the creek,
and down the forks of the creek,
the old schoolhouse there,
a-n-d—on a Sunday afternoon—
and he was a gambling down there with the boys.

And his father and his mother they come and they threaten what
    they was going to do [!!!}
for going down there and a-getting into meanness.

Jack never minded it.
He just went on down there anyway.
And he gambled with those boys and played,
pitching sticks and rocks,
and jumping rail fences.

And finally one day he was down there,
and Jack felt awfully lucky,
because he won nearly everything, nearly all those boys had around
    there.
And he was feeling pretty good.
    (He was just about fourteen years old.)
W-e-l-l,
first thing he knew some man stepped in a booth there.
And he begin to banter with Jack and says,
"Ah, Jack, I'll have to play you some."

A-h-h-h, Jack felt lucky.
He just played him a few hands,
and shot a few dice.
Won everything the old man had.
Well, that old man said, "Now Jack,
I'll tell you now what I've got.
I've got a very pretty daughter.
Now I'll bet you my daughter against everything you've got
on the next turn of our dice."
    (Would you've took that up?) [!!!!]

Jack was just a little old chunk of a boy, you know.
Barely raised up.
Well, he felt lucky and he decided he'd play.
    Ay, he played and he played,
        and he played rather skillfully,
and he won that old man's daughter.
Well, the boys got to shaming him and sharping their fingers at him.

And he got to backing off and quarreling with 'em.
And the first thing you know, he looked around,
and that old man was gone.
Well, he didn't know where that girl was.
Now the boys was fussing at him so much,
just made him determined to set out and see if he could find her.

W-e-l-l, he put a little budget on his back,
and he set out.
   And d-a-y-s passed,
   and nights passed,
   and weeks passed,
   and months passed,
   and he traveled along the road.
And he couldn't find any hide or hair
of that old man.
And after he's gone for nearly six months,
w-a-y off in a far away land,
he's decided he'd better come back home,
and give her up.
Maybe he can find another pretty girl.

But just as he was turning back it was getting dark,
and he began to look for a place to stay all night.
And there was just what he was looking, what he was looking for—
   big old house back on the hill,
on the rise of the land there.
And he just went right up there and he just knocked on the door.

Well, he knocked two or three times.
Pretty soon here the door cracked open.
Here come a fellow out,
and Jack took a look at him.
It was that old fellow.

Said, "*A-i-n'-t* you that man I
won that girl off of?" [!!!!]

That old man said, "Well, all right, if you're Jack. [!!!!]
I guess you are."

So Jack said, "Well, where is she, here?
I want to see her."
   (Wanted to see if she was pretty or not.)

That old man said, "Oh no, I, I can't do that. [!!!!]
No.
Go on in and have supper with us and stay all night."

Well, Jack had been looking for a place to stay all night.
And so Jack said, "Oh, well, I don't care if I do."
He went ahead in.
And pretty soon the old woman had the, had dinner ready.
And a very great old big l-o-n-g table, looked like it was twenty feet
   long,
and just covered all around it with the most a-pretty girls.
And Jack just felt at home. [!!!!!!!!]

So he sat down on one side, and he started eating.
And, time he got his hunger a little bit stayed,
he looked over there and saw a pretty girl right across from him.
And he kept eyeing her through most of that dinner.
And that old man kept watching him and hurrying him up a little.
Well, finally they all did get through, and all went in, went off to their
   rooms, and so forth.
So he just put Jack down there on a pallet,
and he had the room by himself right there.

Well, next morning Jack waked up bright and early.
Nice sunshiny morning.
And he went out on the porch
and pretty soon here come that old man.

Jack said, "O-h now, which one's mine?
I'm going to take her home today."

"Naah."
That old man started shaking his head.
"Augh, Jack, I don't believe you won that hand from me fair back
   yonder."

Jack said, "Oh yes, I—I played you fair."

Said, "O-h, you didn't uhh,
but I've got another little job, like to see you do.
And *then*, you can take the girl."

"Well," Jack said, "well, what is it?"

"Well," the old man said, "well now, down there's my big old barn.
It's got fifty stalls in it,
and my horses,
and hasn't been cleaned out in seven years." [!!!!!!]
He threw down an old beat-up shovel and down a big new shovel
    and says,
"Now you have that barn cleaned out
neat as a pin
when I get back or I'll cut your head off tonight."

Before Jack could fuss much he looked around and he was gone
    again.
Well, Jack began to scratch his head,
but there wasn't nothing he could do
except look over those shovels and decide which one'd work.
    (Which one would you have taken?) [!!!!!]
Well, there's that old bent-up shovel.
    (You know, they're sort of turned up on the ends,
    where you've shoveled a lot on 'em.)
So he just got that big new fine, fine new shovel, about number,
    number eight, I guess.
And he went on down there to those—to that barn.
    And then he got in there.
    And he got in the stall and he started shoveling,
    started shoveling.
    And every time he'd shovel out a shovelful,
    a couple more'd jump back in.
And he worked that-a-way up in the afternoon.
And he couldn't clean out but one or two stalls.
Well, he came back out and he was just sitting there, looking at that
    barn,

looking up toward that house,
and he was wondering how he was going to save his head.
Well, about the time he looked up toward the house a time or two,
he saw a—looked like a girl coming down that way.
Here she come just a sailing down through there,
just kind of perky
and smarty.
And she came down there and said, "What! What are you doing
    down here, Jack?"

"Oh," Jack said, "It wouldn't do any good to tell you."

"Oh, go ahead and tell me.
Won't do any harm."

"Well, that old man sent me down here to clean out this barn.
Get it cleaned out tonight or he'll cut my head off.
And I can't shovel out but one or two stalls full."

She looked at him, and said,
"Well, which one of those shovels are you using?"

"Well," he said, "I'm using that *good* shovel."

"Well," she said, "you take that old shovel in that'n's place."

Well, Jack just picked up that old shovel,
and he went in there,
and it just took about two or three shovels to clean out one stall,
shoveling it out.
    He just went all around through there,
    shoveling it out,
    shoveling it out,
    and he got 'em all cleaned out.
And he came over there
and that girl was waiting for him
and they had about an hour there to spark and court [!!!!!!!!]
before they had to go back to the house.
Well, they was a-starting back up the lane there,

going along and this and that,
just as close together as they could get, you know.
    (He was on one side of the road and she was on the other side.)
    [!!!!!!]
And the old man came in.
And he came right up to 'em and stopped 'em.

Said, "How'd you get along today, Jack?"

"Why," Jack says, "I got along just fine."

"Did you really clean my barn out?"

Jack says, "Yeah, I cleaned it out as clean as a pin."

The old man looked and saw the girl slipping to get away.
He says [*gruffly*], "Somebody's been helping you.
I'll get you yet!"
He was just about to jump on Jack.

But Jack, of course, got out of the side of the way, and went and hid
    around, and went and hid around behind the house.
Waited there to just about suppertime before he showed himself.
But he finally came down, and he went in
and there they all ganged around the table
eating and talking and chatting.
And Jack kept looking over there, and there was that same girl again,
over there,
and he'd wink at her a time or two.
And they talked a little bit louder, and so forth, and finally
the old man noticed 'em, till they was nearly all through.
And he sent 'em all to bed again.
Put Jack in his pallet over there on the floor.
Well, Jack slept good that night,
and he got up and went out on the porch.
Nice sunshiny morning.
Just raring to go,
and the old man came out.

Jack says, "Which one's mine, and I'll go right now."

The old man said, "A-h-h, Jack,
you're not winning 'em fair. [!!!!!]
I got one more little job, like to see you do."

Jack said, "Like to know what that is."

"Well," the old man said,
"now you've got my barn cleaned out,
way back here in these mountains is my big fine horses.
And the leader of my big fine herd of horses is named old Raglif
    Jaglif Tetartlif Pole.
You go back there and you get all those horses and get 'em down
    here and put 'em in that barn
tonight or I'll cut your head off."

Then he threw out a little old halter there
and a big fine bridle
and he disappeared.

Jack began to look 'em over.

"Now, which one to use?" [!!!!]

Well, he'd heard about that old big horse,
and it looked like that little old halter wouldn't hold a calf.
    Well, he just grabbed up that big new bridle and he took right up
        that hill.
    And he saw that herd of horses and began to run, run through
        them.
    And there's old Raglif Jaglif was a leading 'em across hillside to
        hillside.
    And run 'em, right a-w-a-y up in the afternoon, and couldn't
        catch a one.
Well, he just had to come back down there to the barn,
where he was.
Sit down.
Sitting there worrying about his head. [!!!!!]
And he saw the girl coming up that-a-way.
Time she got up there, and her walking, her tossing her head,

he knew who it was.
He's going a time trying to presist [?] her and she came up behind
   him.

"H-e-y, whattaya say there?"

"Oh-h, it doesn't do any good to tell you."

"Go ahead and tell me.
Won't do any harm." [!!!!!]

Jack said [*teary voice*], "Oh-h, well,
he sent me out here to catch his herd of horses.
And I can't get old Raglif Jaglif to take the bridle at all.
'Bout run me to death.
Said he's gonna cut my head off."

She said, "Which one of those bridles are you using?" [!!!!!]

"Why, I got the big *new* bridle."

"Oh, take this old bridle and go back there and see what happens."

Why, Jack, he just grabbed up that halter
and he ran up there.
And run on up on through that big herd of horses.
And he held it out and old Raglif Jaglif just saw it down there
and put his head through,
put his head in that old halter.

Jack jumped up on his back
and grabbed a-hold of his mane, and started riding him out of there.
And of course all the rest just followed,
and they just came right on down there.
Jack just filed 'em all in the barn,
filled up all those fifty stalls,
and buttoned the doors.
Came on back out, and
had about an hour or two there to court a little bit. [!!!!!]

So he started sparking the girl,
and talking 'bout this 'n that,
t'other thing.
Finally, looks like it was getting late enough for them to go toward
    the house,
and they met that old man.

He came a-roaring out,
and he said, "How'd you get along today, Jack?"

Jack, of course, said, "I got along just fine."

"You got all my horses in that barn?"

"Heh-heh, got 'em every one in the stalls
and the doors buttoned."

The girl kept on going, of course.

"Oh-h, somebody's helping you, and I'm going to catch you in it
    yet!"

Jack had to run this time to get out behind the house.
Waited till supper was nearly over before he went in.
Sat down and got eating.
And the girl over there,
nearly through,
she kept looking at him
and talking to him.
He tried to keep his head down and eat.
Finally, it's all over,
and went back to his pallet again.

Next morning, of course
    (you know this was the third time:
    something's got to happen), [!!!!!!!!]
he was out there.
Sunny and nice.
Pretty soon, here come that old man.

Jack said, "Now, which one is mine, cause I wanna take her?"

Man said, "A-h-h, nah, nah.
You're not,
you're not winning my girl fair.
But I'll tell you what.
I've got one more job.
If you can do it,
you can have her."

Jack was getting hard and didn't want to be passive.
But he said, "All right then.
What is it?"

"Well," he said, "now down here, this body of water here you see,
    that's the Red Sea.
And w-a-y o-u-t in the middle of the Red Sea is a little island.
And *on* that i-s-land is a big old tree—it's five hundred feet to the
    first limb.
Just above that limb is a big eagle's nest,
full of eggs and I haven't got those eggs to be gathered in seven
    years.
You go and get those eggs and have them here tonight or I'll cut your
    head off."
Then he pointed down there to that old canoe-like thing and a pretty
    big boat
and he disappeared.
    (Take a drink of water. [!!!!!!!!!]
    Now which one's you going to take?)

Well, I'll tell you, he got in that old thing,
he got in that old thing,
and it was so, it was so darn leaky,
so full of water, it went up under the water.
He had to wade out of there.
Jack couldn't get away from shore.
So he just had to get back out and sit down.
Who should come down that way? [!!!!]
That pretty girl.

"What are you doing down here, Jack?"

"Oh, wouldn't do any good to tell you."

"Go ahead and tell me.
Won't do any harm."

"Well, that old man
put out these boats,
these boats here.
I need to take my choice.
Go a-c-r-o-s-s the Red Sea: here's an island.
Walk b-a-c-k in that island till I see a crooked tree five hundred feet
    high.
In the top of that tree is an eagle's nest with eggs.
I'm supposed to have 'em here tonight or he'll cut my head off."

She said, "Now, which one of those boats you trying to use?"

He said, "Well, I got in this *good* boat."

"Why," she says, "get out and get in this old boat and then see what
    happens."

Well, he got in there
and sat down and started paddling.
And that boat just started a-sizzling and a-singing through the
    water.
And it 'as a-flying.
And pretty soon it was just run up on the sand,
on an island over there.
Well, he just stepped out,
and the girl stepped out,
and they started walking along on that island.

Wasn't much of a road there,
but they were pretty close together.
He was on one side and she's on the other.
They kept going

and as they kept on going that tree kept on looking higher.
Looked like it was a-growing.
Of course, he kept on *looking*.

Finally, he just stopped, says
"I don't see how in the world I'm going to get to the top of that tree."

"Well," she said, "just come along,
come along,
and I'll, I'll think of a way."

By the time they got up there it was so tall he just couldn't
see the top of it.

He said, "I don't know how to do it."

She said, "Well,
I guess I'll have to help you.
I've learned a little magic from this old man.
He's been teaching us there for years,
teaching us to do things.
So I'm going to help you this time.
You do everything I tell you,
or you'll fail."
She just, she just pulled off her fingers.
Like that!
Pulled 'em all off.

"Now you take *all* of these,
and they're just like little staubs.
And you stick one in the tree and it'll stick there
and you stick another up there.
And you step on one, step on the other one, and the other one.
If you keep pulling 'em up behind you,
you can go to the top of this tree."

    (Would you try that?) [!!!!!]

Well, Jack said, "Well, I'll just—
I'll just have to try it."

So he took 'em and he started stepping.
Put 'em up there, and he got a hold of 'em.
He was pretty stout—Jack.
Keeps on going.
Thinking about coming down any moment.
But pretty soon he looked down: he was so darn far up he may as
     well go ahead. [!!!]
So he just kept on a-going,
kept on a-going,
kept on a-going.
Pretty soon he was so far up there, could see a-l-l a-r-o-u-n-d,
almost to his land back where he'd come from.
Finally, he just stuck his head up above this first limb
and there's that eagle's nest.
And so he just gathered up the eggs now,
rather carefully,
and put them in his bosom carefully.

He was tired coming down.
Didn't crush the eggs, though.
Just kept on coming.
Took him about two hours to go up.
He's coming down a little faster.
Kept on coming,
kept on coming.
Finally, he got to the ground about four hours later.
He's just about give out.

And the girl was there, talking to him and saying, "You did fine, you
     did fine.
You all right.
Now give my fingers back."

He climbed back up. [!!!]
They were stuck on there, you see.
And after he went back on up the tree,
finally he came down and found them all, but one missing.

Jack looked up the tree and said, "I'm sorry about that. [!!!!!!!!]
Looks like I've left one in the top of that tree." [!!!!!!!]

"Oh," she said, "don't never mind.
You can't go back up after it."
Says, "Well, yeah, let's go ahead this way.
Of course now, we're gonna have a big masquerade dinner tonight.
Going to have it in that new barn.
Sort of ceremony."
Says, "When we're dancing about, we're gonna be in costumes.
And if you ever happen to see somebody throw a hand out from under a jacket,
where you see one arm with a finger missing,
then you'll know who it is when you pick to dance."

Jack thought that was an awful good idea.
Said, "All right."

So they went walking along,
walking along.
Finally, they came to the boat again.
Jack got in and gave it a little dip of the paddle
and ZIIIP!
they went across and back up on shore.
And they got out,
put the boats up.

Getting pretty dark by now.
A little bit late.
And here, by the time they got started
towards the house,
here comes that old man.
Oh, he was so mad he looked like he was going to cloud up and rain.
    [!!!!!!]

He said to Jack, "How'd you get along today, Jack?"

"Oh, got along just fine."

"You got my eagle's eggs? Yes?"

"I got your eagle's eggs."
Started to pull 'em out of his hat and give 'em to that old man.
Made him so mad he just started slapping 'em against the ground.

The girl by this time had disappeared.

The old man said, "I see,
somebody's been helping you all along.
And I'm gonna cut your head off TONIGHT!"

Jack had to hurry and run away
and get out behind the house before he got his head cut off.
He waited out there till nearly dusky dark
before he came in and had a little bite of supper.
By that time they're all in their costumes going down toward the
    barn.

Well, he followed 'em on down there.
Well, when he got in there,
    there was the barn litened up nice,
    and the hall litened up,
    and a room big enough to have dances in.
    There was music and making noise
    before the square dances begin,
    and swinging, and reels, and jigs, and things. [?]
And Jack just walking all around among them—
he couldn't tell one from another.
And he kept on watching rather careful.
All at once he saw somebody's skirt make a little tremble,
and a hand came out from under it,
and he saw a finger missing.

So he kept dancing around until he finally got her by herself.
Started dancing with her.
And they got to talking.

And Jack said, "You know that man,
he's gonna cut off my head tonight."

The girl said, "Well, now, I wonder what are you gonna do?"

Jack said, "Only thing I can do is to try to run away from here.
Would you go with me, sweetheart?" [!!!]

First time he's ever called her that. [!!!!!!!!!]

Course, she said, "Well, now, all right.
If you, if you can catch that horse,
why I'll, I'll, I'll run away with you."

And so they made it up just right there.
And so they sashayed around a little bit more until they got around
    up on the side,
and they came out of one of those stalls
and went out the front
and went on as fast as they could walk towards the house.
Well, Jack got old Raglif Jaglif,
put that old bridle on him.
And the girl ran in the house,
got her a little budget of clothes,
and picked up some money,
and other things,
and came out there.

Jack got on that horse, and bounced her up behind him,
    and they r-o-d-e away clear out of that kingdom as hard as they
        could go.
    On through the night and way up the next day
before they slowed down and began to look around where they were.
Well, they was going trotting along there feeling pretty good.
And looking this way, and this way.
And finally once Jack looked back.

He said, "Hey, I can see something like a little speck of dust way
    back on the road yonder."

And the girl said, "Well, you keep watching it and see if you can tell
    what it is."

Well, after a while, about half an hour there,
Jack looked back again.
He said, "Looks like that old man riding up on a big horse, just
   about as fast as us."

["Well," the girl said, "you lean forward,
and look in that horse's right ear."

Well, he peeped in there, and said,
"I can't see anything in there,
just a little stick."]

"Well," she said, "you take that little stick
in your right hand, and throw it over your right shoulder.
And you say:

   'GOOD roads before us,
   And briars and grapevines behind us.' "

Well, Jack just reached in there and he got it out and he *threw* it over
   his right shoulder:

   "GOOD roads before us,
   And briars and grapevines behind us."

And he just kept watching it.
   And just as soon as it hit the ground it made a little slew up there,
   and little patch of briar.
   Pretty soon a big clump of briar.
   Pretty soon a big field of briar.
   And pretty soon it just spread out A-L-L over EVERY-where.
And he kept watching, and saw that old man ride in there,
ride into those briars, and get all tangled up.

But then when he turned to the front,
   the r-o-a-d stretched out like a highway.
   And they just r-o-d-e on like the wind
   on old Raglif Jaglif Tetartlif Pole.
   O-n through the night and w-a-y up the next day
   before they slowed that horse down.

And they went ambling along and Jack got to looking around,
  looking at the timber.
He could tell the names of trees and so forth.
Had a batch to do to get back on in his territory.

It was about the time they got the old horse slowed down, he looked
  back.
He says, "*Uh-ohh,*
I see a little speck of dust back yonder again."

But she said, "You keep watching it,
see if you can tell what it is."

Well, they rode on a piece longer, and Jack looked back.
He said, "'That's that old man.
He's got out of that briar patch and he's riding down after us."

"Well," the girl said, "look in that horse's right—" *left ear* is what she
  said.

Well, he peeped in there,
and said, "I can't see anything in there
unless it's a drop of water."

"Well," she said, "you take that drop of water and throw it over your
  left shoulder
and say:

  'GOOD road before us,
  And the Red Sea behind us.'"

Well, he just *flipped* that over his left shoulder:

  "GOOD road before us,
  And the Red Sea behind us."

And just as soon as that drop of water hit the ground
  it made a little pool there

and made a little puddle
and then a little pond
and then a little brook.
And pretty soon it made a *w-h-o-l-e sea.*
And they saw that old man go riding in there,
right out of sight into that brook and into that water. [!!!!!!]

Soon as Jack looked around back to the front,
    there was that r-o-a-d just laid out like a highway.
    And they just r-o-d-e on like the wind
    on old Raglif Jaglif Tetartlif Pole.
Time they looked up again,
next day, after they'd rode all day and all night,
Jack began to recognize his, his territory.
Began to see these little strips of field here and little corn patches.
Looked like he was getting pretty close home.
So he began to talk with the girl,
telling her how he'd been away for about a year, and he didn't
know what they was going to do to him when he got back.

Then the girl began to pout a little bit.

Jack said, "What's the matter, darling?"

She said, "I don't want you to stop home.
I want you to ride ahead a way and marry me."

Jack said, "Now, I don't know whether that is natural or not.
You know [*chuckling*], I want to stop and see my folks, tell them
    where I, where I've been."

And she kept on, she kept on trying to persuade him.
And finally she said, "Well, now I'll let you stop.
And you stay for awhile.
But you're not to let any of them, let anybody hug your neck or kiss
    you,
cause if you do, why you'll forget me.
Maybe I'll have to go back home."

Jack said, "*I'll not.*
I'll just stay here awhile and talk with them.
I won't let 'em do anything to me."

And so she said, "All right, go ahead."

Well, she stayed out there on the horse
and Jack got down and went in
toward the house and they began to yell,
saying "H-e-r-e comes Jack,"
till his father came out with a big stick. [!!!!!!!]
And his mother kept on saying, "Come on. Jack. Jack's back home."
The others came around him,
and Jack kept pushing 'em away,
pushing 'em away.
They didn't know what was the matter with him.

Finally, his little black dog came running out,
just a barking and yelping, "Yip, yip!"
and bounced up on his knee here,
and bounced a-way up here,
and licked his lips.
And Jack just grabbed up all them hugs,
and grabbed his father and mother and began to hug 'em.
And pretty soon they had him just a-hanging on and a-carrying on
    into the house.
And they sat in there talking and talking.

And there was the girl out there.
And he hadn't come and he hadn't come.
So she knew what'd happened—
he'd let one of them kiss him or something,
and he'd forgot her.
So she just rode old Raglif Jaglif across the fields and roads there
and got her a job around there in a household
for a while.

Well,
Jack—
finally they all called him a great hero,

been gone away so long,
telling all kinds of big yarns.
Girls got to swarming around him so bad,
he did completely forget that other girl.
So he and another girl got sort of thick.
Talking about marrying.
Finally they just norated around the countryside
he was going to marry,
next Friday morning,
at the church house,
forks of the roads.

Well, by the time that time was coming,
the news had reached around the country side,
and the girl had heard it.
And she realized this was maybe the last time she could
use her magic and bring him back.
So she made three magic boxes.
And Friday morning she put them on old Raglif Jaglif's mane
and she got up behind,
up on the horse,
she got up on the horse,
and rode down,
across the road.

People were gathering 'round the church.
There were wagons and mule teams
and people walking.
After she saw some people in the church she went up to the door,
she, she went up to the door,
and looked in.
Looked like a man standing up there,
with some pretty clothes on,
had a book in his hand.
There were some girls and little boys there.
She tried—climbed up the stairs into the front of the door.
And preacher was there, lining 'em up.
He looked like he was gonna start reading from that book.
And she threw down one of her magic boxes.

It broke open.
And the people watching it.
A rooster and a hen just flew out, popped out of that box.
Rooster pecked the hen.
Hen called out [*very fast, high-pitched, and unintelligible*]:
> "Cack-caaaa. You forgot about me cleaning out that barn that
> hadn't been cleaned out in seven years, or off come your head at
> n-i-g-h-t!" [!!!!!]

Jack didn't know what in the world that was.
Looked back there, was turned around.
And preacher said, "Jack, come on over here now.
Stand right here. [!!!!]
Got to get started reading the ceremony."
Jack stood back over there.
The man put the girl [the bride] back beside Jack.

And the girl saw what was happening,
and she threw in another magic box.
It burst open, and the rooster and hen popped out.
Rooster pecked the hen.
The hen called out [*almost as fast, high-pitched, and slurred*]:
> "Cack-caaaa. You forgot about me catching the wild horses,
> hadn't been caught in seven years, or off come your head at.
> n-i-g-h-t!"

(Did you catch on yet?)
Jack looked back there and he turned around,
moved around a little bit.
Yep, and the preacher said, "Here, Jack, stand back over here." [!!!!!!]

Then the girl popped down another box.
It popped open and a rooster and a hen popped out.
Rooster pecked the hen.
Hen took her time, and says:
> "Cack-caaaa. You forgot about me getting these eagle eggs, hadn't
> been got in seven years, or off come your head at n-i-g-h-t!" [!!!!]

So Jack understood it,
the girl understood it,

and nearly everybody understood what it was.
Jack looked back there and saw that beautiful girl that he'd had those
　　long escapes with.
He just told the preacher, said, "You take the bride and get her back
　　home, if you will, please." [!!!!!!!]

And he walked down to that girl
and he pushed her out the door,
and they ran to that horse,
and Jack got up on that horse
and bounced the girl up behind him
and they just r-o-d-e away from there,
on through two or three county seats,
before they slowed down.

At one county seat they stopped.
Jack got a pair of licenses there.
And he got the minister there to marry them.
And they settled down on the outskirts of that little village.
And they lived pretty happily there.
Had about six children, last time I went by.

CHAPTER 8

BETWEEN
WORLDS

▼ ▼ ▼ ▼ ▼

DONALD DAVIS

▼ ▼ ▼ ▼ ▼

Joseph Daniel Sobol

The swapping ground at the National Storytelling Festival in Jonesborough, Tennessee, consists of a reproduction old-time medicine show wagon, with a single hay bale on it, fronted by a semicircle of hay bales. Behind the wagon is the old First Methodist Church, built in the 1840s. To the right, dividing the swapping ground from the throngs along Main Street, is a two-story log cabin, dismantled at its original site in the woods two miles from town and reassembled here on Main Street as the figurehead of Jonesborough's drive to revitalize itself by reclaiming its past. To the left of the swapping ground is the main festival tent, which has swelled in size year after year and today holds over a thousand people.

It was from the little swapping ground stage in October 1983 that I first heard Donald Davis tell a Jack Tale. The location provides an appropriate image of Davis's storytelling world. Behind him stood a parody of a turn-of-the-century snake-oil salesman's traveling stage; behind that, the Methodist church, the denomination in which, until quite recently, he was a full-time minister. To his left was a piece of the world of storytelling festivals and conferences, in which he is a prominent performer and workshop leader. To his right was a traditional home, uprooted but intact, its form carrying our imaginations to the first European settlement of the Appalachians, and beyond to the settlers' northern European origins—but greatly altered now in its function and meaning.

The story he told that day was one I had not heard before as an Appalachian Jack Tale, though I remembered it from related Scottish and Irish versions (K. Briggs 1970, 2:424; MacManus 1908). It was the tale of a storytelling contest, the winner being the first one to make the king call him a liar. He told it with a wry vividness that held the outdoor audience rapt. I wondered if he had adapted this particular story into the Jack Tale family himself; but I had no chance to ask him about it until the following year, when I took one of Donald Davis's workshops. His answer then surprised me: he had heard it from his grandmother in Haywood County, North Carolina, and she had told him many long wonder tales, Jack Tales and others, that neither Richard Chase nor other folklorists seemed to know anything about.

As a graduate student in folklore at Chapel Hill at that time, I felt I was being given a remarkable opportunity to study the Jack Tale tradition in transition. Here was a multidimensional storytelling artist, a man who was articulate and at home in the modern world of the storytelling revival, yet whose memory was steeped in an ancient world of tales. That no other folklorist had yet studied his stories seemed incredible, like a purloined letter, sitting open under the eyes of researchers who yet kept blindly searching for something lost.

Over a period of several years, through several interviews and innumerable performance occasions I pestered Davis about the traditional roots and contemporary branchings of his storytelling. (For a fuller treatment of Donald Davis's life and career, see Sobol 1987; for a wider selection of Donald Davis's Jack Tales, see Davis 1992). Davis is a man whose work is public, yet whose sources and processes are deeply private. His art is based almost entirely on traditional themes, forms, and techniques; yet his approach to it is highly personal, reflective, and creative, and he has adapted it to contexts that carry few of folklorists' cherished earmarks of tradition. The stories and their backgrounds are his own, yet he is involved in a lifelong work of restoring and transforming them in order to make them, and the values he derives from them, available to a wider community. Donald Davis is no custodian of antiquated relics, but a creative artist from a folk tradition who has moved beyond the boundaries of his local group, much as musicians like Jean Ritchie or Hedy West have brought their family traditions to urban listeners, borne on a swell of transcultural hunger. As Donald Davis carries Jack out of a vanishing rural South and into the schools and auditoriums of cosmopolitan American communities, his work richly articulates the issues of contemporary storytelling performance.

Davis was born in Waynesville, North Carolina, the Haywood County seat. Both his father's and his mother's families had been landowners in that section of the Smoky Mountains since the late eighteenth century. The Davis family, of Welsh stock, settled the township known as Iron Duff and had been prominent in county politics for several generations. His mother's family was of Scotch-Irish descent—Scottish Presbyterians who came to America from the chaos of the Ulster Plantation. The Fergusons, Williamses, and Walkers of his mother's family had been reclusive, keeping to their rugged farmland high in the mountains north of Waynesville. Davis described the long-term relationship of the Davis and Ferguson families in characteristic style:

> I was born into a sort of a line of youngest children. Because they're the ones who ended up staying on the same land, right down. So there's a small number of generations, and they lived right across the mountain from one another, Welsh and Scottish. This kind of story [Jack Tales] I heard mostly from my grandmother, though there's very much interrelationship between the families through the years. In that, see, my great-great-grandfather and my great-grandfather are the same person. In a certain particular kind of way. Which, Uncle Frank said, "meant I was my own uncle comin' and my own nephew goin'." Which, he says, "accounts for the fact that you look so much like yourself." (Davis 1985, 30 April)

During the course of his childhood, within the branches of his family, Donald Davis was able to experience several divergent worlds. His father had been forced to leave farming because of an accident that left him with a weakened leg. He had taken a business course in

Charlotte and eventually became an officer in a Waynesville bank. It was a small country town, but one that was assembling the infrastructure of postwar America: banks, businesses, transportation, schools. Davis spoke of his father's, and his family's, transition to "city life" thus:

> When he finally came to town to work, he never really trusted jobs. So we always kept farming at the same time. We always still had cows and pigs and chickens and a big garden and all kinds of stuff. He'd get up at four o'clock in the morning and go out and do all his farm work, and then go work in the bank. And then come home in the afternoon and do the rest of it. 'Cause, you know, you really can't depend on that job, that may . . . that may go.

> So it was really sort of growing up on the edge . . . between going back to Grandmother's house on weekends, which was a big log house with no water in the house, no electricity. Featherbeds. And then coming back home and going to school where you heard that there was a man in Hazelwood who had a television. He could get one channel. And that was real fascinating. To be between those two worlds. And I remember always feeling that Grandmother's house was the safe one . . . where you know what's happening. (Davis 1987)

Davis stayed at his grandmother's for long stretches during his childhood, and during those sojourns he absorbed most of his repertoire of wonder tales. "Storytelling was never set apart time," he often says. "It was what was going on in the background instead of television." I asked Davis at what age was he much in his grandmother's keeping. He said, "That was probably . . . all through elementary school. Up until I was maybe getting into junior high school when that kinda wasn't interesting anymore. . . . We got a television when I was about in the sixth grade. And that probably spoiled a lot of that stuff after that" (Davis 1985, 30 January).

Moving from childhood into youth and early manhood also meant spending more time at his uncle Frank's. Donald Davis credits his uncle Frank (Frank Madison Davis, 1903–1972) with being the next essential influence on his storytelling. Introducing his cassette tape, *Favorites from Uncle Frank*, he says, "In my father's family, the main storyteller from whom I learned, not stories, but story*telling* was my

uncle Frank. My uncle Frank was absolutely unafraid to try anything, which was the first secret of how to tell stories" (Davis 1983a).
Davis told me,

> The stories from my daddy's family, like the tall tale things, are the
> stories I remember more from high school. 'Cause they were hunt-
> ing stories, and pure out fool stories and that—the kind of stories
> that a kid in high school would be more interested in. Also when I
> was in high school I started going out squirrel hunting and camp-
> ing out at my uncle Frank's a whole lot . . . because that was an
> environment for teenage boys. My grandmother's had been kind of
> an environment for children. (Davis 1985, 30 January)

Frank Davis also told some tales with Jack as their hero, but, Donald
says, "They mostly were Jack as the main character, say, in a tall tale
or in a hunting story or something like that, and what I feel as being
the real, sort of magical kind of Jack Tales just about all, completely,
came from my Grandmother Walker." Uncle Frank's Jack Tales, like
his tall tales, and like the incidents that Davis retells about his uncle's
life, are focused on active, manipulative responses to physical world
problems, while Grandmother Walker's stories feature much more
the otherworldly, passive-aggressive, and long-suffering heroes and
heroines of the classic wonder tales. An exception, perhaps, is the
story included in this volume, "Jack's Biggest Tale," which features
Jack as the teller of a tall tale within a typical wonder tale frame. Davis
remembers it as coming from his grandmother; yet in its form and
style it blends the best features of his maternal and paternal story-
lineages.

After graduating from high school in Haywood County, Davis
went away to college, first at Davidson, then to seminary at Duke. In
literature courses he began to read stories from the Brothers Grimm
and other folktale collections that contained echoes of his oral up-
bringing. "I went to Davidson in 1962. . . . And at that time I began to
discover that some of the stories I'd heard and had grown up with
were Western European in origin. I began to meet some of that in
places like the Canterbury Tales, and in certain kinds of themes in
Shakespeare, like the King Lear story. . . . It was just kind of interesting to notice that I already knew a lot of that stuff" (Davis 1985, 15
July). After graduating from Duke and being ordained in the Methodist ministry, his second parish assignment was at Andrews, deep in

the North Carolina mountains, and not far from the John C. Campbell Folk School. Davis was invited to the school to teach folkdance (he is still occasionally active as a dance caller), and there he first encountered storytelling as a profession. "Richard Chase would come by, or . . . then I'd go up to Berea, up to a dance thing and there'd be some storytelling going on, and I began to realize that I knew all this stuff too. And would occasionally volunteer to tell something. And it just kind of began from that, where I would tell something somewhere and people would invite me to come and do it" (Davis 1985, 15 July). This first adult experience with storytelling was, he says, around 1973 or 1974—also the time of the first national storytelling festivals in Jonesborough, Tennessee, which did so much to popularize the revival of storytelling as a performing art.

Davis's growing storytelling practice in the 1970s and 1980s has recapitulated his early training. He began by telling mostly the long wonder tales as he had heard them from his grandmother, mostly to groups of children or to adults in specially prepared concert or workshop settings, such as those at the folk schools—a context that could well be called remedial childhood (Davis 1992). Later, as he began taking his art to outdoor festivals with less specialized audiences, he began to reach into his repertoire of attention-grabbing tall tales from his father's side of the family—the adolescence of his storytelling career (Davis 1991). In the 1980s, as he began to tour more widely, performing for general, mostly adult concert audiences, he began to craft his own personal stories. These stories are more reflective, more descriptive, and less generic than the traditional tales in his repertoire. They are humorous local character sketches of members of his family or community, but with complex structures, fully developed narrative points of view, and an articulated sense of place. What would be implicitly shared by a backporch storyteller and his ingroup listeners, Davis must make explicit in his performances for mixed and anonymous concert audiences. It is just this dual point of view, of Davis the narrator and Davis the child-character in the stories, that gives them much of their poignancy and power. To create images through which a modern audience can simulate the imaginative community of a traditional group, he conjures up his childhood in the glass of a storyteller's maturity (Davis 1986 and 1990).

Thus as Davis's storytelling practice has expanded and grown more general, these reflective, relatively realistic, medium-length

"Donald Davis stories" have taken their place alongside the long, fantastical tales from his mother's family and the shorter, outrageous tales from his father's side, in his regular concert presentations. The wonder tales are still performed mainly for elementary school children—the age range he was in when he was absorbing the stories. The tall tales and fool tale sequences provide the bulk of his repertoire in junior high and high schools—again corresponding to the ages in which the stories were developmentally active for him. For mostly adult concert audiences, he relies now on his recent, original stories.

Donald Davis's role in the present storytelling revival is therefore a pivotal one. Throughout his repertoire, and in his workshops and his writings, he remains a key example and spokesman for the oral-traditional approach to the art. Whether his stories have actually been passed down intact in his traditional community, or have been reconstructed after a lapse of decades, or have been woven himself from memory and imagination, they are all developed, stored, and re-created through what Davis calls a "picture-centered approach"—which he opposes to the "word-centered approach" of oral-interpretive performers:

> The revival comes from a couple of directions. It comes in one direction from sort of a folklore perspective, in which people from a folklore base learn traditional stories and tell them. It sometimes comes from a sort of a theater perspective. In that people learn theater—literary stories—and basically perform stories, or do oral interpretation of stories. One of the problems with both of those approaches is that the manuscript comes to be identified as being the story. The script. This is the story. And in a real traditional sense that was never true. (Davis 1987)

Davis holds that stories are preserved in his memory, not in words and sentences, but in images and sequences of images. The key for Davis, just as for Jack and the old king in "Jack's Biggest Tale," is to "see it in his mind":

> What is the biggest difference between the way I learned stories and learning from a book? Well, the biggest difference is that I never learned a story, I just soaked it up. What that means is that by hearing the same story told over and over in slightly different ways, what you finally absorb is not one particular version of a story, but instead the underlying picture. . . . Remembering the words is

irrelevant, because, once you have the picture in your mind, you can describe it many different ways until you see that the people who are listening see it too. (Davis and Stone 1984, 6)

For the group of Chapel Hill folklore students who had just heard him tell it, he illustrated with a section of his story "Jack's Biggest Tale":

You got the picture of Jack jumping across the ocean to get the corn. Then you got the picture of him getting a ride with the geese and bringing it back. You got the picture of him falling on the rock and getting stuck. . . . And you got the little picture of cutting the head off and chasing the fox. You got four little pictures. And you can tell 'em with different words every time. You can tell it long, you can tell it short. You can put in a lot of detail, you can keep out a lot of detail. It's not scripted at all, in no sense is it scripted. (Davis 1987)

The version of "Jack's Biggest Tale" included here is an excellent, representative example of Donald Davis's storytelling style. One of the most immediately appealing Jack tales, "Jack's Biggest Tale" incorporates elements of several subgenres within the Jack cycle—Jack the Trickster (the slayer of giants, in this case the old king), Jack the Wonder Tale Hero (he of the magical helpers, he who always marries the princess), and Jack the Shaman (who understands the languages of birds and beasts, who dismembers and remembers himself)—and gathers them all under Jack the Storyteller. It can aptly stand as a totem tale for Donald Davis the storyteller, as it can for many whose work would bring the storyteller's voice back into the conscience of our culture.

For an alternative telling of the story, crafted by the teller with a reading audience in mind, it would be well to seek out Donald Davis's recent (1992) collection from his own Jack Tale repertoire. The contrast between the two versions highlights key issues raised by this entire volume. In the introduction to the Jack book by Davis, I wrote: "We had talked for several years about collaborating on a book of transcriptions of oral performances of these stories. These would have been faithful documentations of the live performance context: but, ironically, they would have been less faithful to the actual, intended context of the tales—the leisurely converse of reader and book" (Sobol 1992, 21). The transcription that follows here does indeed document the texture and context of a particular oral performance—asides, hesitations, repetitions, slips, and all. These intrusions force readers to use their imaginations in a peculiarly split-screen fashion. Readers must picture the procession of the narrative itself, filtered through their best attempt to imagine a particular performance event.

There are important advances in performance ethnography to be made in this effort. But the ultimate discovery may be that we are opening a Chinese box. Can this latest method of inscribing a folklore text actually bring us to the heart of the told story? Or does it simply force us by refraction to view the imaginative process in the light of its levels of meditation? The pointing finger will never be the moon, for all our confusion, but neither will the rocks in the astronauts' specimen boxes ever tell us what made the poet shiver. We will not locate the soul more efficiently by CAT scan than we did by dissecting corpses. We may find that the story, Horatio, is not in the text, nor in a particular performance, but in ourselves—and in the endlessly renewable, endlessly transferable potential of the story to make us "see it."

JACK'S BIGGEST TALE

as told by Donald Davis

This version of "Jack's Biggest Tale" was created for Dr. Charles G. (Terry) Zug's folk narrative class at the University of North Carolina, Chapel Hill, on 16 March 1987. A variant of AT 852, Davis's tale includes a unique blend of tall-tale elements but retains the self-decapitation motif often associated with the tale.

Metanarrative commentaries that Davis interjected in response to the specialized interests of the audience are indented and in parentheses. About a third of the way into the story occurs an interesting "breakthrough into performance," at the end of one of these parentheses. Davis had been summarizing what might happen in a longer telling of the story, in which Will and Tom try to impress the king, and so on, "until finally everybody's been but Jack." Grammatically the phrase here quoted is part of the preceding summary sentence, but during it Davis swings back into the narrative mode. By the end of the sentence he is fully performing again, and he does not leave the narrative mode any more in the course of the story.

▼ ▼ ▼

(I thought today I'll tell you a fairly short Jack Tale which is
somewhat unusual,
in that it's a Jack Tale
in which Jack himself
tells a story.
Uh, a little, little bit
unusual.)

Jack was living one time with his Mama—
his Daddy was already dead and gone—
but he was living with his Mama,
and his two brothers, Tom and Will. They were real poor.
They were living on this—little ol' house sort of on the side of a
    creek,
in this little town.

And of course a-w-a-y up on top of the mountain above the town
was the king's house.
(I never really heard it called "a castle," just always called—
"the king's house.")
G-r-e-a-t big ol' house where the king lived.

And Jack and his two brothers and his Mama, they were—
they just didn't have much to eat on;
they were awfully poor.

The king, though, was rich, of course—
he was the richest man anywhere around there:
he owned a-l-l kinds of lands, and had gold,
and treasure, and everything—
but he was getting *old.*
He was getting *real* old.
In fact, he was just down to where he was staying in bed
just about all the time,
and he knew one of these days pretty soon he was gonna *die.*

He wasn't real scared of that.

But there was one thing he was worried about.
He didn't have any sons.

He just had one daughter.
And she was fairly young for him to be as old as he was.
And he was worried about who was gonna be the king after he was
gone.

He thought,
Now, my daughter, she's not old enough to know what she's doing;
she's gonna go out here and get married to some old no-good
somewhere,
and then there'll be just an old no-good king,
that'll waste all my stuff
that I've built up,
and saved,
and accumulated,

and get rid of all my gold,
and so forth.
Before I die,
I better pick somebody for her to marry,
to be sure the next king's gonna be all right.

(Course, in all the Jack tales the kings always
would choose who their daughters would marry, 'cause
often that was the prize Jack would get,
would be to marry the king's daughter.
And, course, my grandmother used to say,
that's why back then,
people stayed married so much longer than they do now. [!!!!]
Because, if you
marry somebody you don't know . . .
you don't know enough about them
to be disappointed. [!!!!!]
You think you know everything about somebody,
you know,
you find some surprises
pretty soon.)

So the old king decided he was gonna pick somebody for his
  daughter to marry.
And since that's the way things were always done it suited her just
  fine:
she knew he was gonna pick out somebody for her.

So he got all of his, all of his, sort of wise men in there,
and he talked to them,
about this whole thing: they [*sic*] said,
"Now, we need to have some kind of contest . . .
to see who's gonna get to marry my daughter."

And they talked about it for a while:
they could try this,
they could try that,
they could try different things—

But, see, the king's problem was
that he had to stay in bed all the time.
And he couldn't get up and go out here
and see them cut wood,
or see them hoe corn,
or see who could be the best
at one thing or another.
And he finally decided, all on his own, he thought,
Now if I just have to stay here in bed all the time . . .
I might as well get some good out of this.
Says, "I'll tell you what let's do.
Let's have a—
let's have a contest [to] see who's the best *storyteller*.
And that way they can come in here,
and just entertain me,
one day after another.
Just d-a-y . . .
right here while I'm laying in the bed.
Everybody that wants to marry my daughter,
tell them to come in,
and tell me stories.
And I'll pick the one
that tells the *best story*.
And that's the one that'll get to marry her."

Well, the word went out everywhere, and of course everybody came,
because they all wanted to marry—
whether they wanted to marry the king's daughter or not,
they wanted all that land and all that gold and everything,
and that went along with it.

And so, the old king was entertained just for *weeks*, for weeks.
Finally people began to ask one another, *How do you win this thing?*
    [!]
'Cause some of them had been up there two or three different times.
And nobody had said anything yet about how you win.

The old king thought things were going along so well,
he hadn't even thought about that himself—
he was just enjoying all of it.

But finally people started complaining,
and he had to get his wise men back in there again,
and talk about—
how somebody wins this contest now.

He thought about it for awhile, and he thought,
Now let's see,
I've got a *g-o-o-d imagination.*
And I've been hearing some g-o-o-d stories.
O-h, people just tell me stories and I just sit there and close my eyes
     and I can just *see it.*
Said, "But I'd like—
I tell you what, I'd like to—
I'd like to see somebody
who could tell a story so *good*
that I couldn't believe it."
Said, "Now *that* would be a good one,
if somebody could come in here and tell me a story
that is s-o-o *fan*-tastic,
s-o wonderful,
s-o out of this world,
that right in the middle of it,
I just stop them and say,
That's not true!
that person'll be the winner [!]
—if they can do that—
I'll let my daughter marry them right then and there."

Well, he did start getting some good entertainment now after that. [!]
Because when people found out about that,
oh, everything got *wild,*
I mean, it really did, it just went everywhere,
and the old king would lay back there in his bed and say,
"*A-w-w, I can just see it now!* [!]
I can see it now."

He wore everybody out!
He wore out old Tom and Will—
     (And if we had long enough, see, I could tell you all about

Tom going up there,
and everything that happened,
and all about Will going up there,
and everything that happened—
But that's one of those
kinds of parts of the stories that could come in or out,
sort of come or go.
Um, a lot of people who've studied folklore think that
traditional storytellers are like tape players.
Un-unh. Not at all.
There's a *lot* of variability
in the way a story's told one time or another,
and in terms of the episodes that come in or out.
Uh, a good storyteller could make a story twice as long,
if the time's there for it.
Or shorten it up a lot.
And
—this is sort of an aside, but—
one way of doing that would be to tell about
Tom going up there, and telling his stories,
and the king believing all of it,
and Will going up there and telling all his stories,
and the king believing all of it)
until *finally* everybody's been but Jack.

And everybody sort of teases old Jack,
and says, "Why don't you go up there? Why don't you go?"
And they know old Jack, he's just a little old half-grown boy,
he's not old enough to even know any stories, much. [!]

But one day, he decides,
he's gonna do it.
And he figures,
Now, if I'm going up there to the king's house to tell a story,
I'd better be dressed up right for it.
So he goes back in his Daddy's room,
gets, gets back in his Daddy's old clothes,
and he gets out one of his Daddy's old hats,
put it over his head, it comes way down over his ears.

Gets out one of his Daddy's old coats, it's a great big old coat,
overlaps in the front, hangs way down towards the floor.
And he thinks, Now, if I'm going up to the king's house,
I ought to have a sword with me. [!!]

But they don't have a sword.

So he goes out here down under the cellar in the house,
and his Daddy's got a big old mowing scythe [!!]
that's hanging up there.
And he takes the blade off of that mowing scythe,
big long curved blade,
and he sticks it in his belt,
so that the end of it hangs out down there below his coat.
And he goes marching like that, up there to the king's house.

He knocks on the door.
Some of the king's men come and open the door.
They just start laughing at him.
"Just look at him!
That old hat hanging down over his eyes!
Old coat hanging way down over his hands!
End of that mowing-scythe blade hanging out there dragging the
    ground! That—"

He says, "What 're you laughing at?"

They said, "YOU!"

He said, "Well, you better quit laughing,
'cause I've come up here to tell the king a story
he won't believe." [!]

They said, "You might do it,
'cause he won't believe you could even tell a story." [!!!!!!!]

He said, "I can! Let me in there.
I'm gonna do it."

[When] he got in there, the king,
the old king, laid out there in the bed,

the old king laughed:
he hadn't laughed like that for a long time.

Finally he says, "Okay, Jack.
Jack," he says, "Jack, you're gonna try this."
Said, "I knew your Daddy."
Said, "Your Daddy used to live down there.
He grew about forty acres of corn on some of my land.
You can't tell a *story*!"
Says, "You just grew up down there on the side of the creekbank.
Aw, let's hear you try."

Well, old Jack got started.

He says, "Well, king, you said
you knew my Daddy.
And that he used to raise forty acres of corn
down there on some of your land.
And look at me, how old do you think I am?"
He says, "King, I'm just about half-grown—
Do you know,
that I raise,
all by myself,
without any help,
eighty acres of corn
every *year*?
And when it's time to cut that corn down,
I cut it all down
in one hour,
without moving from the place I'm standing,
and without any help
from any living human being?" [!]

King says, "I know that's true. [!]
I know that's gotta be true. [!]
But, Jack, you're just gonna have to tell me a little bit more about it,
so I can sort of see it a little better."

Jack says, "Well,
this is the way it happened,

the first time.
I had me down there my great big eighty-acre field full of corn.
Oh, it just went on as far as you could see it.
And one afternoon, Mama says,
'We don't have anything to fix for supper.
Go out and see if you can't find us something.'
And I took a butcher knife, and I went out there to the cornfield—
I was gonna just cut a little corn to feed the cow while I was out
    there.
And when I got out there to the edge of the cornfield,
up jumped a rabbit.
And it ran out there about—
about ten feet and stopped.
And I thought, If I could kill this rabbit,
we could cook it and eat it for supper.
And I drew back,
and I threw that butcher knife at that rabbit.
And it went end over end, right toward that rabbit,
and it—
I thought it was gonna hit it!
And just about the time it got there,
that rabbit jumped back,
and reached out,
and caught that butcher knife in its teeth,
by the handle. [!!!]
And when it did, it started running.
And it ran right down a row of corn,
with the knot—blade—of that butcher knife sticking right out,
and corn was just falling,
right down through there, [!!] like that.
And I thought, Look at that!
Look at that!
And when it got to the other end of the row,
and was about to run out of the field,
I just *smacked* my hands, and it—
scared it, and it jumped, and started back down the other way. [!!]
And I just stood there in that one place,
and every time that rabbit got to the end of a row,
I'd smack my hands and it would jump and go—

in an hour's time,
without moving from one spot,
without any help from any living human being, you see,
I cut that whole eighty acres of corn."

The old king says, "Ah, I can just see it now! [!]
Ah, I can just see that rabbit going back and forth, just
oh, I can just see that corn falling."

Jack thought, Well, this is gonna be harder than I thought. [!]
Thought, If he'd believe something like that—
I guess he'd believe about anything!
I'm going, thought, I'm going to have to work hard!

He thought a minute, sort of scratched his head a little bit,
walked around there on the floor.
King says, "*Go on*, now, Jack! Come on!
Tell me something else I won't believe!"

Jack says, "Well, king, you remember three or four years ago,
when we had a *real, bad* dry spell?
And all the crops dried up,
and there was a famine,
and everybody was starving to death?"

King says, "Oh yeah, I remember that."

Jack says, "Well, did you know that I was the person that brought all
that corn and saved everybody's life?"

King says, "Well, no.
But it must be true!
Must be tru—I know it's true.
You, you just sort of tell me about it,
so I can—
so I can see it a little better."

Jack says, "Well, you know it was so dry around here—
and it was dry *all the way* as far as anybody could see, everywhere,

and, and we heard around here that they were having a *lot* of rain,
over, way across the ocean, in other lands.
And I said to everybody,
'I'll go get corn!'
And I backed up to the end of the little street, down town there,
and I ran down through there,
and I got me a g-o-o-d running start,
and I jumped over the ocean." [!!]

King says, "I can see it now! [!!]
Aw, what a jump. I can just see you,
sailing through the air,
over the clouds across through there!
Where'd you land?"

Jack says, "Well, uh, let's see.
Um. Well, I landed in Africa.
Landed right on the side of the ocean, over there in Africa.
And this big king, dressed-up, African king,
came out of the jungle there,
and I walked right up to him and I said,
'We need corn!'

"And he said, 'I can give you five hundred bushels of corn.
Do you have anything to carry it in?' "

Jack says, "I started to say no—at about that time I felt something
    biting me on the neck.
And I reached back and grabbed it,
and it was a *flea*.
And I thought, Oh, yeah, I, I, I,
I've got something to carry that corn in,
just wait a minute.
I'll skin this flea and make a bag out of its skin. [!]
And I'll use that fleaskin bag to carry those
five hundred bushels of corn in."

The old king says,
"I, I believe I can just see that, now."

Jack says, "I got my knife out, and I skinned that flea.
And I turned that fleaskin wrongside-out,
and the king got some of his men to start bringing corn.
And I started stuffing corn in that—"
Said, "It was hard to start with, the getting started [!] was the hard
    part.
And then that fleaskin bag started stretching,
and it got bigger and bigger,
and finally,
I loaded a bu—
finally, I loaded five hundred bushels of corn."

King says, "Boy, that's something!
I can just see it now!
I can just see that fleaskin bag
just stretching and getting bigger and bigger and bigger!"

Old Jack thought, I'm not gonna do this!

King says, "How'd you get home with it?!"

Jack says, "Uh, how'd I get home with it?
Well, let's—
Oh yeah! Let's see—
I started to jump back with it.
But that was such a load, I was afraid I'd go down in the ocean.
And I stood around there for a little while
with my fleaskin bag with five hundred bushels of corn in it.
And I looked up in the sky and I saw this w-h-o-l-e big flock of geese
    coming over.
And I threw a little corn out and I called them to come down, and I
    says, 'Geese—
You're gonna have to fly me home.'
And I got them real close together, about a thousand of them,
and I got my fleaskin bag with my five hundred bushels of corn up
    on their backs,
I got up on their backs.
And they all flapped their wings at one time,
and all thousand of them took off *together*—

just like the whole land coming up in the air.
And they lifted me
and my, my big fleaskin bag full of corn, right—
and we started back right across the ocean."

King says, "I can see it now!
Isn't that wonderful, Jack!
—They could have lifted *anything* for you!
—Oh, that was a *wonderful* ride!" [!]

Jack says, "Yeah. [!!]
And we flew back across the ocean [*sigh*].
And we got back almost home.
And those geese started wanting to know
where they were supposed to land
with me and my corn.
And I knew we were pretty close to home,
and I thought, Well, let me look down here and spot a good place.
So," he says, "I reached down, and I pulled the wings,
sort of open on some of those geese.
And when I did—
the air sort of pulled through there—
and I fell through.
And I fell out of those geese.
There they were left,
flying around up there with my five hundred bushels of corn,
and here I was falling,
down, down, down, out of the sky.
And I hoped—
I, I, I said to myself, I hope I land close to *home*! [!]
And I did.
I landed about a mile from my house up here."

Says, "You know up here on the side of the mountain up here,
where there's a g-r-e-a-t big old flat rock up there?
I landed on that flat rock. [!]
But I landed feet first. [!]
And I was falling so hard and so fast,
that when I hit feet first on that flat rock,

I sunk in it up to my neck. [!]
Just like sinking in mud.
And I was stuck."

Says, "There I was stuck, up to my neck in that flat rock.
I couldn't move anything but my head.
And I thought, I'll never get outa here,
I'm gonna have to get Mama to come help me get out.
What am I gonna do?"

The old king's eyes were just getting bigger and bigger.

And Jack says, "I noticed right there on that flat rock,
my sword, here, had landed.
And I thought, I know what I'll do.
And with my chin,
I reached over there,
and got my sword.
And I pulled it up,
till it was right up
against my neck.
And then,
I started
cutting my head off." [!!!!!]

Old Jack watched the old king: he wasn't saying anything now, his
    eyes were just getting bigger [!] and bigger all the time.

He said, "I kept on
till I cut my head off. [!!]
And my head r-o-l-l-e-d
right down in the road. [!!]
And," he says, "then I says,
'Let's head for home!' [!!!!!]

"And," he said, "my head started rolling toward home.
And it was going just as hard and fast as it could,
going to get *Mama*!

"And on the way I passed a den where this old fox lived.
And it was an old fox I'd been trying to kill for a long time;
I mean, it had been getting in our chickens and everything, all over
  the place,
and when I went by, it recognized my head. [!]
And it started chasing it. [!]
And it was chasing—
and my head was rolling as hard and fast as it could roll,
and that fox was getting closer and closer and closer and closer,
and I thought, What am I gonna do? What am I gonna do?
And all of a sudden I got an idea,
and just about the time that fox almost caught me,
my head stopped.
And it looked up at that fox.
And it said:
'You come
any closer,
and I'll
stomp you to death.' [!!!!]
And that old fox just put his tail right between his legs, [!]
and turned around,
and walked off in the other direction,
and was gone."

The old king says,
"That sure was a stupid fox, wasn't it?" [!!]

Jack says, "Not half as stupid as you are." [!!!!]

The old king says, "That's not true!" [!!]

And then all of a sudden he realized what he had said. [!]
Jack had become the first person
to tell the king something
he wouldn't believe:
that he was stupid. [!]
But he had done it.
And so old Jack got picked
to be the one

to marry the king's daughter.

And he got half of a-l-l the treasure in the kingdom.

He didn't care a whole lot about marrying the king's daughter, but
that's the way things went: if you didn't do that you didn't get the
rest of it.

So as far as anybody knows he did marry the king's daughter.

And, uh, he may still be living there

to this day.

With his head back on and everything. [!!!]

CHAPTER 9

A JACK TALE
TRADITION IN
PENNSYLVANIA'S
NORTHERN TIER

▼ ▼ ▼ ▼ ▼

BONELYN LUGG
KYOFSKI

▼ ▼ ▼ ▼ ▼

Kenneth A. Thigpen

"Grandma Hess's Story about Jack, Bill, and Tom" provides evidence that a Jack Tale tradition is part of the folklore of the Pennsylvania mountains as well as of the southern mountains. It also provides evidence of how the contemporary storytelling movement has helped shape a community's sense of its local tradition and how it has affected the storytelling style of a legitimate heir to that tradition. The narrator, Bonelyn Lugg Kyofski (whose first name is pronounced Bon'-ĕ-lyn), first told me about this Jack Tale at a party in 1975, when we were discussing folklore in Pennsylvania. Bonelyn Lugg was at that time a graduate student at Penn State. She told me how she had learned this tale from her grandmother Pearl Hess, who had learned this tale and others as a child in northern Pennsylvania. Hess, I later found out, also knew songs sung at the end of the nineteenth century in the logging camps of the Northern Tier area of Pennsylvania. She had learned logging songs and tales as a very young woman from the children and adults she taught in a one-room schoolhouse in a logging community but recalled the Jack Tales as a family tradition.

Kyofski recalls storytelling in general as a definite family tradition. She remembers that her father was a "terrific storyteller. He told about the hoop snakes, Indian stories, and other local tales he picked up from God knows where." He did not tell the Jack Tales particularly, but other family members did. After her grandmother's funeral, Bonnie and some of her relatives told the "Jack stories" and other tales and songs their grandmother had told them years before.

A few months after I heard the first, impromptu telling, I traveled to Nelson, Pennsylvania, to record tales and songs known to Kyofski's grandmother, who was still living at that time. Grandma Hess was in her nineties and had difficulty remembering the songs and stories, but she did tell the same rapid-fire formulaic set piece that begins Kyofski's tale. Kyofski remembered that she had occasionally heard this tale as a child but could only remember parts of it until she coaxed her grandmother to teach her the tale as an adult.

Taking advantage of the fact that Bonnie could now tell the tale completely, I also recorded her telling it. This early performance was rather unadorned, an attempt to present the tale as her grandmother had always told it. When Kyofski was a child, she had tried to learn the first part of the tale, the long formulaic set piece, but had never persisted. Grandma would tell of her own brothers and sisters challenging each other with the tale to see who could continue through the whole set piece without taking a breath. In Kyofski's childhood, Grandmother Hess would always continue the story to the end, leaving her grandchildren breathless. This first tale, Kyofski said, could lead into the second tale, with the comment that "Jack was the natural leader," though "Grandma would rarely take center stage long enough to tell the long Jack Tale."

After her grandmother's death, Kyofski, now living in Kentucky, became involved with the Corn Island Storytelling Festival as an organizer. She worked with Lee Pennington, a well-known storyteller; she heard Ray Hicks tell stories; and she even discussed with

Leonard Roberts the fact that she had a Jack Tale tradition in her family. She never performed these tales in Kentucky, though. It was not until she returned to Pennsylvania in 1980 that she began to tell the stories she had learned from Pearl Hess.

Since returning to the Nelson area, Kyofski has become fairly well known as a performer. She has been in several local theater productions, she teaches in the regional state university, and she has been actively performing the Jack Tales, along with other songs and stories, gleaned from books as well as oral tradition.

The impetus for telling the Jack stories to children outside the family came as a result of her new job as a district school administrator. When she would enter an elementary classroom, she would try to put the children at ease by talking to them and telling them stories. She found the Jack Tales especially useful as an ice breaker. The children seemed to like the parts of the tale that addressed the issue of being a youngest child and therefore ignored by older relatives. They also responded to the local references to the logging traditions, still part of the north-central Pennsylvania local identity.

The tale as here transcribed was performed from a stage in the middle of the town of Elkland in front of thirty or forty people, as part of the community's 1990 Heritage Days celebration. Kyofski's Jack Tale is divided into two parts structurally, and three tale types. The first part, which is part of the performance but which also could stand alone, is a cumulative tale based on humorous contradictions (AT 2014). In her performances now she explains how this tale was passed down and how the quick and breathless telling of the cumulative tale is essential to telling the tale correctly.

The two tale types of the second part of the performance are "The King's Tasks" (AT 577) and the "Eating Contest" (AT 1088). In the present text the motif of the stretching bag cleverly unites these two tale types so that there is no sense of two separate stories. Baughman (1966) reports both of these types in the southern Appalachian Jack Tale tradition, although not combined as in the Pennsylvania text. In Leonard Roberts's *South from Hell-fer-Sartin* (1955) there is a Kentucky version of "The King's Tasks." Versions of "Eating Contest" appear in Richard Chase's *Jack Tales* (1943) and in Vance Randolph's Ozark collection, *The Devil's Pretty Daughter* (1955). Herbert Halpert, in notes to Randolph's collection, points to chapbook as well as oral sources and states that it is "combined with other giant tricking incidents in other American versions," although Chase's tale is the only other version reported with this incident.

In any case, the present tale is the only version reported in Pennsylvania. In fact, the Jack tradition has not been considered part of a Pennsylvania tradition heretofore. Is this text an isolated case derived from chapbook sources, or was it carried by oral tradition into the Northern Tier of Pennsylvania? Kyofski believes that the Jack Tale tradition came into northern Pennsylvania with the early settlers. The northern counties of Pennsylvania were once claimed by Connecticut: Kyofski's ancestors moved into Tioga County from Connecticut in the early 1800s. Pearl Short Hess, Bonelyn Kyofski's grandmother, born in 1884, was a granddaughter of these settlers. When I spoke with Hess in 1975, she told me of a man who lived in the area whose great-uncle "knew many Jack Tales and other old stories." She also mentioned that telling stories and singing old songs was common in the logging towns in Pennsylvania when logging was the main occupation of the area. It was at this time that she told me how she had learned new tales and logging songs from the children and adults she taught as a young woman.

For Kyofski, performing her grandmother's story and other local lore is a contribution to the preservation and enrichment of local culture and tradition. It is especially important to her that the children grow up with these stories. The younger audience is a teaching audience. She sees special significance in the identity of Jack as the youngest son. The unpromising hero motif points to a specific moral and provides an uplifting lesson for children, who "need a boost in self-esteem," Kyofski says. "Jack gives that."

To get some idea of how Kyofski has developed her story, we might compare the following excerpt from her 1976 performance with the rather fuller rendition of these episodes in the complete 1990 text that follows this essay.

Jack was just swinging along, fairly happy about the whole thing, and all at once he heard a strange noise out in the forest, sounded like chopping. It went:

Chop, chop; chop-chop-chop;
chop, chop; chop-chop-chop.

And he thought, "Well, I have a little time. I'll run off into the forest to see what is there."

And he got into the forest, and here was this magical ax. And the ax was just chopping down trees all around it, all by itself. Nobody was there. And it was just chopping them down and just stacking them right up into neat little firewood.

Jack thought, "My, what a handy thing to have."

And so he went over and grabbed the ax right by the handle and the ax came right along. Jack had this little rubber pouch around his neck that somebody had given him once. And it was a very handy little thing. So what he did was stick the ax down into the little rubber pouch around his neck and took it along. . . .

So he went off on down the road and all at once he heard:

   Gurgle, gurgle.
   Gurgle-gurgle-gurgle.

"My that's a strange noise."

And he looked up, and here was this enormous stream of water coming right out of the hill, but he'd never seen it before. So he went up to see what was the source of this water. And he found a little hickory nut, not any bigger than that. And all of this water was just springing right out of the hickory nut.

He thought, "My, what a handy little thing."

So he grabbed a piece of wood and whittled a plug quick away and he plugged it in the hickory nut, and he dropped the hickory nut in his bag and went off down the road.

As he went down the road he could see he was coming in view of the castle, because there was a castle and he could see the tree which was just almost overpowering the castle, and the longest line of men all lined up and ready to chop down that tree. . . .

The tree didn't have a single scar in it. It was right there. And right over beside it was one of the strangest sights. There was this block, and beside it a pile of left ears where people had come along and been trying to chop down the tree and lost their left ears.

So anyway, Bill knew he was going to do it though, cause he was the best woodsmen anywhere around.

And so he chopped and he chopped and he chopped and he chopped and he chopped. He got finished and he couldn't chop down the tree either. So he had to go over and put his head down on the block. *Thunk!* There went his left ear. He went off with his hand over where his ear had been.

If we compare these episodes from the earlier performance with the relevant episodes in the full 1990 text, we note differences in detail, of course. Jack's pouch, for instance, which is a special gift from his mother in the later version, is just something that he has in the earlier version. More important than minor details, however, is the difference in style. In the earlier performance the tale is clearly Grandma Hess's tale. It is told matter-of-factly. The text is spare and rests within the tale. This, we may assume, is the older style. But styles are changing. Kyofski's role in the storytelling revival and her exposure to active young audiences seem to have encouraged her to develop a more participatory and dramatically elaborated style. In the later performance the tale has become Kyofski's own tale. She is aware of some changes in style and context. She knows that she makes the text and performance more dramatic. In fact, she notes that the "old-time" storytellers "aren't very expressive—how could kids in a large group be expected to listen to such dry renditions?" Having been involved in dramatic productions, she regards her storytelling as a kind of dramatic performance. Having been involved in storytelling festivals, she sees her own style developing along more appropriately modern lines.

A major motive in this shift seems to be a new sense of audience. Not only are the new storytellers addressing larger audiences, they also seem to be addressing younger audiences. Even though there were adults in the audience when Kyofski performed the present text, the questions were directed to the children in the audience. Many of the young people at this performance had heard her Jack Tale before, more than once, in fact. Because of a familiar audience, Kyofski was inclined to emphasize the participatory and dramatically elaborated aspects of her style still more. The audience had "learned" the tale and expected to be a part of the performance. When she asked questions ("And do you know—?"), young boys would respond with the "correct" answers. When these young boys called out answers, adults in the crowd laughed. Kyofski feels that getting the children involved is important not only to keep their attention, but also to develop in them a sense of ownership of this tradition.

Realizing the focus of the performance on a child audience, one notices some interesting variations in the development of the tale during the fifteen-year period involved here. Already pretty brutal in its description of the ear losses, the tale becomes even more graphic in the description of blood and gore. The earlier version presents only one mutilation. Even then, the conclusion to the scene is relatively mild: "He went off with his hand over where his ear had been." In the 1990 text the scene is much more gory. The narrator dwells with relish on the blood pouring over the edge of the stump, the bloody axe, "all these men running around with hands stuck up against their heads," and finally Bill, "standing there with the blood oozing around his hands." When Tom gets his ear cut off, she cries, "*Chop*! Oooh!" and the children in the audience squeal in delight (at which the adults laugh). Clearly the narrator has been around children long enough to appreciate their less than delicate sensibilities.

The gore is not the only element of the tale that has developed over the years. As mentioned earlier, Kyofski has also found that children—and not only children—respond to references to the logging traditions that are still part of the local identity of the Pennsylvania Northern Tier. The newer variant reinforces the localizations appearing in the older text, especially an appeal to the understood in-group knowledge of logging lore. Now Jack does not have to grab the ax handle. The magic ax comes to Jack's hand when he puts it out, as if to the place where it belongs. When Jack whittles out a plug to stop up the hickory nut, the audience is reminded that "good old Jack always has his knife right here beside him, you know—he's a woodsman." When Bill tries to chop down the magic tree, he first takes out a wedge, like loggers take, "you know, that first great big chip they take to make sure which way the tree's going to fall down." The more recent text also has Jack's magic ax cut the tree into a greater variety of commercial wood products: "It was chopped into timbers, it was chopped into kindling wood, two-by-fours, firewood, the whole business, right there, stacked up alongside the castle wall." The audience continues to appreciate this logger image of Jack and his brothers, even though the great days of the logging industry are long gone.

Events like the Heritage Days at Elkland, Pennsylvania, and others in all towns throughout the region speak to a need for a community identity. Such spirit depends on recognition of common lore and a nostalgic sense of a shared past, often described, in fact, as heritage. Bonelyn Kyofski's public performances of her localized Jack Tales constitute a significant part of her region's heritage and have become increasingly recognized as such.

GRANDMA HESS'S STORY ABOUT JACK, BILL, AND TOM

as told by Bonelyn Lugg Kyofski

This text was recorded at Heritage Days in Elkland, Pennsylvania, 7 July 1990. Most of the audience—children, teenagers, and adults—had heard Kyofski tell this tale and other, more "local" stories many times. Her participatory style elicits verbal responses from the audience. These responses, when they can be detected on the recording, are enclosed in brackets. After this performance Kyofski said that she usually has even more active involvement when she tells the tales to kids. This performance begins with commentary by Kyofski about her grandmother's songs and story. After singing a song, "My Grandmother," she goes on, "That was what Grandma was like. Some of the stories she used to tell were famous stories, though. Stories about Jack."

This story about Jack, though drawn from three tale types, falls into only two parts, the initial nonsense run (AT 2014) and the subsequent narrative. In the second part Jack's stretching pouch provides a connecting link between two tale types (AT 577 and AT 1088), forging them into a single organic narrative.

In the present performance an aside to the audience separates the first and second parts. When Grandma Hess told both stories, she apparently used to connect the initial all-in-one-breath nonsense piece smoothly to the following narrative. Her granddaughter the present storyteller, in the performance recorded in the mid-1970s, made the connection in these words: "Even though Jack was the youngest of these three boys, he was the natural leader; and one of the reasons he was, was because of an adventure all three of these boys had gotten into at one time." In the second part of her story Kyofski's delivery is still quite rapid, but closer to extemporaneous prose than to the cadenced delivery of the southern Appalachian storytellers in this volume. Pauses for breath are generally dictated by grammatical breaks. Transcribing that part of her story in paragraph form seems to represent this style more accurately.

▼ ▼ ▼

(You know, sometimes we hear about Jack living with his widowed mother—just the two of them? Well, the stories I tell about Jack had to do with his two brothers as well. Jack had two brothers, one named Bill and one named Tom. And the first story goes . . .)

[*Speaking very rapidly, as if in one breath:*]
Once there were three boys named Jack, Bill 'n' Tom.
They told their mother to have dinner ready by noon
cause they was goin' huntin'.
When they got home they found their mother
sittin' on a three-one legged stool
cryin' as hard as ever she could.
"Why, what's the matter, Mother?" said Jack.
"Can't you see?" said she.
"The house's gone, blowed clear away in a gust of wind."
"So it did," said Jack.
So Jack left his brothers to take care of his mother
and off he went, down the road
with his shin bones in his pockets and his eyes wide shut,
starin' ahead till he saw Jophus th' Coach Driver
drivin' four dead horses,
fast as ever they could split.
"H'llo, Jophus th' Coach Driver.
Seen anything of Mother Clinton's house?" said Jack.
"Noooo," said Jophus th' Coach Driver,
and off he went, drivin' four dead horses
as fast as ever they could split.
And off Jack went, on down the road
with his shin bones in his pockets and his eyes wide shut,
starin' ahead till he saw John Ironsides
shootin' straws [hay] off a crowstack
with his straight crooked-barreled gun.
"H'llo, John Ironsides.
Seen anything of Mother Clinton's house,
blowed clear away in a gust of wind?" says Jack.
"S-u-r-e," said John Ironsides.
"Blowed clear the other side of everywhere,
where the mad dog bit a hatchet
and the pigs run around with knives and forks in their back,
yellin', 'H-o-l-d the P-o-r-k!' "

(Well, that's one of those kind of joke stories, simply because you tell it so fast. My grandmother said when they were little kids, that's what they did: they just loved to tell stories as fast as they could, and then they'd count how many breaths it would take. I never tell kids that I'm telling that story with breaths, because they'll count it, and they'll say at the end of it, "You did it in thirty-seven breaths!" and supposedly my great-aunt Edith could do it with only two.

But, that story kind of shows how Jack was a little bit the leader of those brothers. But, you know, he didn't start out being the leader. He ended up—he started out being the baby in that family. Is there anybody in here who's ever been the baby in a family?

[*Children in Audience:* Yeah.]

Do you know what they say to you? When you're the baby in the family, what do they tell you?

[*Children:* "Poor Baby!"]

"Poor Baby!" Yes. They're gonna say, "You can't go, you're too little." Is that what they say?

[*Children:* Yeah.]

Yeah. What else do they say?

[*Children:* "Wait till you're bigger."]

"Wait till you're bigger! When you're bigger, you can do it!" OK. Poor old Jack. That's the way it was at his house.

Well, this is a story about Jack, Bill, and Tom, who lived with their widowed mother up on the mountainside. Up on the mountainside, and they were loggers. (It wasn't very far from here.) But they were good loggers.

Bill was the oldest of those brothers, and he was a great big strapping guy, and he was one of the best loggers anywhere around. When Bill would larrup into a tree, you really knew that tree had been hit. He'd haul off with that ax, and everything would just shake when he hit that tree.

Tom was bigger than Bill [Jack], too. Now Tom wasn't quite as big and strong. But Tom had a little bit of flair to him. Everybody liked to watch Tom when he was cuttin' down a tree, because he'd come out, and he'd swing around the ax a couple of times, you know. He'd lick his thumb, run it along the blade—eeeeep—to make sure it was sharp enough, and t-h-e-n he would swing into the tree with a whole lot of style about him. Everybody liked to watch Tom.

But of course, Jack was a pretty good, pretty good wood chopper himself. But he was the littlest one, you know, so people just didn't pay too much attention.

But something very, very important happened one day in the lives of Jack, Bill, and Tom. Word went out from the king. The king says, "Oh, I've got myself a terrible problem. And any man that can come and chop down this great big tree that's giving me troubles, well, he can marry my daughter, and have half my kingdom."

Well, both Bill and Tom decided that's what they had to do. They were gonna take right off, and they were going to chop down that tree just as fast as they could. And both of them were going to have half the kingdom, and both of them were going to marry the king's girl. How were they gonna do that?

[*Audience:* Don't know.]

I don't know either, but they were plannin' on doin' it.

And Jack says, "I'm gonna go, too." And the boys said to him, "Jack, you can't go." What'd they say?

[*Audience:* "You're too little."]

"You're too little. You've gotta' stay home with Mom." That was exactly what they said. But Jack just waited until they'd gone on down the road, and he went to his Mom, and he says, "Mom, I've got to go." And she says, "I know you've gotta go, Jack. A man's gotta do what a man's gotta do. You go off there. And you—you have my blessing. You also have a gift. I have a very special thing for you." And so she gave him this little pouch, this little stretchy pouch to put around his neck, on a leather thong. And she gave him a kiss, and she said, "You have my blessing, Jack! You go off and do it!"

And so Jack went off down the road just as happy as you could please, on a beautiful day like today, and he was whistling along, having a wonderful time, swinging along, and having just the best time in the world, when all at once . . . he stopped for a minute and he heard a very strange noise:
[*Italicized words on a higher pitch, here and throughout.*]

Chop, *chop*. Chop-chop-*chop.*
Chop, *chop*. Chop-chop-*chop.*

He said, "My, that's a strange noise. Well, I'm not in very much of a hurry. I think I'll go and investigate that." And so he went off the road, and went off into the woods, and followed the noise, and he heard it getting louder:

Chop, *chop*. Chop-chop-*chop.*
Chop, *chop*. Chop-chop-*chop.*

And the first thing you knew, he came to this beautiful clearing. And in that beautiful clearing was an ax all by itself. That ax was just going all over the place. It was going

Chop, *chop*. Chop-chop-*chop.*

And it was chopping down trees just as fast as you please. And it was lining them up into two-by-fours, and timbers, and all sorts of firewood and kindling, just as nice as you please. And Jack looked at that ax, and he said, "My, but that would be a handy thing for a man to have. I wonder how you'd get your hands on something like that."

Well, he reached out like this, and that ax handle came right over into his hand like this, and he had that ax. So naturally, he just opens up his little pouch, and sticks the ax down there, and pulls it shut, and goes on down the road.

And he's swinging along having a wonderful time because it's a beautiful day. And he said, "Well, well, it's such a beautiful day," stopped for a minute, and heard this very strange noise:

Dig, *dig*. Dig-dig-*dig*.
Dig, *dig*. Dig-dig-*dig*.

"My, a shovel, you say!"

Well, he had to investigate; he just couldn't take anybody's word for it. So he went, sure enough, out through the woods, and he looked, until all at once he came to a hearing—to a clearing, and sure enough, he found—what did he find?

[*Audience:* A shovel.]

A shovel! A magical shovel, and it was just digging by itself. It was going

Dig, *dig*. Dig-dig-*dig*.
Dig, *dig*. Dig-dig-*dig*.
Dig, *dig*. Dig-dig-*dig*.

And it was digging trenches, and it was digging holes, and it was digging all sorts of things, all by itself. And Jack says, "My, but that would be a handy thing for a man to have. I wonder how you'd get your hand on something like that?" And so he reached out his hand, like that, and sure enough, the handle of that shovel came right over into his hand, and he opens up his pouch, sticks the shovel down there, pulls it shut, and goes back to the road, and goes on swinging down the road, whistling away.

But it's such a beautiful day, all at once he stops, and takes a deep, deep breath, and he hears a very strange sound:

Gurgle, *gurgle*. Gurgle-gurgle-*gurgle*.
Gurgle, *gurgle*. Gurgle-gurgle-*gurgle*.

"My, that's a strange sound," says Jack. "I think I'm gonna go investigate that and see what that's all about. I'm not in any very much of a hurry."

And so Jack wanders off through the woods until he hears

Gurgle, *gurgle*. Gurgle-gurgle-*gurgle*,

much louder. He was getting closer. Pretty soon, he comes out to a side hill, where he sees the most beautiful cascade of water, just tumbling right down from the side of the hill. He said, "My, that's the strangest looking waterfall I've ever seen. It's coming from a little tiny spot, way up there on the hill. I think maybe I'll go investigate that." So sure enough, Jack climbs up the hill till he comes to that little spot, and he looks, and that wonderful cascade of water is coming out of a little tiny hickory nut. Not any bigger than that. "My," he says, "I think that'd be a handy thing for a man to have. I wonder how you'd get your hands on something like that." Well, good old Jack always has his knife right here beside him, you know—he's a woodsman—so he takes a piece of wood and whittles himself out a little plug, and sticks it right in that hickory nut, like that, really good and tight, and then he puts that hickory nut down in his little pouch, goes back down to the road again, and wanders on off down towards the king's place.

Well, by this time he's getting very, very close to that castle. In fact, he can look out there at that castle and he can see all the problems the king is having. There's this great big tree that's growing and growing and growing and growing. This tree is knocking down the wall of the castle, for pity's sake.

"Well," Jack says, "somebody ought to do something about that." And then he looked and he saw a whole line-up of men. There had to be at least four hundred and twenty-nine men lined up there, waiting to chop down that tree because *they* wanted to marry the king's girl and get half the kingdom too.

W-e-l-l, when Jack got a little closer he saw not only was there a great big tree there, but right—beside—that—tree—was—one—of—the—strangest—things—he—had—ever—seen.

It was a stump.

A great big stump.

And there on the stump . . . was b-l-o-o-d.

All this red stuff coming down over the edge.

And beside that stump was an ax.

And on that ax was all this red runny stuff, too, blood all over that ax.

Well, beside the stump was the strangest thing he *had* ever seen.

Ears.

Left ears.

The problem about this was, if you tried to chop down that tree and you failed, you had to go over there and put your head down on that block, and they'd take an ax and go *thawaak!* and take off your left ear.

There were all these men running around with hands stuck up against their heads [!!!!] with blood oozing out around the fingers. Ooohs.

Anyway, Jack saw that, and he said, "Well, a man's gotta do what a man's gotta do."

You know, Jack had taken his own good time about this, and Bill and Tom were right up at the head of the line. It was Bill's turn. So Bill gets up there and he takes his ax, and he chops an enormous chunk out of this tree—you know, that first great big chip they take to make sure which way the tree's going to fall down. Well, Bill whacked out an enormous chunk, and it looked just fine until all at once, *zip*. Would you believe that that chunk just grew right back again. Every time anybody took a chip out of that tree, why the tree would grow right back.

Well, Bill was a really big strong logger. He chopped and he chopped and he chopped and he chopped. He went on for eight hours, just chopping away. And, sure enough, he'd take chunks right out of the tree, and the minute he'd take the chunks out, they'd grow back again. Well, didn't take very long. Eight hours was just about enough, and Bill says, "Just can't do it any more." So Bill goes over and puts his head down on the chopping block, and sure enough, they take the ax and *thwaak!* There go one of the family ears! [!!!]

Well, Jack felt pretty bad, you know. Tom—Bill gave him a bad time some of the time, but he was really pretty fond of Bill, and the boys only had six ears among them, you know, and . . . there went one of them.

Well, Bill was standing there with the blood oozing around his hands, and it was Tom's turn. And Tom was no coward, you know. He had to go on and do the same thing. And so sure enough, Tom comes up, and in his usual way, takes his ax and he does his swirls with it, comes up and licks his finger, goes *eeeep!* across the ax to make sure it was sharp enough—it was very, very sharp—and hauls off and with his usual flair, larrups into that tree. Takes the first chunk out, and guess what?

[*Audience:* It grows right back.]

It grows right back. Right you are. Yes. And, anyway, that's what happened. It grew right back, and he chopped and he chopped. Now Tom wasn't quite as big and strong as Bill. Didn't take him quite as long. Probably about six hours, and that was as much as he could do. And so, anyway, poor old Tom has to go over and put his head down on the block. And *chop!* Oooh! There goes another one of the family ears. And there he is.

By this time both Tom and Bill have seen Jack there. And they're really concerned. They come over to him. And you know what they say to him?

[*Audience:* "You're going to get your ears chopped off."]

Yes: "You don't think you can chop down anything that Bill and Tom—Bill and I can't chop down, do you? You're too little. You should have stayed home with Mother. Why didn't you stay home? Don't you do this."

And Jack said, "A man's gotta do what a man's gotta do." And, so he stood right there in line.

Well now there were some other people in line who were all at once beginning to realize that maybe it wouldn't be such a good idea to be chopping that tree down after all. Or trying to. Because, after all, they'd been in lots of competitions with Bill and Tom before. And some of them were saying, "Well, if Bill and Tom can't do it, I don't reckon I can do it." Well, there was something to that, all right. But, this time most of the men just decided that they would turn around and leave.

And it was Jack's turn. He was right there in front. And so, Jack turned his back to the audience, just a little bit, and he whips out his wonderful ax. And that ax just started on that tree. And it went

Chop, *chop*. Chop-chop-*chop*.
Chop, *chop*. Chop-chop-*chop*.

The first thing you knew, that tree was down. It was chopped into timbers, it was chopped into kindling wood, two-by-fours, firewood, the whole business, right there, stacked up alongside the castle wall.

Well, Jack was very proud of himself. And he went over to the king. Bowed. And he was all ready for the king to say, "Good job, Jack. You can have half my kingdom and marry my girl."

But you know how kings are. This king looked at him, and says, "Well, now, Jack, that's a pretty good job. But I don't think, somehow, it's quite worth half a kingdom and marrying my girl. Now I've got this other problem, Jack, that might be pretty important." He says, "We've got a terrible drought in the kingdom. Hasn't rained in so long. Now you make it rain, Jack, and then, then, we'll see about your getting half the kingdom and marrying my girl."

Jack thinks, "Gee, I can't make it rain, but you know, maybe I could fix him a little river." So Jack goes up the side of the hill, and he takes out his shovel. And the shovel starts:

Dig, *dig*. Dig-dig-*dig*.
Dig, *dig*. Dig-dig-*dig*.
Dig, *dig*. Dig-dig-*dig*.

First thing you know, he's got this wonderful riverbed that's just sweeping down, up through the pasture, and down past the castle,

down into the meadow. And Jack goes up to the top again, and takes
out his little hickory nut, hauls the plug out of it, puts it up at the top
of that river, and

Gurgle, *gurgle.* Gurgle, *gurgle.*
Gurgle-gurgle-*gurgle.*

Well, the first thing you know, there's this wonderful river, that's just
sweeping down through the pasture. You can just see the grass getting greener. You can see all of the cattle just coming as fast as they
can to get a drink of water and get some of that nice green grass. Well,
anyway, it was a wonderful river, and Jack was very proud of himself.

So he goes down to the king, and, uh, very pleased, he says, "OK."
He says, uh, "Yes, sir!"

The king, uhhmm, said, "Well,"—you know how kings are. The king
says, "Well, that's, that's pretty good, Jack. But it doesn't seem to me
to be quite worth half the kingdom and marrying the king's girl."

Uh-oh! Jack was just remembering. He doesn't have anything left in
that little bag of tricks of his.

Empty!

And so the king says, "But I've got a real problem." He says, "It's a
giant."

"A giant?" says Jack.

"A giant!" says the king. Says, "This giant is stealin' my cattle. He's
always into my steers." He says, "Every time I turn around I'm finding that I'm losin' 'em. They're just goin', and that giant is eating
them. I've got to do something about it. Now, Jack, you take care of
that giant, then you can marry my girl and have half my kingdom."

So old Jack says, "Well, a man's gotta do what a man's gotta do."
So, sure enough, he trots up to the edge of the forest. Gets up there,
and takes a d-e-e-p breath. The minute he takes that deep breath he

smells the most wonderful aroma. [*Sniff, sniff.*] Barbecue! He can
smell the steaks from here. And so he starts wandering into the forest,
and he hasn't gone very far before, sure enough, he sees this wonderful clearing. And here in the middle of the clearing is a barbecue pit. It
is such a big barbecue pit, well, it's probably about as big as this
porch. And on it are seven cows. They're on spits, and they're just
turning around and around. They're about medium rare, about now,
and Jack has never smelled anything so good in his entire life.

And so, just as he's looking at these cows, he turns around and he sees
two calves, right here [*indicating eye level*], with knees on top of them,
and the rest of the giant goes on up from there. It's the biggest fellow
that Jack's ever seen. He has to be fifty or sixty feet high. And he says
to Jack, "And who might you be?"

Jack says there's nothin' to it, and turns around and says, "My name's
Jack."

The giant says, "Can you give me any good reason why I shouldn't
eat you right now?"

Jack looked up and he says, "Well, . . . I reckon I can eat more than
you can eat."

The giant laughed and laughed. He said, "You? You little squirt? You
can eat more than I can eat? That's a good one! Now, I'll tell you what
we're going to do. We're going to sit down and we are going to eat,
and when we are finished eating, and you've eaten as much as you
can eat, I'm—going—to—have—you—for—dessert!"

Mmm!

So Jack and the giant sat down beside all of those wonderful spinning
cows, and each of 'em hanks off a quarter and starts to chew.

Well, they ate and ate—of course, Jack was starved. He hadn't eaten
since he left his mother's place, and the giant was pretty good at
eating, too. Well, the giant just ate and ate and ate. And Jack ate as
much as he needed, and then, he started just spitting his, his meat

right into his little pouch. So the more he ate and the more the giant ate, the less Jack was feeling it because the pouch was filling up and filling up and filling up, and he kept right on eating. And he yanked off another quarter and he kept right on eating. The giant couldn't believe it. He took another quarter and kept on eating.

Well, by the time they'd gone through two-and-a-half cows, the giant said, "Jack, you eat more than any little guy I've ever seen in my whole life. Aren't you getting full?"

And Jack says, "Oh, no." He says, "I don't have much trouble when I start gettin' full—I like to eat, you know." He pulls out his knife and sticks it into that little pouch that his mother had given him, rips it open and dumps the meat out on the ground, settles it around him again, and takes another big bite of beef.

The giant looked at him and he says, "Well, you little shrimp. Anything you can do, I can do!" Grabs his knife, and sticks it in his stomach, and goes *rrrip*. [!!!!!!]

And so, Jack went off on down the mountain, and said hello to the king, and the king said, "Good job, Jack. I think maybe you can marry my daughter *and* have half my kingdom." And he lived happily ever after, of course.

[*Applause.*]

(Oh, thank you.)

CHAPTER 10

JACK'S
ADVENTURES IN
TORONTO

▼ ▼ ▼ ▼ ▼

STEWART CAMERON

▼ ▼ ▼ ▼ ▼

Kay Stone
with Stewart Cameron

"Once upon a time in Scotland there was a king, and
he had a very, very prosperous kingdom, and he had three healthy,
strong princes, sons, to look after—and to look after him. But he was
getting on in years, and his mind was bending towards just who he
was going to leave this kingdom to." These words open Stewart Cameron's story about Jack, the unlikely hero in a story known to folklorists as "The Frog Bride" (AT 402). Cameron used his son as a living
model for unworldly Jack; but when he spoke these words in Toronto
in 1988, he did not know that he would soon find his own mind
"bending towards just who he was going to leave this kingdom to."[1]

Cameron, of Sudbury, Ontario, a self-trained urban performer,
appeared at clubs and folk festivals, contributed songs and tales to the
Canadian Broadcasting Company's national program *Identities,* and
served as one of the artistic directors of the Northern Lights Festival

at Sudbury. He began his performing career in the 1960s as a singer who favored "the ballads with their long and complicated plots full of blood and mayhem" (1979 program, Toronto Festival of Storytelling). His fascination with "complicated plots" led him to traditional tales, which began to demand a place in his repertoire in the 1980s when he became a regular contributor to the annual Toronto Festival of Storytelling and to the weekly festival-sponsored Friday night gatherings. Cameron did not come to ballad singing and storytelling from a traditional background in a rural community, as did other narrators included here, though both he and his wife, Dianne, learned some of their songs and music from their respective "pan-Celtic" families (Dianne's description). As she wrote to me on 8 March 1990, about a year after his death, "We were certainly exposed to people in our families and immediate neighborhood who could sing, relate anecdotal stories, or talk about family history. Stew played accordion and guitar as a child, and was very early involved in doing Scottish songs for his family gatherings." As a mature performer, Stewart, unlike many other urban, nontraditional performers, preferred to appear with his family. Dianne was an experienced singer, and their son, Duncan, and daughter, Moira, were gradually brought into the act as they matured.

Dan Yashinsky, one of the founding members of the Storytellers School, recalls Cameron performances at the weekly Friday night gatherings: "There would be singing, funny stories, ghost stories. The audience would join in—and I'd leave feeling like I'd been to a party in a very warm, friendly living room." These performances were closer to the intimate oral traditional model than to the more usual theatrical model of many urban storytelling events, possibly because they grew naturally from the family setting. Daughter Moira Cameron remembers that storytelling was always important: "At home, storytelling came naturally to my father. Having two story-minded kids certainly gave him ample inspiration to learn and tell stories in the home environment. My father would tell me a story almost every night before bed. Often, because his stories were so long, he would have to tell them in several installments—one each night—until the story ended. 'The Three Feathers' was one of my favorites" (letter, 6 February 1990).

Because storytelling and singing began at home, Stewart Cameron (and the Camerons as a whole) developed a strong sense of performance as a communal exchange in which tellers and listeners were not separated by a "fourth wall." Cameron was always aware that any single story or song was only one link in a complex chain of artistry. He never viewed "Jack and The Three Feathers" as his own story, even though it became one of his favorites and took on unique features as a result of his frequent retellings.

I first heard Cameron tell "Jack and The Three Feathers" in 1985, at a story-swapping session at the annual Toronto festival. A pleasant, bearded man in his late thirties had wandered in, smiled, and found a place. He sat quietly and attentively until everyone else had finished and then offered politely to tell a story. Here began the tale of Jack and his muddy adventures. We were all delighted, those who had heard it before no less so than those (like me) for whom it was a new experience. The tale was so compelling that I began to retell it after I returned to Winnipeg, and my curiosity as both storyteller and folklorist was aroused. The next year I had the chance to hear his story again and to ask how he had learned it and why he loved it so. He said he had first heard Jim Strickland tell the story in Toronto, recorded that performance, and got permission from Strickland to retell the story. In a letter of 29 January 1988, he explained further: "The story when I first heard it [from Strickland] had an immediate appeal. I won't bother to analyze why—it just did. When I began telling it, it developed a life and purpose all its own."[2]

In 1988 I returned to Toronto and was able to tape Cameron's retelling of the story as it had evolved after several years of performances at home and in public. The annual Toronto Festival of Storytelling, with dozens of tellers and large crowds of avid listeners, was taking place all around us, but we managed to find a quiet room with no one else present. We shut the door hoping for complete privacy, but as I turned on the machine and Cameron began to speak, three boys (I would guess their ages as eight, ten, and eleven) came in noisily and sat down at a table near the door, across from where we were sitting. I tried to ignore their presence, hoping that they would realize we were taping a story and would quiet down, but Cameron acknowledged them with a nod and launched into his story. They went on with their own loud conversations, pretending not to listen but casting glances in our direction. Cameron turned occasionally and addressed parts of the story to them directly, and they began acting out the roles of the three sons among themselves.

Thus, instead of being a distraction, the presence of those three boys inspired Cameron to add details not included in his earlier telling and to act out more of the story with broad gestures, facial expressions, and changes of voice. These elaborations made the story much longer than the one I had heard in 1985 and considerably richer.

About halfway through the story the door opened again and a man wandered in and sat quietly in the opposite corner, paying no obvious attention to what was going on. I was surprised to see that Cameron seemed, momentarily, to lose his concentration. The casual conversational tone and natural pace shifted into a more formal and elaborate style, which lengthened his tale even more. (In my memory the story as told in 1985 was not more than ten minutes long, but this telling took up the full side of a half-hour tape.) When he finished the story, he addressed the three boys, who had stayed to the very end, each keeping in character within the story. He then turned to the man in the corner, who, as it turned out, was Jim Strickland himself. I understood why Cameron had become concerned after Jim's entry: telling a story in the presence of the one who "owns" it is a daunting feat, for both traditional and nontraditional tellers.

Cameron was aware of his response both to the boys and to Jim Strickland. He commented that the story "wasn't very tight," noting that he had not told it for a while. He admitted that Strickland's presence had affected his telling of the tale, and he seemed to feel that he had not "done as well" as usual. He did not discuss the three boys, though he had obviously enjoyed their presence and benefited from their indirect participation.

The process of evolution is enlightening even when it is seen in the fleeting history of a single folktale variant told by one person. Cameron was aware of the evolution of the story over the few years in which he told it. He was sensitive to the immediate effects of audience on performance, and of his own response to the differing contexts of storytelling within his own family and in public performances. For example, he described how the motif of Jack's "mucking about in the mud" came to take an increasingly central part in his telling because both he and his audiences found it compelling. (Strickland's variant has Jack "puttering about in the back garden.")

When I began telling it to my kids I found that it changed considerably [according] to my audience's response. My son Duncan was heavily into the wonders of mud at the time and spent many hours mucking around in our "back garden." I naturally enlarged the importance of this part of the story and Duncan became the role model for my Jack. (letter, 29 January 1988)

When I told Cameron that this was precisely what held the lengthy story in my own memory after a single telling, and made me want to tell it myself, he modestly commented: "The story seems remembered well by those who hear it. You are not the only one who has made note of that tale and remembered it on one hearing only. Very gratifying to the teller."

Another memorable feature of the story is the convincing vitality of Jack and his opportunistic brothers. In the same 1988 letter, Cameron wrote:

The characters within the story gradually assumed their own peculiar personalities as I told the story. Jack becomes not so much a fool as an absent-minded child, too full of his own world and imagination to be overly concerned with the "real world" around him. His brothers, on the other hand, are worldly wise and socially conscious. They do the right things, go to the right schools and generally excel at doing what princes are supposed to do.

Cameron understood that such narrative developments were a natural part of the storytelling process and did not try to hold himself rigidly to Strickland's text, commenting in his letter that "other things have crept into my telling of the tale as well." His critical portrayals of the ambitious brothers and of the two kings, human and frog, contrasts with his sympathetic portrayal of Jack, who simply refuses to play the worldly game offered to him by his position as prince in a royal family, and of the frog princess who allows him to continue his adventures in the mud. Indeed, Cameron emphasizes that even marriage and regal responsibilities do not squelch Jack's love of play. It was this conclusion that expressed his sense of the story most fully. He ended his 1988 letter to me by quoting it fully, and poetically:

The ending of my tale is different also. Jack ends up marrying the princess and inheriting the kingdom, but:
She is as wise as he is foolish,
    As industrious as he is lazy.
And she is quite understanding

When he slips away from his kingly duties
And putters about in the back garden;
For after all, considering her background,
She knows just how much fun that can be.

Tellers of tales in all times and in all places have always faced the challenge of making their stories convincing for their audiences and for themselves without losing the integrity of the story. Cameron understood that the creative balance between teller and audience was by its nature a risky venture in which the teller's interpretations were destined to be acclaimed by some listeners and rejected by others. He noted, for example, that he was sometimes faulted for digressions and anachronisms, such as his elaborately detailed descriptions of Jack "mucking about in the mud" as well as playing with Lego, and for "side allusions to the [British] Royal Family" that were not always complimentary. He felt that his responsibility to his listeners was to create an immediately entertaining story without denying his own faith in the deeper realities of the tale. "This approach *is* a tricky business. I do not *require* my audience to believe in what I tell, but I make damn sure they know that *I* believe in it. My characters *are* real and the story I tell *is* important, no matter how far-fetched, fantastic, or ridiculous" (letter, 29 January 1988).

In his desire to remain true to a story as well as to the audience, he struck a balance between stability (telling it as he heard it from Jim Strickland) and innovation (responding to his own aesthetic sense, his own life experiences, and the immediate performing context). He believed in the inner truth of the story, but he did not demand this of his listeners. As he put it in his letter: "Anachronisms abound in all my telling. Some consider this a fault. They say a storyteller should create a self-consistent world conducive to a willing suspension of disbelief. I don't even attempt to do that in many of my tales. I find that I can draw more people into a tale if I don't insist on 'suspension of belief' as a prerequisite." Cameron himself *was* willing to suspend belief, to see Jack as a convincing human being and not merely a quaint character to be manipulated for theatrical effect. Therein, perhaps more than anywhere else, lies the secret of his power as a storyteller.

Like the aging king in his story and like master narrators everywhere, Cameron has passed on a living legacy to those who have heard his stories. Ruth Stotter and Bill McCarthy end Chapter 6 of

this volume by asking whether nontraditional storytellers can play a
vital role in preserving all those boys named Jack of whom Carl Lindahl writes. The answer seems clear. Because of Cameron and others
like him, Jack and all the Jacks will retain their place as ordinary heroes, far removed from traditional rural settings perhaps, but no less
adaptable to challenge and adversity, and utterly lacking in worldly
ambition.

NOTES

1. Cameron died little more than a year later. Wife Dianne and son Duncan carry on the performing tradition of the Cameron family.

2. Cameron, in this same letter, also credited a version from Andra Stewart, printed in *Tocher*, the journal of the School of Scottish Studies, as influ-
encing his telling. Strickland told me his own source was Jeannie Robertson,
the Scottish Tinker singer and storyteller.

JACK AND THE THREE FEATHERS

as told by Stewart Cameron

*Stewart Cameron told this Scottish version of "The Three Feathers" (AT 402, Grimm nos. 63 and 106), to Kay Stone during the 1988 Toronto Festival of Storytelling. They began the recording in an empty room but were soon joined by three boys and, later, one atten tive adult—who turned out to be Jim Strickland, from whom Cameron had first heard the story. This performance is more than twice as long as the first performance that Stone heard Cameron present, in 1985. Stone has transcribed the story in longer blocks, resembling paragraphs, rather than in lines, judging such a transcription more appropriate for this storyteller and his story (see Note on the Texts). One slip, an inconsistent personal pronoun (*he)*, has been replaced by the correct noun reference in brackets.*

▼ ▼ ▼

Once upon a time in Scotland there was a king, and he had a very, very prosperous kingdom, and he had three healthy, strong princes, sons, to look after—and to look after him. But he was getting on in years, and his mind was bending towards just who he was going to leave this kingdom to. He wanted to leave it to the right man. Which of his three sons would do?

Well, I tell you, two of his sons were everything that you could expect as far as princes were concerned. You couldn't tell one from the other. They were great at all of the things that princes were supposed to do. They went to the polo and they went to the tennis matches and they went to the horse races and one thing and another, and they always did well in their lessons, as far as courtly bowing is concerned, and politics, and everything. A-1 students they were. You couldn't wish for better. And they dressed to the teeth. No doubt about it— they looked the role of princes. And all of the young girls, ah, they were falling head over heals in love with them, vying for them right, left, and center.

But . . . the third son now, if you must know, was somewhat different. Jack was his name, and the king would say, rather, ahhhm, [un]easily, that Jack spent most of his time tending to the back garden. But, the truth be told, the back garden was nothing but a marsh full of muck, rain, drizzle, bulrushes, frogs, toads, and all manner of weeds. And that's where Jack liked to spend his time, just mucking around in the back garden.

Well, the king made up his mind that, yes indeed, he would have to decide, and he could not decide between his three sons—well, at least between two of them—just who he was going to leave his kingdom to. So, as all good kings do, he had a number of good advisors, some wise men, and he assembled them around him and asked the big question of them:

"How can I decide who I am going to leave my kingdom to?"

And they gave it some long and hard thought and came up with a solution:

"Just set your sons a quest. Set them a quest."

"What's a quest?" said the king.
[*Cameron is now beginning to tell the story to the boys off to the right, who pretend to be uninterested, though they have become silent.*]

"Oh, just send them to hunt something up or to do something within a period of time, and the one that either gets it or doesn't, to your satisfaction, is the one that wins the kingdom in the end."

"That's a great idea," said the king.

And he summoned his three sons in front of him. And he had an idea in mind, yes indeed. And, they stood in front of him. And the king said:

"I am going to set you three lads a quest. Each one of you is to go off, where the winds will take you, and to come back with the most beautiful tablecloth in the entire world. And the one that comes back with the most beautiful, finely made tablecloth—that is the lad that will be the king after I go."

[*Here he turns and addresses the three boys as if he were the king, and to this they respond by giggling and pretending to take on the character of each brother. They actually leave the room briefly and return, still laughing.*]

"Fair enough."

The three lads were ushered up to the topmost turret of the castle, and each one of them was given a white feather. The first lad, the oldest prince [*Cameron points to the boy on the left*], he was told:

"Go over to the turret and throw it, and cast that feather to the wind. And whichever direction that feather goes, that's the direction you shall go to find the finest tablecloth in the entire world."

Well, the eldest son, he took the feather, and he *threw it* over the turret of the castle, and it caught in the breeze—whshhhshhut—and off to the east it went.

"Fair enough."

He saddled and he bridled, and he got his bags and gold and his suit of clothes upon his back, and enough provisions to last him a good long time, and he set off to the east after that feather and after that prize of a tablecloth.

Well, the second son [*Cameron points to the middle boy*], he came to the topmost turret, he too was given a feather, he too cast it to the side, and away it went—whshhhshhoo—to the west. He too saddled and bridled and dressed appropriately, and away he went in search of the finest tablecloth in the west.

And of course . . . Jack too must be given a chance at this. "After all, you have to be fair about these things," said the king.

"Fair enough."
[*Cameron indicates the remaining boy, who is already in character, acting silly and grinning.*]

"Jack!"

"Yes."

Up he steps. And he was given a feather too. Jack took the feather in his rather grubby hands and *threw it* over the edge of the castle. Whshhshhhhh-shthud: right down into the mud in the back garden.

[*The boy imitates Jack's actions.*]

"Hu, well," says Jack, but he didna' mind.

Well, I tell you, a year and a day was the length of time these princes had to fulfill their quest. And just about that time—it was just about a year later—Jack found himself mucking about in the back garden. [*He addresses himself to the boys again.*] You know, he had his rubber boots off to the side there, and he was mucking around in this little pool of brown, yucky water, squishing the mud up between his toes—Ach, there's no more beautiful feeling in the world than to have that mud sort of shshsh up through the big toe and the little toe—it's just marvelous. But he was squishing around, and trying to do a sword-fight with a little bit of a bulrush he had in his hand, slicing back and forth, pretending that he was the prince that he should have been anyway, when there, in front of him, he hears this little bit of a voice.

[*A high-pitched, quick, broad Scots voice:*] "Jack! Jack my man!"

Well, Jack looks around, you know, but there's nobody there what-soever. And he says:

"Ach, it's just the wind."

But then, as he's mucking around, squishing back and forth with his blade of grass, the voice says again:

"Jack, Jack my man! You've no left us much time!"

And Jack looks down, and sure enough there's a tiny, wee frog, talking to him.

"Jack, Jack my man, you've no left us much time. You've got to hurry. What about your quest?"

And Jack, he'd never seen a frog talk before, but he said in answer, quite amiably:

"Why, I've forgotten all about my quest."
[*He looks at the three boys, who are paying somewhat closer attention, waiting to see what will happen next.*]

"What, what! You've forgotten about your quest! Well, your time is almost up. Follow me! Follow me!"

And the frog hopped over to the tail end of the garden and there was a great big rock. And the frog said:

"Tap that three times, Jack." And Jack took the bulrush that he was holding and tapped it three times and [*squeaking*], *eeeaaaeee*, the boulder opened right up and this great big tunnel went down, down, down into the center of the earth. And the frog said:

"Come on Jack! Come on Jack!" and leapt and hopped right down the tunnel.

Well, Jack, he followed after, for what could he do, you know? He was curious. He went down and down and down, and lo and behold, this tunnel opened up into a great, big, huge cavern that was filled to the brim with frogs and toads and lizards and snakes. They were writhing about like it was, like it was, ach, I don't know, *Raiders of the Lost Ark*, or something. [*Giggles from the boys, for whose benefit this reference was added.*] And there at the foremost end of it was this huge, great bullfrog setting on this stone throne, with a tiny wee crown on his head. And he shouts to the back as Jack enters, and says:

"Jack, Jack, my man, you've made it at last! Why, you didn't, you didn't leave us much time, Jack. Come here, come here."

And Jack steps forward, and—minding where he's putting his feet— and he bows before the king of the frogs, and the frog says:

"Jack, what is your quest? How can we help you this time?"

"Oh, my quest," says Jack. "Uhhh . . . I'm supposed to bring back a—tablecloth! Yes, a tablecloth."

"A tablecloth?" said the frog. "My, my, my, we don't use tables down here. But I tell you what—we have this wee bit of a rag that we, we hang up, over top of the walls, just to, to keep the moisture in, you know. So, uh, you can take that—I'm sure it will do. Over there, Jack."

So Jack goes over to the corner of this great, big, huge cavern and takes down this cloth, bundles it up, and shoves it inside his shirt. And away he goes, to the cheers of the frogs, the lizards, and the toads, up, up, up the big tunnel.

And as soon as he gets out, out in the air again, the rock closes behind him. And he is just in time, I tell you, because his, his brothers at just that moment have returned. And in fact, his eldest brother was up there in the throne room in front of the father himself, and spreading out on this table the most beautiful piece of Holland linen you have ever seen in all your born days. Not a stitch out of place, perfect in every regard: a little trim of lace around the edge, and embroidery all the way through it. Ach, the king was feeling the texture of it—as fine as silk it was—and he said:

"Och! this is beautiful, absolutely beautiful. This is the best tablecloth I have ever seen. Ah, it's going to take a heap of beating," said the king. "But, to be fair we must see what your brother has brought in."

Well, the second brother with much ceremony came forward and spread out the most beautiful piece of Irish linen that you have ever seen—lacework like you wouldn't believe, in and out woven with little bands of silver and gold. Ah, it sparkled in the sunlight.

"Och," said the king, "I've never seen a ta—have you ever seen a tablecloth so beautiful, now! That's marvelous, marvelous! I don't know how I can tell the difference between them. Oh, what a choice. What can I do? But . . . to be fair," said the king, "we must give Jack his chance as well."

"Jack?"

Jack had just come to the throne rooms. He had his boots on, but of course he shouldn't have, because they were caked with mud and he was leaving a track like you wouldn't believe across the velvet carpet there. But the king ignored them as he usually did, and said:

"Jack, Jack, have you managed to complete your quest?"

And Jack said:

"Well, ahh . . . I have something here."

And he opened up his shirt and, since all the tables were used, he just sort of spread it out in front of the throne. [*Voice hushed in wonder:*] And I tell you, it was beautiful! It, it had a picture on it like a, a mural, and every time you moved from one location to the other, the picture seemed to move. Around and around. And the, the cloth was made of the finest, finest silk, never before seen in that land. Transparent, it was so fine. And not a stitch out of place. And the king stood transfixed. And he said:

"Jack, my man, that's the finest piece of work I have ever seen. You've won!"

"WAIT A MINUTE! WAIT A MINUTE!" said the other princes. "No way is Jack going to win the kingdom from us! No way! We've been away for a year and a day. I don't know where he found that piece of rag, but there's no way one could've . . . We demand a rematch! No! Another quest!"

"Well, it does seem a little peculiar" said the king. "Well, you're only right. It's only fair. Ok. Another quest. Let me think now. All right, all right. You three are to go out and find the finest ring in the entire world. The most beautiful, the most priceless ring."

"Right enough!"

Up to the topmost turret of the castle they went. Each of the sons was given a white feather. The eldest son [*Cameron again points to the tallest of the three listening boys*], the big tall one with the brown hair and the sparkling eyes, he went over there and very proudly tossed it over the edge of the castle [*the boy imitates the tossing*], and the wind caught it— whshhhshh- shhhwshhh—and off to the north it went.

The second son, he took his feather, he threw it over the turret of the castle and—whshhhshhwipt—off to the south it went. [*The second boy imitates the first, and follows his feather out of the room.*]

And Jack, he took his feather, and he threw it over the turret of the castle—shhhwhh-ssssssspuhp—right down into the mud in the back garden.

"Ohh well."

The eldest son, he saddled and bridled, got his pants and pockets filled with gold, and away to the north he went. The second son, he went out to the south with a caravan of goods behind him. And Jack, of course, went down to muck about in the back garden. [*The third boy sits down on the floor and "mucks about in the mud."*]

Time passed like you wouldn't believe. It was almost a year later, and Jack was busy there. He was making a tiny castle out of the dried muck, and he was putting little flags with the grass around the turrets, arragh, and they kept falling down because they were rather wet. But he had, he had some Lego that he built a bridge, and it was red Lego except for the one piece that was blue, but he put it the other way around so you couldn't see it from that side, and, and uh, uh, he, he was pretending with his figures to go over and underneath the archway, but, but, but then the—well anyways, he was getting into trouble. He decided that he'd better make a moat around the mud castle so that it would sort of drain the mud away and the Lego wouldn't fall into the center, so, so he got this stick and he was digging a trench right around the castle, like so, when, what do what do you think happened next? This tiny wee frog hops right up to him and says:

"Jack, Jack my man! Jack, Jack my man! You've no left us much time!"

"Oh," says Jack, "Is that you again?"

"Yes, yes, I'm here to help you."

"Hey, great! Would you mind getting another stick and pulling it 'round to the . . ."

"No, no, no, no! Your quest! Your quest, Jack. I'm here—"

"Oh, my quest. I've forgotten all about my quest," he says. "Yes."

"Sure. Hop. Here Jack, follow me, follow me."

Hip, hip, hip, hop, hop, hop, over to the big rock at the end of the garden.

"Hit that three times with your stick, Jack."

And Jack did, one, two, three. Aaaeeeheeee, the boulder opened right up, and this great big huge tunnel went right down into the center of the earth.

"Come on Jack, come on Jack."

And down [the frog] went, and Jack right after, lickety-split. And there he was, right into that great, big, huge cavern filled with all the toads and frogs and snakes and lizards, and all sorts of things. And the bullfrog, the great big bullfrog, sitting on his throne at the end of the cavern, says:

"Jack, Jack, my man, it's nice to see you. Now, what can I do to help you on your quest this time, Jack?"

Well, Jack sort of sat himself down, and he said:

"Well, this time I'm supposed to bring back a . . . I'm supposed to bring back a . . . what am I supposed to . . . ? Ah, a ring! I'm supposed to bring back a ring, a beautiful ring. That's what that is, yes. I remember now, all right."

"A ring," said the frog. "Well, I know just what to do. You see that big chest over in the corner? Bring it here, Jack." And Jack goes up and he lifts up this big, big, heavy chest, and he says:

"Here."

"Well, open it up, Jack."

And Jack did. Oh, then, I tell you, the priceless gems, the rings, all of the things that you wouldn't believe were there. And the frog said:

"Choose whatever you like, choose whatever you like."

So he dishes himself back into the bottommost corner of that chest, pulls out a ring, which he can't see very well because they don't have too many lights down there, in the cavern, and he sort of rubs it off and puts it in his shirt pocket. And, to the cheers of all the toads and lizards, he goes up the tunnel, comes out into the daylight, the rock closes up behind him, and he's off, up to the chamber of the king.

And, sure enough, the eldest brother had just come back, with a velvet cushion, and was just kneeling in front of the king, saying:

"I've got the ring for you."

And the king picked it up and looked at it and said:

"Ho, that's a beautiful golden ring. It's marvelous, marvelous." And it was all inscribed with little Celtic knotwork and stuff. "Och, that's beautiful—very, very, very, fine. That's going to take a heap of beating." And he put it back down.
[*Jim Strickland, the man from whom Cameron learned the story, has entered the room and seated himself at the back, well behind Cameron and the tape recorder. Cameron seems to be searching more carefully for words and momentarily stops playing to the boys.*]

"Now,"—the second son—"You. What have you got for me?"

And with much ceremony, the second prince came forward and opened up this little jewelry box. And there, sitting on a piece of velvet, was the most beautiful silver ring, with a big, big pearl sitting right in the center.

"Och, that's marvelous—marvelous work," he says, the king. "Och, that's beautiful. Ach, I don't know, I don't know which is better," he says. "My, my, what a decision."

Just at that point Jack comes through the door, and the king catches his eye and says:

"Well, Jack, my man,"—hem, ah-hem, just to be fair, of course—"uh, have you got anything for me?"

"Uhh, yes, I do," uh, said Jack.

[*By now Cameron is again including the boys in his audience.*]

And he takes out this ring, polishes it off on his shirt, and hands it to the king. And I tell you, it was the most beautiful ring the king had ever seen. It was a band of gold, true enough, but it was studded and encrusted with diamonds and pearls, and the inside edge of it was inscribed with all of the most beautiful flowered pattern you've ever seen. The workmanship! You'd need a magnifying glass just to see the detail in it. The king was struck dumb. He says:

"Jack, my man, you've won again!"

"WAIT A MINUTE! WAIT A MINUTE!" said the two princes. "There's NO WAY we're going to have the kingdom go to Jack just because he—I don't know where he found that ring down in the muck in the back garden, but that's NO FAIR at all. WE DEMAND AN-OTHER QUEST!"

"WAIT A MINUTE!" said the king. "FOR HEAVEN'S SAKES! I'm getting on in years. I'm going to DIE before you guys come back with your quests! NO!"

"YES! YES!"

"NO!"

"YES!"

"All right. One, one more quest. Just one. And that's IT! I've had enough! I want you and you and you [*Cameron points to each boy*] to go out and find yourself a wife. [*They giggle at this.*] Yes, and the one that comes back with the most beautiful princess to be his wife . . . after all, when you inherit the kingdom you're going to need a wife, the kingdom is going to need a queen. Therefore I give you one week."

"ONE WEEK!"

"One week to go out there and find yourself a wife, come back here, and I'll decide."

Up to the topmost turret of the castle they went. The eldest son, he threw his feather. Wshhhhhhshewt. Off to the east it went. The second son, he took his feather. Wshhhhhhshww. Off to the west it went. And Jack, he took his feather. Wshhhh-shhew. Right down into the muck in the back garden.

"Oh, well."

Well, the sons went off in opposite directions, dressed as handsomely as they possibly could—even combed their hair and brushed. They put on their finest hats with a feather in the back. They put on their jewelry and all their crests. They even brushed down their horses to make their skin all shiny. Och-a, they were beautiful—Och! They even put on a little bit of rouge, you know, just to make them look a little bit more healthy than they actually were. Hup! And off they went, off they went, and everyone was looking at them.

And Jack, of course, he was about to go down into the back garden but . . . he was a little bit hungry, you know. So he spent his time in the kitchen, down in the scullery of the castle—because, you know, the people there, they didn't mind him. He was an all right chap, you know. And if they were making up some cakes and pies and batter and whatnot, they'd, they'd let him lick the spoon, and, and clean out the stuff from the bottom of the bowl.

([*Winking at the boys:*] Oh, great stuff. Have you ever had that? Ach, great.)

But he was always—you know, they were always making things here, and there, and Jack would be picking up this and picking up that, you know, and just getting in the way no way whatsoever.

"Go, go away, go away Jack!" they would say, and they'd shove him out the door.

Well, no problem for Jack. He went out to the back garden to play a little bit further. And, sure enough, he was going to make an entire village. There he had this road that he'd built up, and sort of piled it up. And he had this Tonka truck that he would drive over the edge, and into a little circular area where they were—it was the parking lot to the castle that he'd built—but, of course, it fell down, but he still had the Lego bridge that went over there, and he got one of the platforms from—the gray pieces, you know, with the crisscross on it— and, well, anyways, he was just about to make that into an airport, and had this, this, well anyways, he got interrupted. That always happens, you know, just when you get something interesting going:

"Jack, Jack, my man! Jack, Jack!"

And sure enough, there was the frog, the tiny wee frog. "You've no left us much time! Come on, Jack, come on. Hurry! Hurry!"

Well, Jack, he goes over to the rock, taps it three times, it opens up, he goes down the big long tunnel, and there is the bullfrog sitting at the back of this hall. And he says to Jack:

"Jack, what is your quest this time?"

"Och, I don't think you can help me this time," said Jack.

"And why not?" said the bullfrog.

"Well, I'm supposed to come back with the most beautiful bride, the most beautiful princess in the entire world."

"No pro-blem," said the bullfrog [*sounding very froglike, then resuming a normal voice*]. "As a matter of fact, my daughter happens to be the most beautiful woman, the most beautiful princess you could ever care to marry. And I would be more than happy to grant my consent to your marriage."

Well, Jack was sort of taken aback at the king's—uh—kindness? and said:

"Well . . . , where is this, uh, princess of yours?"

"Why, Jack, my man, she's sitting right there in the palm of your hand. Isn't she the most beautiful princess you've ever seen?"

Sure enough, he had to admit she was, she was *really* beautiful—for a frog. And, all the cheers that happened. The lizards, the toads, they had a fanfare, and they were cheering them—they almost picked them up bodily, he and the princess, as they went up this great big long tunnel. And all Jack could think of was that he wasn't even sure if his father approved of mixed marriages [*smiling; laugh from Kay Stone*].

But he got outside, got outside, to the tumultuous roar of turtles and lizards—do they roar tumultuously? They did THIS time! For sure! You wouldn't believe it! And Jack, as he turned around . . . this great huge turtle turned into a coach and four. A coach and four! He was dumfounded! And he looked around. And that tiny wee green frog turned into the most beautiful princess he had ever seen. Why she was BEAUTIFUL! His mouth dropped open and his tongue hung out. But, she said:

"Come along Jack" as she stepped into the carriage, in a green gown.

And Jack followed her, and, and closed the door.

Well, I tell you. Just at that time the king was up in the throne room, and the two princes, the elder brothers had come back with the most mean, miserable women you could ever imagine. They, being princesses, wanted to buy all sorts of things. You know, they wanted to have a big fancy wedding and invite their hundreds of relatives, just as you would want. But one week? You canna do that in one week! It takes that amount of time just to get the invitations printed, and to say nothing about ordering the trousseau and the whole—they had to elope. In one week, they had to elope. And here they were, already arguing with their husbands. Married only one week—for heaven's sakes! And just then the butler said:

"Och! Stations everyone! I think we've got visiting royalty. Hurry! Hurry!"

And the king and the princes and their wives looked out the window of the castle room, and what did they see but this huge, great emerald carriage pulling up to the front gate. And weren't they dumfounded when out should come . . . Jack. Jack! Little tiny Jack, with the most beautiful woman, the most beautiful princess, anyone had ever seen.

Well, there was no doubt about it—no doubt about it at all. Jack won the day. And in time Jack became the king. And a good thing it was, too, for his wife was as smart as Jack was a little bit . . . soft. She was as industrious as he was, well, maybe a tiny bit lazy. And besides that, every time when the affairs of state got a little bit beyond his control, he would nip out the back door and go play in the mud in the back garden. But she let him do that because, you know, considering her background, she understood how that might be a nice thing to do. And that's the end of the story.

REFERENCES

▼ ▼ ▼ ▼ ▼

Aarne, Antti, and Stith Thompson. 1961. *The Types of the Folktale.* F F
Communications 184. Helsinki: Academia Scientiarum Fennica.
Addy, Sidney Oldall. 1895. *Household Tales and Other Popular Remains.*
London: D. Nutt.
Adler, Thomas A. 1980. Record reviews. *Western Folklore* 39:147.
Bakhtin, Mikhail. 1984. *Rabelais and His World.* Translated by Hélène
Iswolsky. Bloomington: Indiana University Press.
Baughman, Ernest W. 1966. *Type and Motif Index of the Folktales of En-*
gland and North America. Indiana University Folklore Series 20. The
Hague: Mouton.
Bauman, Richard. 1984 [1977]. *Verbal Art as Performance.* Prospect
Heights, Ill.: Waveland Press.
Ben-Amos, Dan. 1972. "Toward a Definition of Folklore in Context." In
Toward New Perspectives in Folklore, edited by Américo Paredes and
Richard Bauman, 3–15. Publications of the American Folklore So-
ciety, Bibliographical and Special Series 23. Austin: University of
Texas Press.
———. 1976. "Analytic Categories and Ethnic Genres." In *Folklore Genres,*
edited by Dan Ben-Amos, 215–42. Publications of the American
Folklore Society, Bibliographical and Special Series 26. Austin: Uni-
versity of Texas Press.
Bennett, Louise. 1979. *Anancy and Miss Lou.* Kingston: Sangster's.
Bolte, Johannes, and Georg Polívka. 1913–32. *Anmerkungen zu den*
Kinder- und Hausmärchen der Brüder Grimm. Leipzig: Dieterich'sche
Verlag. 5 vols.
Botkin, B. A. 1949. *A Treasury of Southern Folklore.* New York: Crown.
Brians, Paul. 1972. *Bawdy Tales from the Courts of Medieval France.* New
York: Harper and Row.
Briggs, Charles L. 1988. *Competence in Performance: The Creativity of*
Tradition in Mexicano Verbal Art. Philadelphia: University of Pennsyl-
vania Press.
———, ed. 1990. *The Lost Gold Mine of San Jaun Mondragón: A Legend*
from New Mexico Performed by Melaguías Romero. Tucson: University
of Arizona Press.
Briggs, Katharine M. 1970. *A Dictionary of British Folk-Tales in the En-*
glish Language. London: Routledge and Kegan Paul. 4 vols.
Bruford, Alan. 1978. "Recitation or Re-creation?: Examples from South
Uist Storytelling." *Scottish Studies* 22:27–44.
Burrison, John A. 1989. *Storytellers: Folktales and Legends from the South.*
Athens: University of Georgia Press.
Campbell, John C. 1924. *The Southern Highlander and His Homeland.*
New York: Russell Sage.

Campbell, Joseph. 1944. "Folkloristic Commentary." In *The Complete Grimm's Fairy Tales*. New York: Pantheon.

Campbell, Marie. 1958. *Tales from the Cloud Walking Country*. Bloomington: Indiana University Press.

Campbell of Islay, John Francis. 1890. *Popular Tales of the West Highlands*. New ed. Paisley: Alexander Gardner. 4 vols.

Carrière, Joseph M. 1946. Review of *The Jack Tales*. *Journal of American Folklore* 59:74–77.

Carter, Isabel Gordon. 1925. "Mountain White Folklore: Tales from the Southern Blue Ridge." *Journal of American Folklore* 38:340–74.

Chambers, Robert. 1870. *Popular Rhymes of Scotland*. 4th ed. Edinburgh: W. and R. Chambers.

Chase, Richard. 1939. "The Origin of the Jack Tales." *Southern Folklore Quarterly* 3:187–91.

———. 1950. *Jack and the Three Sillies*. Boston: Houghton Mifflin.

———. n.d. *Richard Chase Tells Jack Tales*. Sharon, Conn.: Folk-Legacy Records.

———, ed. 1943. *The Jack Tales*. Boston: Houghton Mifflin.

———, ed. 1948. *Grandfather Tales*. Boston: Houghton Mifflin.

———, ed. 1956. *American Folk Tales and Songs*. New York: New American Library.

Chase, Richard Volney. 1949. *Quest for Myth*. Baton Rouge: Louisiana State University Press.

———. 1957. *The American Novel and Its Tradition*. Garden City: Doubleday.

———. 1958. *The Democratic Vista: A Dialogue on Life and Letters in Contemporary America*. Garden City: Doubleday.

Crowley, Daniel J. 1966. *I Could Talk Old-story Good: Creativity in Bahamian Folklore*. Berkeley: University of California Press.

Curtin, Jeremiah. 1890. *Myths and Folk-Lore of Ireland*. Boston: Little, Brown.

———. 1895. *Tales of the Fairies and of the Ghost World Collected from Oral Tradition in South-west Munster*. Boston: Little, Brown.

———. 1943. *Irish Folk-Tales*. Edited by James H. Delargy [Séamus Ó Duilearga]. Dublin: Educational Company of Ireland.

Davis, Donald D. 1981. Storytelling workshop. Charlotte Public Library, Charlotte, N.C., October.

———. 1983a. *Favorites from Uncle Frank*. Cassette tape. Issued by performer.

———. 1983b. *Traditional Tales for Children*. Cassette tape. Charlotte, N.C.: Issued by performer.

———. 1984. "Inside the Oral Medium." *Storytelling Journal* 1, no. 3: 7.

———. 1985. Interviews by Joseph Daniel Sobol. 30 January, 30 April, 15 July. High Point, N.C.

———. 1986. *Miss Daisy and Miss Annie*. Cassette tape. Issued by performer.

——. 1987. Classroom guest lecture-performance. 16 March. University of North Carolina, Chapel Hill.

——. 1990. *Listening for the Crack of Dawn*. Little Rock: August House.

——. 1991. *Barking at a Fox-Fur Coat*. Little Rock: August House.

——. 1992. *Jack Always Seeks His Fortune*. Little Rock: August House.

Davis, Donald D., and Kay Stone. 1984. " 'To Ease the Heart': Traditional Storytelling." *Storytelling Journal* 1, no. 1: 3–6.

Dégh, Linda. 1969. *Folktales and Society: Story-telling in a Hungarian Peasant Community*. Bloomington: Indiana University Press.

Delargy, James H. [Séamus Ó Duilearga]. 1945. *The Gaelic Story-teller*. London: Proceedings of the British Academy.

Donoghue, Denis. 1987. *Reading America: Essays on American Literature*. New York: Knopf.

Dorson, Richard M. 1959. *American Folklore*. Chicago: University of Chicago Press.

Dotterer, Peggie. 1988. Interview by Bill Ellis. 30 May. Hot Springs, N.C.

Dundes, Alan. 1972. "Folk Ideas as Units of World View." In *Toward New Perspectives in Folklore*, edited by Américo Paredes and Richard Bauman, 93–103. Publications of the American Folklore Society, Bibliographical and Special Series 23. Austin: University of Texas Press.

——. 1980. "Texture, Text, and Context." In *Interpreting Folklore*, by Alan Dundes. Bloomington: Indiana University Press.

Duval, John, and Raymond Eichman. 1982. *Cuckolds, Clerics and Countrymen*. Fayetteville: University of Arkansas Press.

Edwards, C. L. 1895. *Bahama Songs and Stories*. Memoirs of the American Folklore Society 3.

Ellis, Bill. 1987. "Why Are Verbatim Transcripts of Legends Necessary?" In *Perspectives on Contemporary Legend*, edited by Gillian Bennett, Paul Smith, and J. D. A. Widdowson, vol. 2. Sheffield: Sheffield Academic Press.

El-Shamy, Hasan. 1990. "Oral Traditional Tales and the *Thousand Nights and a Night*: The Demographic Factor." In *The Telling of Stories: Approaches to a Traditional Craft*, edited by Morten Nøjgaard et al., p. 100. Odense: Odense University Press.

Fine, Elizabeth C. 1984. *The Folklore Text: From Performance to Print*. Bloomington: Indiana University Press.

Fischer, David Hackett. 1989. *Albion's Seed: Four British Folkways in America*. London: Oxford University Press.

Furrow, Monica. 1985. *Ten Fifteenth-century Comic Poems*. New York: Garland.

Gardner, Emlyn E. 1937. *Folklore from the Schoharie Hills, New York*. Ann Arbor: University of Michigan Press.

Georges, Robert A. 1969. "Toward an Understanding of Storytelling Events." *Journal of American Folklore* 82:313–28.

Glassie, Henry. 1964. "Three Southern Mountain Jack Tales." *Tennessee Folklore Society Bulletin* 30:88–102.

———. 1982. *Irish Folk History: Texts from the North.* Philadelphia: University of Pennsylvania Press.

———, ed. 1985. *Irish Folk Tales.* Pantheon Fairy Tale and Folklore Library. New York: Pantheon.

Glimm, James York. 1983. *Flatlanders and Ridgerunners: Folktales from the Mountains of Pennsylvania.* Pittsburgh: University of Pittsburgh Press.

Gmelch, George, and Ben Krout. 1978. *To Shorten the Road.* Toronto: Macmillan.

Goffman, Erving. 1974. *Frame Analysis: An Essay on the Organization of Experience.* New York: Harper and Row.

Gurko, Leo. 1953. *Heroes, Highbrows, and the Popular Mind.* Indianapolis: Bobbs-Merrill.

Gutierrez, C. Paige. 1975. "The Jack Tales: A Definition of a Folk Tale Genre." Master's thesis, University of North Carolina, Chapel Hill.

———. 1978. "The Jack Tales: A Definition of a Folk Tale Sub-genre." *North Carolina Folklore Journal* 26:85–110.

Halpert, Herbert. 1943. "Appendix and Parallels." In *The Jack Tales*, edited by Richard Chase, 181–200. Boston: Houghton Mifflin.

Halpert, Herbert, and J. D. A. Widdowson. 1986. "Folk-Narrative Performance and Tape Transcription: Theory versus Practice." *Lore and Language* 5:39–50.

Hancock, Joyce. 1987. "The Emergence of Jack Tales in Our Times." Manuscript.

Haring, Lee. 1972. "Performing for the Interviewer: A Study of the Structure of Context." *Southern Folklore Quarterly* 36:383–98.

Hellman, Robert, and Richard O'Gorman. 1965. *Fabliaux: Ribald Tales from the Old French.* New York: Crowell.

Hicks, John Henry, Mattie Hicks, and Barnabas B. Hicks. 1991. *The Hicks Families of Western North Carolina (Watauga River Lines).* Boone, N.C.: Miner's Printing.

Hicks, Ray. 1963. *Ray Hicks of Beech Mountain, North Carolina Telling Four Traditional "Jack Tales."* Sharon, Conn.: Folk-Legacy Records.

———. 1989. "Telling 'Jack and the Old Bull.'" *North Carolina Folklore Journal* 36:73–120.

Hoffman, Daniel. 1961. *Form and Fable in American Fiction.* New York: Oxford University Press.

Hook, Frank S. 1970. Introductory notes to *The Old Wive's Tale* [George Peele]. In *The Life and Works of George Peele*, edited by Charles Taylor Prouty, vol. 2. New Haven: Yale University Press.

Hymes, Dell, 1981. *"In Vain I Tried to Tell You": Essays in Native American Ethnopoetics.* University of Pennsylvania Publications in Conduct and Communication. Philadelphia: University of Pennsylvania Press.

Jacobs, Joseph. 1890. *English Fairy Tales*. London: David Nutt.
———. 1895. *More English Fairy Tales*. London: David Nutt.
Jekyll, Walter. 1907. *Jamaican Songs and Stories*. London: David Nutt.
Jones, Steven. 1979. "Slouching towards Ethnography: The Text/Context Controversy Reconsidered." *Western Folklore* 38:42–47.
Kercheval, Samuel. 1902 (orig. 1833). *A History of the Valley of Virginia*. Woodstock, Va.: Gatewood Press.
Lang, Andrew. 1889. *Blue Fairy Book*. London: Longmans, Green.
———. 1890. *Red Fairy Book*. London: Longmans, Green.
Lindahl, Carl. 1987. *Earnest Games: Folkloric Patterns in the Canterbury Tales*. Bloomington: Indiana University Press.
Long, Eleanor. 1986. "Response to Niles." *Western Folklore* 14:106.
Long, Maud. 1955a. *Jack Tales (I)*. LP record (AAFS L47). Washington, D.C.: Library of Congress.
———. 1955b. *Jack Tales (II)*. LP record (AAFS L48). Washington, D.C.: Library of Congress.
Lord, Albert B. 1960. *The Singer of Tales*. Cambridge, Mass.: Harvard University Press.
McClosky, Herbert, and John Zaller. 1984. *The American Ethos: Public Attitudes toward Capitalism and Democracy*. Cambridge, Mass.: Harvard University Press.
McDermitt, Barbara. 1983. "Storytelling and a Boy Named Jack." *North Carolina Folklore Journal* 31, no. 1: 3–22.
———. 1986. "Comparison of a Scottish and an American Storyteller." Ph.D. dissertation, School of Scottish Studies, Edinburgh, Scotland.
MacDonald, D. A. 1978. "A Visual Memory." *Scottish Studies* 22:1-26.
McDowell, John H. 1974. "Some Aspects of Verbal Art in Bolivian Quechua." *Folklore Annual of the University Folklore Association* 6:68–81. University of Texas at Austin.
McGowan, Thomas, ed. 1978. "Marshall Ward: An Introduction to a Jack Tale." *North Carolina Folklore Journal* 26, no. 2: 51–53 (Jack Tales issue, edited by Thomas McGowan).
MacManus, Seumas. 1908. *In Chimney Corners*. Garden City: Doubleday.
May, Jim. 1986. *Purple Bogies and Other Ghost Tales*. Cassette tape. Woodstock, Ill.: Issued by performer.
Moser, Joan. 1988. Interview by Bill Ellis. 29 May. Swannanoa, N.C.
Mullen, Patrick B. 1981. "A Traditional Storyteller in Changing Contexts." In *"And Other Neighborly Names": Social Process and Cultural Image in Texas Folklore*, edited by Richard Bauman and Roger D. Abrahams, 266–79. Austin: University of Austin Press.
Newell, W. W. 1888. "English Folk-Tales in America." *Journal of American Folklore* 1:227–34.
Nicolaisen, W. F. H. 1978. "English Jack and American Jack." *Midwest Journal of Language and Folklore* 4:27–36.

———. 1980. "AT 1535 in Beech Mountain, North Carolina." *Arv: A Journal of Scandinavian Folklore* 36:99–106.

———. 1984. "Names and Narratives." *Journal of American Folklore* 97:259–72.

———. 1990. "Variability and Creativity in the Folktale." In *D'un conte . . . à l'autre: la variabilité dans la litterature orale,* edited by Veronika Gorog-Karady, 39–46. Paris: Editions du C. N. R. S.

Opie, Peter, and Iona Opie. 1951. *The Oxford Dictionary of Nursery Rhymes.* Oxford: Clarendon.

———. 1974. *The Classic Fairy Tales.* London: Oxford University Press.

Oxford, Cheryl Lynne. 1987. " 'They Call Him Lucky Jack': Three Performance-centered Case Studies of Storytelling in Watauga County, North Carolina." Ph.D. dissertation, Northwestern University.

Painter, Jacqueline Burgin. 1987. *The Season of Dorland-Bell: History of an Appalachian Mission School.* Asheville, N.C.: Biltmore Press.

Paredes, Américo, and Richard Bauman, eds. 1972. *Toward New Perspectives in Folklore.* Publications of the American Folklore Society, Bibliographical and Special Series 23. Austin: University of Texas Press.

Perdue, Charles L., Jr., ed. 1987. *Outwitting the Devil: Jack Tales from Wise County, Virginia.* Santa Fe: Ancient City Press. Identical with *Appalachian Journal* 14 (Winter 1987).

Radin, Paul. 1915. "Literary Aspects of North American Mythology." Canada Geological Survey *Museum Bulletin* 16 (15 June): 35.

Randolph, Vance. 1952. *Who Blowed up the Church House? and Other Ozark Folktales.* New York: Columbia University Press.

———. 1955. *The Devil's Pretty Daughter and Other Ozark Folktales.* New York: Columbia University Press.

———. 1957. *The Talking Turtle and Other Ozark Folktales.* New York: Columbia University Press.

———. 1958. *Sticks in the Knapsack and Other Ozark Folktales.* New York: Columbia University Press.

———. 1976. *Pissing in the Snow and Other Ozark Folktales.* Urbana: University of Illinois Press.

Roberts, Leonard. 1955. *South from Hell-fer-Sartin: Kentucky Mountain Folktales.* Lexington: University Press of Kentucky.

———. 1969. *Old Greasybeard: Tales from the Cumberland Gap.* Hatboro, Pa.: Folklore Associates.

———. 1974. *Sang Branch Settlers: Folksongs and Tales of a Kentucky Mountain Family.* Austin: University of Texas Press.

Rourke, Constance. 1931. *American Humor: A Study of the National Character.* New York: Harcourt, Brace.

Saucier, Corinne. 1962. *Folktales from French Louisiana.* New York: Exposition Press.

Schlesinger, Arthur M. 1986. *The Cycles of American History*. Boston: Houghton Mifflin.

Smith, Jimmy Neil. 1988. *Homespun: Tales from America's Favorite Story-tellers*. New York: Crown.

Sobol, Joseph Daniel. 1987. *Everyman and Jack: The Storytelling of Donald Davis*. Master's thesis, University of North Carolina, Chapel Hill.

———. 1992. "The Jack Tales: Coming from Afar." Introduction to *Jack Always Seeks His Fortune*, by Donald D. Davis. Little Rock: August House.

Stivender, Ed. 1983. *Ed Stivender Live*. Cassette tape. Issued by performer.

Tatar, Maria. 1987. *The Hard Facts of the Grimm's Fairy Tales*. Princeton: Princeton University Press.

Tedlock, Dennis. 1972a. *Finding the Center: Narrative Poetry of the Zuni Indians*. New York: Dial.

———. 1972b. "On the Translation of Style in Oral Narrative." In *Toward New Perspectives in Folklore*, edited by Américo Paredes and Richard Bauman, 114–33. Publications of the American Folklore Society, Bibliographical and Special Series 23. Austin: University of Texas Press.

———. 1983. *The Spoken Word and the Work of Interpretation*. Philadelphia: University of Pennsylvania Press.

Thomas, Gerald. 1983. *Les deux traditions: la conte populaire chez les Franco-Terreneuviens*. Montreal: Editions Bellarmin.

Thompson, James W. 1987. "The Origins of the Hicks Family Tradition." *North Carolina Folklore Journal* 34: 18–28.

Thompson, Stith. 1946. *The Folktale*. New York. Dryden Press.

Thompson, Stith, and Antti Aarne. *See* Aarne, Antti, and Stith Thompson.

Toelken, Barre. 1969. "The 'Pretty Languages' of Yellowman: Genre, Mode, and Texture in Navaho Coyote Narratives." *Genre* 2:211–35.

———. 1979. *The Dynamics of Folklore*. Boston: Houghton Mifflin.

Torrence, Jackie. 1984. *Mountain Magic—Jack Tales II*. Cassette tape. Chicago: Earwig Music.

Turner, Victor. 1967. "Betwixt and Between: The Liminal Period in *rites de passage*." In *The Forest of Symbols: Aspects of Ndembu Ritual*, by Victor Turner, 93–111. Ithaca, N.Y.: Cornell University Press.

Ward, Donald, ed. 1981. *The German Legends of the Brothers Grimm*. Philadelphia: Institute for the Study of Human Issues. 2 vols.

Warner, Anne. 1984. *Traditional American Folksongs from the Anne and Frank Warner Collection*. Syracuse, N.Y.: Syracuse University Press.

Webster, Dixon. 1941. *The Hero in America: A Chronicle of Hero-worship*. New York: Scribner.

Whisnant, David, E. 1983. *All That Is Native and Fine: The Politics of Culture in an American Region*. Chapel Hill: University of North Carolina Press.

Williamson, Duncan. 1983. *Fireside Tales of the Traveller Children: Twelve Scottish Stories.* New York: Harmony Books.

Williamson, Duncan, and Barbara McDermitt. 1978. "Duncan Williamson." *Tocher* 33:141–48.

Williamson, Duncan, and Linda Williamson. 1987. *A Thorn in the King's Foot: Stories of the Scottish Travelling People.* New York: Penguin.

Wolfenstein, Martha. 1965. "Jack and the Beanstalk: An American Version." In *The Study of Folklore*, edited by Alan Dundes, 110–13. New Jersey: Prentice-Hall.

Yaskinsky, Dan. 1989. "Stewart Cameron" (obituary). *Appleseed* 4 (Fall): 5.

TALE AND SONG INDEX

▼ ▼ ▼ ▼ ▼

Page numbers in boldface indicate the primary discussion.

"Barbara Allen" (Child 84), 99
"Berangier of the Long Ass," 8
"Big Claus and Little Claus"
   (AT 1535), 107
"Big Jack and Little Jack"
   (AT 1000/1007/1011/1563), 8
"Billy Peg and His Bull"
   (AT 511/530), xx, xxxiii (n. 5)
"Boy Steals the Giant's Treasure,
   The" (AT 328), xxv
"Brave Little Tailor, The"
   (AT 1640), 100
"Bremen Town Musicians, The"
   (AT 130), 156
"Broken Token, The," 99

"Cat and Mouse" ("Jack and the
   Animal Bride," AT 401), 5

"Dance among Thorns, The"
   (AT 592), xiv
"Dungbeetle" (AT 559), 65

"Eating Contest" (AT 1088), 231
"Enchanted Lady, The"
   (AT 570), 97

"Fill, Bowl, Fill" (AT 570), 8

"Grandma Hess's Story about
   Jack, Bill, and Tom" (AT 2014/
   577/1088), 229–37; comparison of two versions, 232–36

"Hardy Hard-Ass" (AT 513B),
   xix, 6–10, 101, 142

"Hardy Hard Back" (AT 513B),
   100, 103
"Hardy Hardhead" (AT 513B),
   6–10, 98
"History of Jack and the Bean-
   stalk, The," xv
"History of Jack and the Giants,
   The," xv
"Huddon and Duddon and
   Donald O'Leary" (AT 1535),
   168–69

"Jack and His Step-Dame"
   (AT 592), xiv
"Jack and King Marock" (Chase,
   AT 313C), 69 (n. 3), 171
"Jack and Old King Marock"
   (Shores, AT 313C), 171, 173,
   177
"Jack and the Animals" (AT 130),
   156–63
"Jack and the Beanstalk"
   (AT 328), xv, 100, 154, 167
"Jack and the Bean Tree"
   (AT 328), 167
"Jack and the Bull" (AT 511/530),
   xl, 69 (n. 3)
"Jack and the Calf Hide"
   (AT 1535), 94, 98, 99
"Jack and the Doctor's Girl"
   (AT 1525), 8, 28, 30
"Jack and the Firedragon"
   (AT 301), 133
"Jack and the Giants' New
   Ground" (AT 1640), 101
"Jack and the Heifer Hide"

(AT 1535), 8, **94–107, 126–49,** 156; possible British origins of, 126–27, 142; food in, 138–40; gender issues in, 139–40, 148
"Jack and the Old Rich Man" (AT 1525), 8, **27–34;** comparison with earlier version, 30–33
"Jack and the Three Steers," xiv
"Jack and the Varmints" (AT 1640), 101
"Jack and the Witch's Bellows," 177–78
"Jackie's Gone A-Sailing," 99
"Jack in the Lion's Den" (AT 853/559), **60–70,** 133
"Jack's Biggest Tale" (AT 852), xix, **204–13**
"Jack the Giant Killer" (AT 1640), xiv–xv, xxxiii (n. 3), 101

"King's Tasks, The" (AT 577), 231

"Little Peasant" (AT 1737), 127
"Little Red Ox, The" (AT 511A), xxv, xxvii

"Man in the Kraut Tub, The," 7
"Master Thief" (AT 1525), xxv, 8, 178; comparison of British and American versions, **xxix–xxxii,** 32

"Meunier et Les Deux Clers, Le," 8
"Moine Segretain, Le," 7

"Old Bluebeard" (AT 301A), 97, 103
"Old Dry Fry," 7

"Pack Down the Big Chest," 7

"Quare Jack" (AT 853), 62–63

"Raglif Jaglif Tetartlif Pole" (AT 313C), xxxiii–xxxiv (n. 10), **169–80;** layers of composition, 171–79; comparison with version from Columbia Roberts, 176–77; comparison with version from Nancy Shores, 177; comparison with Scots and Irish tales, 177–78
"Reeve's Tale," 8

"Sheep for the Asking" (AT 1535), 126
"Soldier Jack" (AT 330/332), 69 (n. 3), 156, **163–65**

"Table, the Ass, and the Stick, The" (AT 563), xxv, xxvii
"Three Feathers, The" (AT 402), **250–57**
"Tom Thumb," xvi
"Tree in the Woods, The," 99

PLACE AND NAME INDEX

▼ ▼ ▼ ▼ ▼

Page numbers in boldface indicate the primary discussion.

Addy, S. O., xl
Adler, Thomas, 165–66
Albuquerque, N.M., ix
Allen, Cornelius, xxx
American Folklore Society, ix
Amherst, Nicholas, xvi
Andersen, Hans Christian, 107
Andrews, N.C., 208
Appalachian State Teachers College, 57, 58
Arthur, King, xv
Asheville Folk Festival, 102
Asheville Normal Teachers' College, 97
Ashley, Edgar A., xx, xxxiii (n. 5)

Bahamas, xvi
Bakhtin, Mikhail, 63, 66
Batcheller, Irving, 97
Baughman, Ernest W., xxv, 231
Bauman, Richard, xxxvii
Beech Creek, N.C., 56
Beech Mountain, N.C., 3, 10, 125. See also Hicks-Harmon family tradition
Ben-Amos, Dan, 166
Berea College, 209
Boccaccio, Giovanni, 7
Boswell, James, xvi
Botkin, Benjamin A., 99, 100
Briggs, Charles L., xxxvii
Briggs, Katharine, xxv, xxix, xxxiv (n. 11), 126
Bruford, Alan, 148
Burrison, John, xl

Cameron, Dianne, 251, 256 (n. 1)
Cameron, Duncan, 251, 253–54, 256 (n. 1)
Cameron, Moira, 251
Cameron, Stewart, 250–57
Campbell, Marie, xxvi, 179 (n. 1)
Campbell of Islay, John Francis, xvi
Canadian Broadcasting Company, 250
Carrière, Joseph, xxiii
Carter, Isabel Gordon, xxi, xl, 7, 94, 97
Chambers, Robert, xvi
Charlotte, N.C., 207
Chase, Richard, ix–x, 57, 68, 95, 102, 131, 132, 205, 209; collecting technique, 59, 98; and folkdancing, 98, 101
—American Folk Tales and Songs, xxiii, 7
—Grandfather Tales, xxiii, 100
—Jack Tales, The, xiii–xxxii passim, xxxiii (n. 8), xl, 6, 7, 8, 10, 27–28, 34, 69 (n. 3), 94, 97, 98, 100, 101, 104, 125, 133, 140, 142, 149 (nn. 1, 2), 154, 170, 171, 231–32; stylistic alterations in, xxv; Marshall Ward's contribution to, 58–60, 69 (n. 4), 70; influence of on Beech Mountain tradition, 149 (n. 1)
Chase, Richard V., xxii

Chaucer, Geoffrey, 7, 8, 208
Corinoran, xv
Corn Island Storytelling Festival,
153, 230
Crockett, David, xxiii
Curtin, Jeremiah, 170
Cushing, Frank, xxxvi

Davidson College, 208
Davis, Donald, xix, xxxiii (n. 6),
xxxviii, 7–8, 156–63, 204–13;
influence of Grandmother
Walker, 207–8; influence of
Uncle Frank, 207–8; ordained
as Methodist minister, 208;
role in storytelling revival,
209–10; "picture-centered"
approach, 210–11
Dégh, Linda, xviii, 95
Delargy, James H. (Séamus
Ó Duilearga), xix
Disney, Walt, 100–101
Dorland Institute, 95–107 pas-
sim; storytelling at, 95–97;
becomes Dorland-Bell School,
97; merges with Wilson Col-
lege, 102
Dorson, Richard M., xxii, xxxiii
(n. 9)
Dotterer, Peggie, 96, 98, 101,
103–4
Douglas, Jane, 103, 105
Duke University, 33, 208
Dundes, Alan, xxxv–xxxvi

Edwards, C. L., xvi
Elkland (Pa.) Heritage Days,
231, 236, 237
El-Shamy, Hasan, 149 (n. 1)
Emrich, Duncan, 94, 99–101

Fielding, Henry, xv
Fine, Elizabeth, xxxviii–xxxix,
xli, xlii
Fink, Mike, xxiii

Fischer, David H., xxxii

Gentry, Jane Hicks, xxi, xl, 94–
97, 101, 102, 103, 104, 105,
107, 126–49 passim
Gentry, Pat, 97
Geoffrey of Monmouth, xv
Glassie, Henry, xx, xxv, xxvi,
xxvii–xxviii, 168–69
Goffman, Erving, xxxvii
Greeneville, Tenn., 98
Grimm, Jacob, xxxv, xxxviii, 156,
170
Grimm, Wilhelm, xxxv, xxxviii,
156, 170
Gurko, Leo, xxii
Gutierrez, C. Paige, 69 (n. 2)

Halpert, Herbert, xxxviii, 231
Hancock, Joyce, 154
Haring, Lee, xxxix
Harley, Bill, 159, 165
Harmon, Council, 27, 56, 61,
68–69 (n. 1), 95, 107, 125,
127, 131, 142, 148; genealogy,
128–29
Harold, Ky., 179 (n. 2)
Harvard University, xxiv
Haywood County, N.C., 205
Hebrides, Scotland, 148
Hess, Pearl, 229–30, 231, 232,
234, 237
Hicks, Ben, 4, 28, 131, 132–33,
140, 142
Hicks, David, Sr., 126, 127, 131,
142
Hicks, Leonard Ray, xiv, xix,
xxx, xxxviii, 3–10, 27, 29, 30,
33, 34, 126–49, 154, 163–65,
177, 230; style, xxxvii, 30;
comparison with Chase, 133
Hicks, Nathan, 4, 131
Hicks, Ransom M., 127, 131
Hicks, Roby Monroe, 131, 132
Hicks, Rosa, 3, 4, 5, 6, 10

Hicks, Samuel, I, 126, 127, 131, 142
Hicks, Stanley, xxxiii (n. 3), 131
Hicks-Harmon family: genealogy, 125–31
Hoffman, Daniel, xxii–xxv
Hook, Frank S., xv
Hot Springs, N.C., 94–107 passim
Hymes, Dell, xxxvii

Identities (TV program), 250
Iron Duff, N.C., 206

Jack: and Jacks, x, xiii–xxxiii, 211, 256; name, xvi, 9, 154; as American folk hero, xvii–xxxii, xxxiii (n. 9); as reflection of narrator, xlii, 33, 158–59; persona/archetype, xlii, 105, 166–67; as trickster, 8, 9, 67, 146, 211
Jackson, Andrew, xxxii
Jacobs, Joseph, xl
Jamaica, xvi–xvii
Jekyll, Walter, xvii
John C. Campbell Folk School, 209
Johnson, Samuel, xvi

Kendal, England, 126
Kercheval, Samuel, xvii
Kilgore, James, 163
Kirkland, Edwin, 98
Korson, Rae, 94, 104
Kyofski, Bonelyn Lugg, xxxiii (n. 6), 229–37; style, 234–36, 237

La Fontaine, Jean de, 7
Lang, Andrew, xl
Lees, Durham, 126
Library of Congress, xiii, xxxvi, 93–94, 99–102, 103, 107
Lindahl, Carl, 167, 256

London, England, 126
Long, Eleanor, 165
Long, Grover Cleveland, 97–98; death, 100
Long, Maud, xiii, xx, xxxiii (n. 6), xxxviii, 93–107, 126–49 passim; Library of Congress recordings, 93–94, 99–102, 103; compared with Chase, 101–5; style, 103–6; genealogy, 130
Lord, Albert Bates, 172
Los Angeles, Calif., 4

McDermitt, Barbara, 31, 34, 95
MacDonald, D. A., 148
McDowell, John H., xxxvii
McLuhan, Marshall, 6
Marshall, Peter, 101
May, Jim, 163–65
Mededović, Avdo, 172
Moser, Artus, 94, 98–99, 100, 106
Moser, Joan, 102, 105
Mountain Life and Work, 169
Muncie, Jane, 179

Nashe, Thomas, xv
National Association for the Preservation and Perpetuation of Storytelling (NAPPS). See National Storytelling Festival
National Storytelling Festival, xiv, 3–4, 153–54, 155, 157, 163, 204–5, 209
Nelson, Pa., 230
Nerelich, Mim, xix
Newell, W. W., xl
New York, N.Y., 97
Nicolaisen, W. F. H., xxv, 158, 166
Nolan, Hugh, 168–69
Northern Lights Festival, 250
Notre Dame University, 158

Oxenholme, England, 126
Oxford, Cheryl, 133
Oxford Dictionary of Nursery Rhymes, The (Opie and Opie), xxxiii (n. 2)

Painter, Jacqueline Burgin, 101
Patch, Sam, xxiii
Pecos Bill, 101
Peele, George, xv
Pennington, Lee, 230
Pennsylvania Northern Tier, 229, 232, 235
Pennsylvania State University, 229
Perdue, Charles L., Jr., xxvi, xl, 98, 179 (n. 2)
Perrault, Charles, xxxv
Phillips, Julia, 95–96
Pikeville College, 180
Pond, Caroline, 100, 107
Power, Oney, 178
Presnell, Hattie, **126–49**
Primitive Baptist church, 5
Proffitt, Frank, Sr., 28–34
Proffitt, Frank, Jr., xxxiii (n. 3), xxxviii, 4, **27–34**, 149 (n. 1), 177; style, 30–32, 34
Proffitt, Wiley, 28, 30, 31, 32

Radin, Paul, 165
Randolph, Vance, xxi, xxiii, xxxvi, 8, 61, 63, 231
Redfield, Robert, xviii–xix
Ritchie, Jean, 206
Roberts, Columbia, 169–79 passim
Roberts, Leonard, xiii, xxi, xxiii, xxvi, xxxiii (n. 6), xl, 61, 63–64, **169–80**, 231; *Old Greasybeard*, 169, 172; *South from Hell-fer-Sartin*, 231
Roberts, Olga, 169, 170
Roberts, Rachel, 169, 170
Robertson, Jeannie, 256 (n. 2)

Rourke, Constance, xxii

Schlesinger, Arthur M., Jr., xxviii
Shakespeare, William, xv, 208
Sharp, Cecil, 97, 102, 131
Shores, Nancy, 171, 173, 177, 179 (n. 2)
Smith, Doris, 154
Sobol, Joseph Daniel, 154
Somerset County, England, 127
Stewart, Andra, 256 (n. 2)
Stivender, Ed, **156–63**
Stone, Kay, 154
Storytellers School, 251
Strickland, Jim, 252, 253, 255, 256 (n. 2), 257
Sudbury, Ontario, 250
Sunnybank (inn), 96, 98, 105

Tedlock, Dennis, xxxvii, xxxviii, xxxix, xli, xlii
Thomas, Gerald, xxxiii (n. 4)
Thompson, James W., 125, 126, 128–29
Thompson, Stith, xxxiii (n. 1), 69 (n. 1), 101, 123
Thompson, T. W., 126
Tioga County, Pa., 232
Toelken, Barre, xxxvii, xxxix
Toronto Festival of Storytelling, 251, 252
Torrence, Jackie, **163–65**
Turner, Victor, 66
Twain, Mark (Samuel L. Clemens), xx
Types of the Folktale, The (Aarne and Thompson), xxxiii (n. 1), 69 (n. 6), 123, 135, 141, 169–70

University of Connecticut, 158
University of Kentucky, 170
University of North Carolina, 99, 205, 211, 213
University of Tennessee, 98

Valle Crucis Episcopal School, 59

Ward, Donald, xxxv
Ward, Marshall, xiv, xxxiii (n. 6), 56–70, 98, 126–49, 177; comparison with Chase, 134
Ward, Mary, 131
Ward, Miles A., 56, 57, 60, 95, 133, 140
Ward, Roby Monroe, 28, 95, 125, 131, 140
Warner, Anne, 127
Watauga County, N.C., 27, 94–95, 126

Waynesville, N.C., 206
Webster, Dixon, xxii
Wellesley College, xxiv
West, Hedy, 206
Widdowson, J. D. A., xxxviii
Williamson, Duncan, xvi, 177–78
Winnipeg, Ontario, 252
Wise County, Va., 163, 177, 179 (n. 2)

Yashinsky, Dan, 251
Yeats, William Butler, 168–69

Zug, Charles G., 213
Zundell, Kathleen, 4–6, 10

SUBJECT INDEX

▼ ▼ ▼ ▼ ▼

Page numbers in boldface indicate the primary discussion.

Aesthetics, xxxvi, 171–79, 255
Anachronism, 255
Audience, 30, 158, 161, 205–6, 209, 234–36, 253, 255. *See also* Stories and storytelling
Authenticity, x, 28, 104–5, 134, 155, 165–67, 205, 209, 255
Authority: immigrants' trust in local, xxxii

Ballads and songs, 98, 100, 102, 105, 124, 131, 230, 232, 237, 250, 251. *See also* individual ballad and song titles
Basket weaving, Appalachian, xx
Beech Mountain tradition. *See* Hicks-Harmon family tradition
Bicentennial, U.S., 29
"Breakthrough into performance," 59, 170, 213

Capitalism, xxviii–xxxii
Chapbooks, xiv, xvi, xvii
Civil War, 29
Cloth making, 93–94, 95, 96
Collecting and collectors, x, 60, 124; recording devices, xxxvi–xxxvii, 60, 98–99
Community, sense of, 229–37
Context, for storytelling: classroom, x, xxi, 7, 31, 57–59, 60, 95–98, 102, 134, 142, 180; work, xix, 93–95, 96; family, xx–xxi, 4, 11, 29, 56–57, 71, 105, 229–30, 239, 251, 253; comparison of American and

European, 95; reconstructed, 170
Context, historical, xlii
Coyote tales, 9
Creative stance, 132–34, 147
Creativity. *See* Stories and storytelling

Democracy, xxviii–xxxii
Depression, Great, xxii, xxiv, xxviii, 32
Dialect, xlii, 10, 61, 97
Digression, 255. *See also* Stories and storytelling
Donor, Proppian, xxvii–xxxii

Ethics, 155, 166; and moralizing, 162–63

Fabliaux, 7–8
Federal Writers' Project, x, xxiv, xxviii, xl, 177
Festivals, x, 30, 153–54, 209, 250. *See also* individual festivals
Folkdance, 209. *See also* Chase, Richard
Folk schools, 180, 209
Function, 165, 232

Genre, x
Great tradition and little tradition, xviii–xx, 27, 29, 32–33
Guineas (coin), 142

Hemispheric theory, xxxiii (n. 9)
Hicks-Harmon family tradition,

ix, x, xvii, xl, 30, 34, 56, 58, 68, 95, 97, 101, **123–49**; provenance of tales, 126–27. *See also* Beech Mountain, N.C.
Historic-geographic method, xxxix, xl
Humor, 6, 10, 62, 63, 66–67, 175–76

Interpretation of tales, 9, 32, 62

Jack Tales, x, 58–59; and North American frontier, xvii, xix; distribution and diversity in United States, xxi–xxii; comparison of American and British, xxv–xxxiii, xxxiii (nn. 3, 4, 8, 9); as cycle, 58, 134; and audience, 154

Literary versions of tales, xxxv–xxxvi, xl, 211. *See also* Chase, Richard
Logging, 230, 232, 235–36

Magic, xxvii, xxxii, xxxiii–xxxiv (n. 10), 7, 172–73, 176, 255
Memory, 148
Motific depth, 172

Narrative traditions: Irish, x, xvi, xvii, xix, xxiv, xxxviii, 177; Scots, x, xvi, xvii, xxiv, xxxii, 148, 177; German, x, 56, 68; Appalachian, xiv, xxi, xxv, xxix–xxxii, xxxiii (n. 10), xxxviii–xxxix, xl, 32, 94, 102, 105, 123–49, 167, 171–79; British, xiv–xvii, xxiv, xxxii, xxxiii (nn. 3, 4, 8), xxxix–xl, 68–69 (n. 1), 126; European, xviii, 95; Anglo-American, xviii–xxxiv (nn. 3, 4, 8, 9, 10), xlii; in Kentucky, xxi, xl, 171–

77; Scots-Irish, xxiv, xxxii, 206; Native-American, xxxvi, xxxvii. *See also* Hicks-Harmon family tradition
Nursery rhymes, xvi

Obscene and scatological elements, xiv, xviii, xxxii, xl, 7–9, 10, 60, 61, 65–68, 101, 105, 171
Oikotypes, xviii
Oral medium: free verse, xxxviii–xxxix; prose, xxxviii–xxxix, 237, 257

Parsons: as characters, 140
Performance, xxxix, xli–xlii, 31, 59, 125, 155, 206
Print: authority of, 102–3, 149 (n. 1)
Professional storyteller: defined, 155; re-creative role of, 165–67. *See also* Storytelling revival

Quilting, xx

Repertoire, 124
"Run," 97, 103, 174, 180

Schwank, 140
Self-correction, law of, 165
Sensory deprivation, xix
Stories and storytelling: style and variation, x, xviii, xxii, xlii, 31, 102–5, 123–67, 168–79, 235, 253–55; length, 27, 30–32, 34, 148, 162, 177, 205, 218, 255; metafictional devices in, 65; cultural constraints, 165; levels of composition, 171–79
Storytellers: and the church, 5, 61, 71
Storytelling revival, x, 3, 30, 105, 153–67, 205, 229, 251; auton-

omy of storytellers in, 155, 165–67; performance style and variation, 155–67, 234

Tall tales, xx
Text, texture, and context, xxxv–xxxvi, xxxvii–xxxix, xl–xlii, 212
Tinkers. *See* Travelers
Transcription of tales, x, xi, xxxv–xlii, 135, 211; conventions of, xli, 10, 34, 180, 212, 237, 257. *See also* Literary versions of tales
Travelers (tinkers), xvi, 177–79, 256 (n. 2)

Understatement, xx
Unlimited opportunity, xxvii

Variation. *See* Stories and storytelling

World War II, xxii